⊰ THE ⊱
Grand Inquisitor's Manual

A History of Terror
in the Name of God

JONATHAN KIRSCH

HarperOne
An Imprint of HarperCollins*Publishers*

HarperOne

HarperCollins books may be purchased for educational, business, or sales promotional use. For information please write: Special Markets Department, HarperCollins Publishers, 10 East 53rd Street, New York, NY 10022.

HarperCollins Web site: http://www.harpercollins.com

HarperCollins®, ▉®, and HarperOne™ are trademarks of HarperCollins Publishers.

FIRST EDITION

Library of Congress Cataloging-in-Publication Data is available.

ISBN-13: 978-0-06-081699-5

08 09 10 11 12 RRD (H) 10 9 8 7 6 5 4 3 2 1

I was torn in pieces by the devils that rack the brains of unhappy men. Do God's eyes not reach to the prisons of the Inquisition?

CARCEL, *goldsmith of Seville,*
a victim of the Spanish Inquisition

FOR

Ann Benjamin Kirsch,
Jennifer Rachel Kirsch,
and Adam, Remy and Charles Ezra Kirsch,

AND

Heather Kirsch
and Joshua, Jennifer and Hazel Kirsch

Remember us in life,
and inscribe us in the Book of Life.

TABLE OF CONTENTS

THE PIETÀ AND THE PEAR

Christendom seemed to have grown delirious and
Satan might well smile at the tribute to his power
in the endless smoke of the holocaust which bore
witness to the triumph of the Almighty.

HENRY CHARLES LEA,
A History of the Inquisition of the Middle Ages

L et us imagine a traveler arriving in the city of Rome when the Renaissance was in full flower, a pilgrim or a merchant or a diplomat.
He seeks out the chapel near St. Peter's Basilica where the *Pietà* of
Michelangelo is now on display, and he spends a few moments admiring
the sublime depiction of the body of the slain Jesus in the lap of his griev-
ing mother. *Pietà* means "pity," and the scene is rendered with exquisite
tenderness and profound compassion. Like Michelangelo's frescoes on the
ceiling of the nearby Sistine Chapel—the finger of a very fleshy God touching the finger of an equally fleshy Adam—the *Pietà* celebrates the beauty,
dignity, and grace of the human body and the most exalted emotions of the
human heart.

At the very same moment, however, and not far away, hooded men in
dungeons lit only by torches—henchmen of what would come to be called

the Roman and Universal Inquisition—are applying instruments of torture to the naked bodies of men and women whose only crime is to have entertained some thought that the Church regarded as heretical. The victims' cries, faint and distant, reach the ears of the traveler who gazes in prayerful silence at the *Pietà,* or so we might permit ourselves to imagine. Yet the torturers are wholly without pity, and they work in the sure conviction that the odor of the charred flesh of heretics is "delectable to the Holy Trinity and the Virgin."[1]

The scene allows us to see the Renaissance and the Inquisition as a pair of opposites, the highest aspirations of human civilization coexisting with its darkest and most destructive impulses at the same time and place. Tragically, the genius that Michelangelo applied to the celebration of the human body is matched by the ingenuity of the grand inquisitors in their crusade to degrade and destroy their fellow human beings. Consider, for example, the contrivance known simply and even charmingly as *La Pera*—the Pear.

Fashioned out of bronze, richly and fancifully decorated, and cunningly engineered to open and close by the operation of an iron key-and-screw device, the Pear was the handiwork of a skilled artist and craftsman with a vivid imagination and a certain measure of wit. The first examples of the Pear date back to roughly the same era as the *Pietà.* But unlike the scene depicted in Michelangelo's statuary, the diabolical faces and demonic figures that embellish *La Pera* are the stuff of nightmares, and the object itself was designed as an instrument of torture to afflict the bodies of accused heretics who refused to confess, whether because they were wholly innocent of the accusation or because they were true believers in their own forbidden faith.

Exactly how the Pear was used to insult and injure its victims is a gruesome topic that we will be compelled to examine in greater detail a bit later. For now, let *La Pera* serve as a symbol of the willingness, even the eagerness of one human being to inflict pain on a fellow human being. None of us should be surprised, of course, that otherwise ordinary men and women have always been capable of heart-shaking and heartbreaking atrocities, but the fact that a man with the soul of an artist and the hands of a craftsman should apply his gifts to the creation of something as fiendish as the Pear reveals something dire and disturbing about how we use the gifts we have inherited from our distant art- and toolmaking ancestors.

An even more sinister irony is at work here. What the men in black did to their victims with such tools was *not* a crime. To the contrary, when they tortured and killed countless thousands of innocent men, women, and children, they were acting in obedience to—and, quite literally, with the blessing of—the most exalted guardians of law and order. Significantly, the official seal of the Inquisition carried the Latin phrase MISERICORDIA ET JUSTITIA ("Mercy and Justice"), and all the atrocities of the friar-inquisitors were similarly veiled in pieties and legalisms.[2]

Here begins something new in history, an international network of secret police and secret courts in the service of "Throne and Altar," a bureaucracy whose vast archives amounted to the medieval version of a database, and an army of inquisitors whose sworn duty was to search out anyone and every- one whom a pope or a king regarded as an enemy, sometimes on the flim- siest of evidence and sometimes on no evidence at all except the betrayals and confessions that could be extracted under torture and threat of death. The worst excesses of the agents of the Inquisition—priests and monks, scribes and notaries, attorneys and accountants, torturers and execution- ers—were excused as the pardonable sins of soldiers engaged in war against a treacherous and deadly enemy.

The strange story of the Inquisition begins in the distant past, but it can- not be safely contained in history books. The inquisitorial apparatus that was first invented in the Middle Ages remained in operation for the next six hundred years, and it has never been wholly dismantled. As we shall see, an unbroken thread links the friar-inquisitors who set up the rack and the pyre in southern France in the early thirteenth century to the torturers and ex- ecutioners of Nazi Germany and Stalinist Russia in the mid–twentieth cen- tury. Nor does the thread stop at Auschwitz or the Gulag; it can be traced through the Salem witch trials in the Massachusetts Bay Colony, the intern- ment of Japanese-Americans during World War II, the Hollywood black- lists of the McCarthy era, and even the interrogation cells at Abu Ghraib and Guantánamo.

Another instrument of torture, far less ornate but no less effective than *La Pera,* provides the best evidence that the inquisitor's tools are still in use today. Among the first and favorite forms of torture used by medieval inquisitors was the so-called ordeal by water, that is, pouring water down a victim's throat to simulate the sensation of drowning and thereby extract a confession. As far as the Inquisition was concerned, the ordeal by water was an ideal method of interrogation: it required only a bucket of water and a funnel, it left no telltale marks and no bloody mess to clean up, and yet it produced such agony and terror that the victim would readily tell the torturer whatever he wanted to hear. That's why the ordeal by water was favored not only by the medieval inquisitors but also by their successors in the Gestapo and the Soviet secret police. And the same form of torture is still in use today, although we are asked by its modern users and defenders to call it "waterboarding."

Nowadays, we tend to regard the Inquisition as an object of parody. Indeed, when the Inquisition is recalled at all, it is in the guise of the chorus line of step-kicking Dominicans in Mel Brooks's *History of the World: Part 1* or the Monty Python sketches in which the setup line—"*Nobody* expects the Spanish Inquisition!"—is the occasion for sly but bloodless buffoonery. For that reason alone, a glance into the real face of the Inquisition is not merely surprising but shocking.

The first stirrings of the Inquisition can be traced back to a specific time and place in history. Faced with competition from the abundance of new ideas that appeared in western Europe in the aftermath of the Crusades, so rich and so strange, the Roman Catholic church resolved to impose a theological monopoly by fiat and force of arms. The thoroughly human tendency toward diversity in religious belief and practice had troubled Christianity since the first century of the common era—"For there must also be factions among you," observed Paul in his first letter to the Corinthians—but the so-called lawyer-popes of the Middle Ages resolved to root out heresy once and for all by devising and deploying the new and terrible contraption that came to be known as the Inquisition.[3]

The first target of the Inquisition was a community of dissident Christians known as the Cathars, who were hunted down, tortured, and burned by the thousands in the thirteenth century. To the modern eye, the Cathars appear to be exotic but inoffensive; the Church, by contrast, slandered them as plague-bearing vermin and servants of the Devil.* The Cathars were soon exterminated, but the Inquisition never ran out of victims. Indeed, as we shall see, the inquisitors were perfectly willing to imagine or invent new heresies where none existed to feed the fires of the auto-da-fé. Thus the Inquisition continued to function in fits and starts over the next six centuries—not only in Europe but also in the New World and a few far-flung outposts in Asia and Africa—and its last victim was not put to death until 1826.

Strictly speaking, a vestige of the Roman Inquisition still exists within the bureaucracy of the Church, although it has been renamed several times over the centuries and is now known as the Sacred Congregation for the Doctrine of the Faith. Although the ordeal by water is no longer used at the Vatican, the essential function of the Sacred Congregation is the same as it was among its more fearful predecessors: the detection and elimination of what the Church regards as false belief. The cardinal who until recently directed its affairs was elevated to the papal throne as Pope Benedict XVI in 2005, but he was hardly the first or only inquisitor who went on to serve as the Supreme Pontiff.

The long history of the Inquisition can be conveniently divided into three phases. The medieval Inquisition, which functioned across western Europe for a couple of hundred years starting in the early thirteenth century, finished off the Cathars and then expanded its scope of operations to include a miscellaneous assortment of accused heretics, ranging from radical Franciscan priests to women accused of witchcraft. The Spanish Inquisition was franchised by the pope in 1478 to detect and punish Jewish and Muslim converts to Christianity (known as *conversos*) who were suspected of secretly clinging to their former faiths, and remained in formal existence through 1834. And the Roman Inquisition, which aspired to universal jurisdiction but operated mostly in Italy, was created in 1542 as the papal weapon of choice in the crusade against the Protestant Reformation as well as the freshening winds of secularism and scientific inquiry that accompanied the Renaissance.

---

* "The Church," as the phrase is used here, refers to what is generally called the Roman Catholic church, which regarded itself as the sole and absolute religious authority in Christendom. As we shall see, the Eastern Orthodox church, too, claimed to be the sole source of religious truth, and the two churches regarded each other as heretical.

Some figures and episodes in the history of the Inquisition have a special claim on our imaginations. Joan of Arc is surely the most famous victim of the medieval Inquisition, for example, and Galileo was among the last victims of the Roman Inquisition. But the doomed grandeur of imperial Spain has attracted the most attention in both scholarship and arts and letters, which may explain why we are tempted to think of the Spanish Inquisition as *the* Inquisition. From Goya's heartrending drawings of inquisitorial victims to Dostoyevsky's dreamy account of the Grand Inquisitor in *The Brothers Karamazov*—"I shall burn Thee for coming to hinder us," says the imaginary Grand Inquisitor to Jesus Christ, whose second coming at Seville is treated as the ultimate act of heresy—the Inquisition has been made to serve as a symbol of the arrogance, brutality, cynicism, and hypocrisy of an authoritarian regime that drapes itself in the veils of both law and piety.[4]

The reach and sweep of the Inquisition have discouraged historians from treating it as a single institution. That's why an overview of the medieval, Spanish, and Roman Inquisitions in a single volume like this one is rare. The fact remains, however, that the inquisitors of every nationality and in every age were deputized under the same body of canon law, inflicted the same tortures and punishments on their victims, and devoted themselves to the same terrible mission—the arrest, torture, and execution of any man, woman, or child whom they regarded as a heretic, a term sufficiently elastic to reach *any* victim who happened to excite their anxieties or greed. Thus, for example, the manuals and handbooks composed in the Middle Ages to instruct the first inquisitors in their day-to-day work were still being consulted by the last inquisitors six centuries later.

Then, too, the Inquisition seems almost quaint when compared to the industrial-scale carnage of the twentieth century. Far more ink has been expended in chronicling the events that took place in Germany and Russia between 1917 and 1945 than in telling the story of the Inquisition, a saga that spans a period of six hundred years. Yet, ironically, the moral and cultural DNA of the grand inquisitors can be readily detected in Hitler and Stalin and their various accomplices and collaborators, and the inner workings of the Inquisition help us understand the goals and methods of the Great Terror and the Holocaust. The similarities are so striking that when the Jewish historian Cecil Roth published *The Spanish Inquisition* in 1937, he felt obliged to warn his readers that the book was a work of history and not merely a satire on current events.

As we unpack the inquisitorial toolkit, we will find a set of interlocking ideas, values, and techniques that link all phases of the Inquisition into one great engine of persecution. Moreover, and crucially, we will see how the crimes of the first inquisitors came to be repeated in the twentieth century and even in our own benighted age.

"Fanatic zeal, arbitrary cruelty, and insatiable cupidity rivaled each other in building up a system unspeakably atrocious," writes Henry Charles Lea (1825–1909) in summing up the verdict of history on the Inquisition, "It was a standing mockery of justice—perhaps the most iniquitous that the arbitrary cruelty of man has ever devised."[5]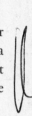

Henry Charles Lea is to the Inquisition what Edward Gibbon is to the Roman Empire, a self-invented historian who was also a gifted phrasemaker and relentless polemicist. The scion of a Quaker publishing family from Philadelphia, Lea set himself to work on a definitive study of the Inquisition after a breakdown confined him to his home and library. More than a century after Lea wrote a three-volume history of the medieval Inquisition and a four-volume history of the Spanish Inquisition, his vast body of work remains the starting point for any conversation about the meaning and effect of the Inquisition. Today, even as the history of the Inquisition is being revised by a new generation of scholars, Lea is still invoked to remind us why and how the Inquisition came to be regarded as an ineradicable symbol of the crimes that are committed when absolute power works its corruptions.

Revisionist historians, for example, have engaged in lively debate over how many men and women were actually tortured and burned alive by the Inquisition. Even though the precise body count remains undetermined, the hard evidence for the suffering of its victims was created and preserved by the Inquisition itself. We have the manuals, treatises, ledgers, and transcripts in which the inquisitors and their minions recorded every detail of their daily labors. We can read for ourselves the questions they asked, the punishments (or as the Inquisition preferred to call them, the "penances") that were prescribed for convicted heretics, and even the precise formulas to be spoken aloud by an inquisitor in Rome or Toulouse, Cologne or Madrid, when sending a condemned man or woman to prison or to the stake.

"The accused are not to be condemned according to ordinary laws, as in other crimes," explains Bernard Gui (ca. 1261–1331), author of one of the most influential and enduring of the inquisitor's manuals, "but according to the private laws or privileges conceded to the inquisitors by the Holy See, for there is much that is peculiar to the Inquisition."[6]

It reveals something crucial about the inquisitor's cast of mind that the Inquisition maintained such meticulous and even boastful records. Every word uttered during interrogation, torture, and trial, every gasp and cry of the victim, were dutifully transcribed by a notary. Bookkeepers toted up the income from confiscations and fines as well as the expenditures for ropes, straw, and wood with which to burn those from whom the treasure had been taken. Since the inquisitors were utterly convinced that they were doing God's work, they collected and preserved the smoking-gun evidence of their own brutality and greed with unmistakable pride as well as an obsessive attention to detail.

The whole point of the Inquisition was to achieve a critical mass of terror by making examples of the men and women who dared to think for themselves, and thereby frightening the rest of the populace into abject compliance. Interrogation, torture, and trial were conducted in strict secrecy, and the inquisitors emerged into daylight only to sentence and punish the victims at the great public spectacle known as an auto-da-fé. But the whispered rumors about what went on in the cells and dungeons of the Inquisition—and the private fears of those whose loved ones had been seized, shackled, and taken away—amounted to a powerful weapon in the war on heresy. "When the Inquisition once laid hands upon a man, it never released its hold," writes Lea. "The Inquisition had a long arm, a sleepless memory, and we can well understand the mysterious terror inspired by the secrecy of its operations and its almost supernatural vigilance."[7]

So we will come to see that the Orwellian future described in *1984*—"Big Brother Is Watching You"—is actually rooted in the distant past. "Naming names," a hateful feature of both the Moscow show trials of the 1930s and the Communist witch-hunt in McCarthy-era America, actually began with the inquisitors, who regarded the confession of an accused heretic as unacceptable unless it included the names and whereabouts of fellow believers. Even the black dunce's cap used to humiliate prisoners at Abu Ghraib bears an unsettling resemblance to the *coroza* that was placed on the heads of the condemned before they were burned alive by the Spanish Inquisition.

So, too, did the Inquisition teach its successors how to use language to conceal their crimes and, at the same time, to inspire terror in their victims. Just as the inquisitors used the ornate Latin phrase *judicium secularum* (secular justice) to refer to torture on the rack and the wheel—and just as auto-da-fé (act of the faith) came to signify burning at the stake—mass murder in the Soviet Union was called "liquidation" and the extermination of six million Jews by Nazi Germany was called "the Final Solution." Even today, kidnapping a suspected terrorist and spiriting him away to a secret prison where he can be safely tortured is known as "extraordinary rendition" by our own intelligence services. When George Orwell coined the word *Newspeak* to describe a vocabulary of euphemism and misinformation—"War Is Peace, Love is Hate, Ignorance is Strength"—he was recalling yet another invention of the Inquisition.[8]

Who were these so-called heretics, and exactly what were their misdeeds? The men, women, and children who suffered and died at the hands of the Inquisition, as it turns out, did not do anything that we would recognize as a crime; they were guilty (if at all) of wrongful thoughts rather than wrongful acts. *Heresy*, after all, is derived from the Greek word for "choice," and one could be condemned as a heretic for choosing to believe something that the Church regarded as impermissible. Perhaps the best way to understand the function of heresy in the workings of the Inquisition is to borrow again from George Orwell's *1984*: heresy is the original "Thought Crime," and the agents of the Inquisition were the world's first "Thought Police."

"You are accused as a heretic," the inquisitor was instructed to say to the accused in Bernard Gui's handbook, "[because] you believe and teach otherwise than the Holy Church believes."[9] Since the official dogma of the Church was still being fine-tuned by various medieval popes, it was sometimes damnably hard for ordinary Christians to avoid heresy. Christian rigorists, apocalyptic theologians, cloistered women, and church reformers—all of whom thought of themselves as perfectly good Christians—were always at risk of arrest, torture, and death. "Nobody can understand the Middle Ages who has not clearly realized the fact," observes historian G. G. Coulton, "that men might be burned alive for contesting publicly and impenitently *any* papal decretal."[10]

The Inquisition slapped the deadly label of heretic on so many of its victims that the word ceased to have any real meaning. Women were tried and burned as witches simply because of their age, appearance, or personal eccentricities; the evidence against Joan of Arc, for example, included the fact that she dressed in men's clothing. The warrior-monks of the Knights Templar were denounced as heretics and persecuted by the Inquisition because, among other things, their vast wealth provoked the envy and avarice of a French king. Eventually, as we shall see, the maw of the Inquisition would be fed with the bodies of Jewish and Muslim converts to Christianity who were accused of lapsing into their old faiths. And Galileo was famously condemned as a heretic merely because he doubted that the sun revolved around the earth. "Even doubt was heresy," explains Henry Charles Lea. "The believer must have fixed and unwavering faith, and it was the inquisitor's business to ascertain this condition of his mind."[11]

The frantic search for heretics, as we shall see, took on the symptoms of collective paranoia. A woman of North African descent who had converted from Islam to Catholicism was denounced to the Spanish Inquisition as a false Christian merely because she was observed eating couscous at a family meal, and a young woman who had converted from Judaism suffered the same fate because she put on clean underwear on Saturdays. A woman with a facial mole, a bad temper, or no husband—or one who had the misfortune to live next door to someone whose household supply of beer had gone bad—was a likely candidate for arrest, torture, and burning as a witch. At certain ludicrous moments, a text rather than a human being— the Talmud, for example, and the writings of a Christian theologian—was put on trial on charges of heresy and then put to the flames in place of its long-dead authors.

Nor was death itself a refuge from the Inquisition. If an inquisitor had exhausted the local supply of living heretics, he might turn to the graveyard in search of new victims. Charges of heresy were brought against long-deceased men and women whose rotting corpses were dug up, put on trial, and then put to the flames. Since confiscation of a condemned heretic's land, goods, and money was a standard punishment for heresy, the Inquisition would seize the dead man's possessions from his children or grand-children, which is doubtless what inspired the inquisitors to put defunct heretics on trial in the first place. The fact that the heir of a dead heretic was himself a good Christian was wholly irrelevant to the Inquisition; indeed, if he happened to serve the Church as a monk or priest, he would be stripped of his church offices as well as his inheritance.

The appetite of the inquisitors for new victims was so insatiable that they invented heresies where none existed. The so-called heresy of the Free Spirit, a fifteenth-century cult whose adherents were said to engage in all manner of sexual adventure because they regarded themselves as sinless, is now thought to have been a figment of the inquisitorial imagination rather than a real religious community. Precisely because the inquisitors relied on manuals and handbooks that included lists of leading questions to be put to accused heretics, they suggested the answers they wanted to hear from their exhausted, brutalized, and terrified victims. How many women under torture, when asked whether the Devil had ever appeared to them in the guise of a black cat, conducted them to a nighttime orgy, and demanded that they kiss his private parts, were quick to answer yes, thus telling their torturers exactly what they expected and wanted to hear?

Here we find what is arguably the single most dangerous idea that the medieval Inquisition bequeathed to the modern world. "Heretics were not only burned," writes historian Norman Cohn, "they were defamed as well." And these two acts were intimately linked. As the inquisitors grasped, and as history has repeatedly proved, it is far easier for one human being to torture and kill another if he has convinced himself that the victim is not really human at all.[12]

The war on heresy was a total war, and no weapon in the arsenal of the Inquisition was left unused. Among the ugliest was a psychological ploy that the inquisitors used with unmistakable zeal and a certain relish. Lest the accused heretics be viewed with pity and compassion as good Christians who had been wrongly condemned by the Inquisition, they were officially denounced as the vile and wretched minions of Satan, far beyond sympathy or salvation. Thus, for example, the victims were charged not only with the crime of false belief but also with every act of wretched excess that the human imagination is capable of conjuring up.

Ironically, the very same charges that had been laid against the first Christians by their persecutors in imperial Rome were now applied to the Christian rigorists who caught the attention of the Inquisition. Their sober religious services were falsely characterized as "erotic debauches" in which fathers coupled with their daughters and mothers with their sons. The babies who were conceived at such orgies, it was said, were tortured to death and then eaten in a ritual meal that was a diabolical imitation of the Eucharist. Such outrages and excesses existed only in the perverse imaginations of certain friar-inquisitors, but they eventually found their way into one of the papal decrees that served as the charter of the Inquisition.[13]

Sexual slander against accused heretics was so common that we might conclude that the friar-inquisitors protested too much when they charged their victims with sexual excess. The incestuous orgy was a favorite theme, used indiscriminately against heretics of both genders and all religious persuasions, but the accusers' imaginations wandered to even darker corners. Women charged with witchcraft were assumed to kiss the backside and private parts of the Devil before engaging in sexual acrobatics with him. The pious members of the Knights Templar were accused of engaging in homoerotic rituals of initiation and acts of organized homosexuality. *Bugger,* a word still used today to refer to anal intercourse, is derived from a term used in the Middle Ages to identify the Cathars, who were wrongly believed to prefer any kind of sexual activity that did not lead to conception.

Imaginary sexual perversion of various kinds may have titillated the inquisitors, but the routine and unrelenting slander of accused heretics served another purpose as well. The Inquisition understood the danger that its victims might be seen by their friends, neighbors, and relations as pitiable rather than hateful. So the inquisitors sought to convey the impression that they were engaged in a life-and-death struggle against "a monstrous, antihuman conspiracy" under the control of "a devoted underground elite," and that the Inquisition itself had been "called into existence to meet a national emergency," all of which will strike a shrill but familiar note to contemporary readers. Heretics were nothing less than "traitors to God," according to Pope Innocent III (1160/61–1216), and "thieves and murderers of souls," according to Pope Innocent IV (d. 1254). Once the war on heresy was understood as an apocalyptic struggle between good and evil, God and Satan, then the end plainly justified the means—and no means were ruled out.[14] "When the existence of the Church is threatened, she is released from the commandments of morality," declared the Bishop of Verden in a tract published in 1411. "[T]he use of every means is sanctified, even cunning, treachery, violence, simony, prison, death."[15]

So the dehumanization of accused heretics, which provided a theological rationale for their extermination, was an early and constant theme of inquisitorial propaganda. Heresy, according to Innocent III, "gives birth continually to a monstrous brood" that "passes on to others the canker of its own madness." The men and women accused of "heretical depravity," according to the cant of the Inquisition, were not human beings at all but rather "harmful filth" and "evil weeds," and it was the duty of the inquisitors to cleanse Christendom by eliminating them as one would dispose of other forms of waste or infestation.[16] "[They] were the wolves in the sheepfold," a Spanish priest wrote of the Muslim *conversos* in 1612, "the drones in the beehive, the ravens among the doves, the dogs in the Church, the gypsies among the Israelites, and finally the heretics among the Catholics."[17]

Here is yet another linkage between the Inquisition of the distant past and the crimes against humanity that have taken place within our living memory. The better angels of our nature inspire us to look into the eyes of another human being and see a kindred spirit and, according to both Genesis and Michelangelo, the face of God. "When you visualized a man or woman carefully, you could always begin to feel pity—that was a quality God's image carried with it," writes Graham Greene in *The Power and the Glory.* "Hate was just a failure of the imagination."[18]

It is also true, however, that some men and women are capable of acting with appalling cruelty once they convince themselves that their victims are filth or vermin or, at best, miscreants with some incurable disease or congenital defect that compels them to serve the Devil rather than God. That's how the Inquisition instructed good Christians to look on those it condemned as heretics, and it is the same moral and psychological stance that has always served as a necessary precondition for crimes against humanity. Not coincidentally, Zyklon B, the poison used to kill Jewish men, women, and children in the gas chambers at Auschwitz, was the brand name of an insecticide.

Strictly speaking, the Inquisition exercised its authority only over professing Christians who had deviated from whatever the Church defined as its
current dogma. This explains why the only Jews and Muslims who fell into
the hands of the Spanish Inquisition were those who had formally converted to Christianity after Ferdinand and Isabella offered them the choice
between conversion and expulsion from Spain. Jews who refused to convert were expelled from Spain in 1492, the year that the same monarchs
famously sent Columbus on his fateful voyage across the Atlantic. Since
the inquisitors followed the conquistadores, however, a Jewish or Muslim
converso who managed to escape the Inquisition in the Old World was at
risk of torture and burning in the New World, too. The first Jews to reach
North America, in fact, were some two dozen refugees from Brazil who
were fleeing the long reach of the Inquisition.

Accused heretics who confessed to their crime, recanted their false beliefs, and managed to survive the "penances" imposed by the Inquisition
would be welcomed back into the arms of the Mother Church, or so insisted the pious friar-inquisitors. The official theology of the Inquisition
held that the inquisitors never actually punished anyone; they merely corrected the errors of repentant Christians who had strayed from the Church
and then freely returned to its maternal embrace. Thus, for example, a convicted heretic who had managed to escape from an inquisitorial prison is
described in an inquisitor's handbook as "one insanely led to reject the salutary medicine offered for his care." By contrast, the truly repentant Christian was likened to a patient who took his medicine by performing without
protest all the penances that had been prescribed by the "good doctors" of
the Inquisition.[19]

The Inquisition in practice was never as benign as it advertised itself to
be. Confession was required before the sin of heresy could be forgiven, for
example, and yet confession alone was never enough. The confession had
to be abject, earnest, and complete, which meant that it had to include the
betrayal of others, including spouses and children, friends and neighbors.
That's why the naming of names was rooted in both the theology and the
psychology of the Inquisition—the will of the victim to resist had to be utterly crushed, his or her sense of self eradicated, and the authority of the

interrogator acknowledged as absolute. The best evidence that an accused man or woman has been utterly defeated, then as now, is the willingness to betray a loved one or a trusting friend.

At its darkest moment, the Inquisition developed a new and even more dangerous notion: an obsession with "purity of blood" rather than "purity of faith." With the adoption of a Spanish law that distinguished between those who had been born into Christianity and those who had converted to the faith, it was no longer sufficient or even possible for an accused heretic to merely confess and repent the sin of heresy. Under the Spanish Inquisition, the *conversos* were regarded as ineradicably tainted by their Jewish or Muslim origins, a fact that could not be changed by confession, no matter how many names were named. Thus did the Strictures of the Purity of Blood, as a Spanish decree of 1449 was known, prefigure the Law for Protection of German Blood and Honor of 1935, Nazi Germany's formal declaration of war on its Jewish citizenry. The "machinery of persecution," as the Inquisition has been called by historian R. I. Moore, was now driven by race rather than religion.[20]

The Spanish Inquisition marked the zenith of the inquisitorial enterprise and thus the beginning of its long and slow decline. But it also signaled a sea-change in the inner meaning of the Inquisition and its significance in history. Once the Inquisition began to condemn people to death because of the blood that ran in their veins, the groundwork was laid for crimes against humanity that would be committed long after the last inquisitor had donned his hood and uttered the tortuous Latin euphemism—*debita animadversione puniendum* or "he is to be duly punished"—that translated into burning at the stake. By the mid–nineteenth century, the last grand inquisitor was dead and gone, and his successor in the twentieth century was the nameless and faceless man in a field-gray uniform who dropped the canisters of Zyklon B into the gas chambers at Auschwitz.[21]

Remarkably, the Inquisition has always had its defenders and its deniers, then and now. The most stubborn among them insist that it is more accurate to speak of *two* inquisitions, "one uppercase and one lowercase," as historian Henry Ansgar Kelly puts it. The lowercase inquisition consisted of a random assortment of persecutors who were at work at various times and places across six centuries, sometimes as freebooters under papal commission and sometimes as apparatchiks in a fixed bureaucracy like the notorious one in Spain. By contrast, they insist that the uppercase Inquisition is purely mythic, the collective invention of Protestant reformers, Enlightenment philosophers, Russian novelists, and English propagandists, all of whom contributed to the fanciful notion that the Inquisition was, according to Kelly's sarcastic description, "a central intelligence agency with headquarters at the papal curia."[22]

The apologists also urge us to make a lawyerly distinction between the way the Inquisition was designed to work on paper and the atrocities that took place behind the closed doors of its tribunals and torture chambers. They correctly point out that the workings of the Inquisition were subject to canon law and papal oversight; indeed, the men who designed and ran the Inquisition were obsessed with rules and regulations, and that's why the inquisitors consulted the handbooks and manuals in which standard operating procedures were prescribed in meticulous detail. The duration of torture was carefully measured out by degrees: the second degree of torture, for example, was to be applied no longer than it took to recite an Ave Maria. If a sadistic or overzealous inquisitor sometimes disregarded the rules and tortured a victim to death, the apologists insist, we should regard any such incident as an aberration—a crime against the Inquisition, in other words, rather than a crime of the Inquisition.

Finally, the apologists caution us against imposing our values on the conduct of men and women who lived long ago. Criminal defendants enjoyed few rights and privileges in the Middle Ages, they point out, and torture was a commonplace in the secular courts. Why, then, should we be surprised to find that the ecclesiastical courts were no less brutal when it came to those accused of the crime of heresy? They ask us to overlook the question of whether it is ever morally defensible to punish someone for holding a private belief, and they encourage us to credit the Inquisition for following its own dubious rules. Thus, for example, some modern scholars are willing to argue that the victims of the Inquisition were afforded "legal justice" by their tormentors even if the friar-inquisitors failed to supply any measure of "moral justice."[23]

To this day—and, in fact, never more so than in recent years—a state of tension exists between "the Inquisition" as it was chronicled by historians like Henry Charles Lea and "the inquisition" as it has been reinterpreted by the revisionists who came after him. As we confront the crimes that were committed in the name of God, and as we look beyond the friar-inquisitors to their more recent imitators, we will come to see that the Inquisition with a capital *I* is not only a fact of history but also an urgent moral peril to the American democracy.

"It's a remarkable piece of apparatus," says a character in Franz Kafka's *In the Penal Colony*, a boastful prison official who is describing a machine for torture and execution supposedly still in use in some nameless tropical backwater at the turn of the twentieth century.

The condemned men in Kafka's story are never told what crime they are accused of committing. "There would be no point in telling him," explains the official to a foreign visitor. "He'll learn it on his body." Nor are they afforded an opportunity to defend themselves against the accusation: "My guiding principle is this: Guilt is never to be doubted." Once the prisoner is strapped into the elaborate machine, the crime is literally inscribed into his flesh by the mechanical operation of a set of long, sharp needles. A man who defies the authority of the jailors, for instance, is marked with the words "Honor Thy Superiors." The inscription is so ornate in its calligraphic flourishes that it requires six hours to complete and inevitably costs the man his life, but not before he finally realizes what words are being carved into his flesh and thereby learns why he was condemned in the first place. "Enlightenment," the prison official concludes in a moment of unwitting self-parody, "comes to the most dull-witted."[24]

The artful device on display in Kafka's story is an appropriate symbol of the Inquisition, as Kafka himself surely intended it to be, and for reasons that will become increasingly clear as we move forward in history from the origins of the Inquisition to its reverberations in our own world. Like the bewildered defendant whose ordeal is depicted by Kafka in *The Trial*— "You can't defend yourself against this court, all you can do is confess"—the victims of the Inquisition were subjected to the workings of an all-powerful tribunal that operated with "an Alice-in-Wonderland arbitrariness." Indeed, Kafka can be regarded as the poet laureate of the Inquisition, if only because its absurdities and grotesqueries—as it was conceived in the febrile imaginations of the first inquisitors, and as it actually operated in the here and now—can aptly be described as "Kafkaesque."[25]

"[T]he story of the Inquisition reads," observes G. G. Coulton, "sometimes like a tale from a madhouse." Yet we cannot dismiss the Inquisition as a figment of anyone's imagination. It is not merely a myth fabricated by parlor propagandists and the writers of bodice rippers, as its modern apologists argue, nor can we comfort ourselves with the argument that the flesh-and-blood inquisitors never really succeeded in carrying out the master plan for persecution that is writ large in the inquisitor's handbooks. Men, women, and children in the thousands and tens of thousands suffered and died at the hands of the pious friar-inquisitors, and the death toll is immeasurably greater if we include the latter-day inquisitors who followed in their footsteps, and still do.[26]

The Inquisition has imprinted itself on the history of Western civilization in ways that are sometimes overlooked but can never be eradicated. To be sure, it was not the first or only tribunal that acted cruelly and capriciously in the name of "Mercy and Justice," but the routine use of torture under the imprimatur of the Church has been blamed for encouraging the secular authorities across western Europe to do the same. The fact that England and the Netherlands far outpaced Spain, Portugal, and Italy in commerce and technology has been explained by some historians as yet another unintended consequence of the Inquisition; after all, enterprise and invention proved to be more vigorous in places that were beyond the reach of the inquisitor and "the power of fanaticism to warp the intellect of the most acute," according to Henry Charles Lea.[27]

The story of the Inquisition, however, is also the story of flesh-and-blood human beings who suffered at the hands of men whose fears and fantasies were acted out in real life. We know them by name: Jerónima la Franca is the woman who was condemned as a heretic because she ate couscous, Arnaud Assalit is the bookkeeper who added up the cost of ropes, straw, and wood for burning a heretic alive, and Arnauld Amalric is the abbot who, when asked by the soldiers under his command how to tell a Christian from a heretic, answered by issuing the chilling command: "Kill them all; God will know his own."[28]

Into the world where they lived and died, we now go.

2.

THE CATHAR KISS

Kill them all; God will know his own.

ARNAULD AMALRIC,
Abbot of Cîteaux, 1209

At Christmastide in the year 1022, the townsfolk of Orléans in the Loire Valley of France were distracted from their seasonal revelries by an ugly rumor. A strange and dangerous cult had supposedly been detected among the highest-ranking citizens of the town, and the initiates were said to be practicing self-invented rites and rituals that included incestuous sex orgies, infanticide, and cannibalism. The suspects included monks and nuns, gentlemen and ladies, as many as twenty in all, and even a priest named Stephen who had once served as confessor to the queen of France.

The cult at Orléans, as we learn from an obscure medieval text, had been uncovered in the course of a covert investigation by a Norman aristocrat called Arëfast. When word of their heretical beliefs and hateful practices reached the self-appointed spy, Arëfast posed as a potential convert in order to infiltrate and expose the heretics. Arëfast listened attentively to their whispered teachings, "all the time availing himself of the protection afforded by Christ and the Church," as he insisted on pointing out, "praying, making the sign of the cross, and receiving the holy communion every day." Thus shielded from the taint of heresy, he discovered for himself their dark secrets and then hastened to tell what he knew to the church authorities.[1]

The cultists, as we might call them today, embraced an eccentric set of beliefs and practices that were wholly at odds with the dogma of the Roman Catholic church. They claimed to possess a body of secret knowledge—or gnosis—that was miraculously conveyed from one to the other by the laying on of hands. Once initiated into the cult, they were able to discern that the teachings of the Church were based on an erroneous reading of the Bible: "Christ was not born of the Virgin Mary. He did not suffer for men. He was not really buried in the sepulcher and was not raised from the dead." Thus filled with the "Holy Spirit," they rejected all the sacraments of the Church, including baptism, ordination of priests, confession and penance, and the Eucharist. And they convinced themselves that they were cleansed of sin and thus privileged to dine not on the body and blood of Christ like ordinary Christian believers but on a diet of "heavenly food."[2]

Exactly what was the "heavenly food" that took the place of the wafer and the wine for the cultists of Orléans? We do not and cannot know what metaphorical meanings were attached to the phrase as it was used by the initiates, but according to a monk named Paul, who composed an account some fifty years after the events he described, what passed their lips was a "devilish viaticum made of the ashes of a murdered baby." Nor did the monk stop there. Paul insisted that the ritual slaughter of a baby and the cannibalistic communion were followed by a sexual free-for-all in which each of the male participants in the orgy "grabbed whatever woman came to hand" and freely satisfied his own sexual appetites, no matter how cruel or bizarre.[3]

Such was the report that eventually reached the king of France, Robert the Pious, and his consort, Queen Constance, and they were sufficiently alarmed by these wild rumors to convene a council of bishops at Orléans to confront and condemn the heretics. The accused men and women were brought in irons to the Church of the Holy Cross, where the king, queen, and bishops were waiting to hear the evidence and pass judgment. Arëfast was among the defendants, and it was only during the trial that he revealed himself to be an undercover agent and a friendly witness for the prosecution. Confronted with Arëfast's damning testimony, the accused are said to have admitted the charges against them, but they refused to renounce their own cherished beliefs. Indeed, they continued to insist that they alone possessed the divine truth as revealed to them in angelic visions, whereas the Church relied only on "the fictions of carnal men, scribbled on animal skins."[4] "Do with us what you will," they affirmed. "Now we see our king reigning in heaven—He will raise us to His right hand in triumph."[5]

The self-appointed inquisitors were happy to oblige. A bishop stripped the vestments from those of the defendants who held clerical rank, and all the accused were condemned to death. Only a single clerk and a single nun, who recanted at the last moment, were spared. So agitated was the crowd that King Robert stationed the queen herself by the doors "to prevent the common people from killing them inside the church." Even so, someone in the crowd raised his staff and struck out the eye of the queen's former confessor as the convicted heretics were herded by armed guards to the place of execution. The condemned heretics, apparently convinced that their salvation was at hand, are said to have laughed out loud in the face of imminent death.[6]

The execution itself was an improvised affair. The condemned men and women were locked inside a cottage that stood outside the town walls, and the cottage was set afire and allowed to burn to the ground. Paul reports that the "evil ashes"—that is, the remains of the babies who supposedly had been killed and eaten during the cult's orgiastic rituals—were tossed on the flames, too. At last, on the order of the bishop, the bones of one of the cultists, who had died of natural causes before he could be tried and burned alive, were exhumed and dumped into the pits where garbage and human waste were buried.

The trial and execution of the heretics at Orléans took place more than a century before the Inquisition was called into formal existence by the Church. But the incident allows us to see how the mere existence of freethinking men and women was regarded by the guardians of law and order as an intolerable threat, and how brutally and cynically the authorities were willing to act in suppressing any belief they regarded as deviant. We can see, too, that many of the moving parts of the inquisitorial machine were already available for use. The whispered accusations, the testimony of infiltrators and informers, the high drama of the trial, the frenzy of the crowd, the burning of condemned heretics, both dead and alive, the improbable beliefs and practices attributed to the cultists—and even the slanderous charges of ritual murder and incestuous sex orgies—will be seen again and again in the long, terrible history of the Inquisition itself and its successors in later times.

Exactly here we begin to see the footprints of the rude beast that was already slouching toward Bethlehem.

The self-invented gnostics of Orléans, as it turns out, were hardly the only people in medieval Christendom who were inspired to borrow or invent a shiny new set of religious beliefs and practices to supplement those provided by the Roman Catholic church. Contrary to its own shrill claims, the Church was never "catholic" in the literal sense of the word: "one Universal Church of the faithful, out of which there is absolutely no salvation." To the distress of the pope and the princes of the Church, the men and women who lived under their authority were always ready to embrace some rich and strange ideas of their own. To understand the Inquisition at all, it must be seen as a panicky and ultimately futile effort to establish a monopoly in religion rather than as an effort to preserve one that already existed.

Here we find not only the starting point of the Inquisition but also the great besetting irony of *all* religion. The core idea of monotheism is the sure conviction that there is only One True God and only one proper way to worship the deity. Yet none of the three great monotheisms—Judaism, Christianity, and Islam—has ever managed to win the hearts and minds of its own followers, much less the whole world. The gray matter of *Homo sapiens* seems to be hardwired to produce a rich flowering of religious ideas and images, and no amount of brute force has ever been able wholly to suppress them, not now and not at any point since the first Cro-Magnon shaman painted the first totemic image of a bison on a cave wall.[7]

The competition among various strains of true belief in medieval Christianity was sometimes almost comical. The Roman Catholic church and the Eastern Orthodox church, for example, each claimed to be the sole source of religious authority in Christendom, and each church condemned the beliefs and practices of the other as heretical. At one highly theatrical moment in 1054, a papal legate acting in the name of Pope Leo IX, and

Michael Cerularius, the patriarch of Constantinople, pronounced decrees of excommunication against each other. The reciprocal excommunications marked the beginning of the Great Schism between the eastern and western churches, and the decrees were not formally rescinded until 1965.

Nor was the Great Schism merely a game of theological tit-for-tat. A charge of heresy, as we shall see, was always a convenient excuse for bloodshed. The knights of the Fourth Crusade and their Venetian allies, for example, sailed from Italy in 1202 with the pious goal of taking the city of Jerusalem back from its Muslim overlords. But the holy warriors turned instead toward Constantinople, the seat of Eastern Orthodoxy, and the blood they spilled belonged to their fellow Christians. Of course, the crusaders were taught to regard the populace of Constantinople as inauthentic Christians, and the former's religious bigotry served the ulterior motives, both political and commercial, of the men who sent them into battle in the first place.

"For three days the Venetians and Crusaders rushed through the streets, raping, killing and pillaging," writes Karen Armstrong in *Holy War: The Crusades and Their Impact on Today's World,* pointing out that Christian women and children were among the casualties and that the victims of rape included cloistered nuns. "In the great basilica of St. Sophia, drunken soldiers tore down the silk hangings and trampled the sacred books and icons underfoot, and a prostitute sat on the Patriarch's throne singing bawdy songs."[8]

Yet the rape of Constantinople during the Crusades is only one particularly outrageous example of the open conflicts that raged within medieval Christianity. The Roman Catholic church itself was in a state of constant moral and political crisis. Popes contended with kings and emperors over the right to govern the nations of Europe, and the Church was repeatedly shaken by scandals that boiled up in its inner circles. Critics both inside and outside the Church complained about the arrogance and opulence of the pope and the high clergy, the appalling ignorance of parish priests, and the carnality and corruption that could be found in all ranks. All of these stresses and strains played a role in triggering the authoritarian impulse that found its ultimate expression in the Inquisition.

The sorry state of affairs in the Church, in fact, invited the criticism and dissent that eventually came to be called heresy. Holy oil, relics of dead saints, and indulgences—promises on paper that the bearer would be relieved of suffering in the afterlife—were sold for hard cash by avaricious bishops, and at least one priest was accused of putting down penances as bets in a game of dice. Popes as well as priests were known to keep wives or mistresses, or both at once. Even cloistered monks and nuns were rumored to take each other as lovers. Perhaps the best evidence that such sins were actually being committed behind the closed doors of the convents is the fact that the bishops of the Fourth Lateran Council in 1215 found it necessary to specifically forbid them.

No one in the Church openly defended such sexual adventures, of course, but other practices and privileges were equally off-putting to its more pious congregants. Popes, cardinals, and archbishops dressed in silks and other fine fabrics and anointed themselves with rare perfumes; they presided over the rites of the Church in bejeweled vestments, and they collected artifacts and ornaments of gold and silver, ivory and gemstone. Like the nobles whom they aped, they resided in mansions and palaces, lived off the labor of serfs who toiled on lands owned by the Church, engaged in the pleasures of the hunt, and dined at tables where the food and drink were rich and abundant. At a time when hunger and hard labor were the common fate of the peasantry and the urban poor, the men who held themselves up as the moral exemplars of Christendom resembled Herod more than Christ.

"Dumb dogs who can no longer bark, men who will do anything for money, zealous in avarice, lovers of gifts, seekers of rewards" is how Pope Innocent III (1160/61–1216) described the clergy of Narbonne in southern France, ground zero of the Inquisition. "The chief cause of all these evils is the Archbishop of Narbonne, whose god is money, whose heart is in his treasury, who is concerned only with gold."[9]

The lower clergy, by contrast, tended to be as poor, and as poorly educated, as their parishioners. "The ignorance of the priests," complained an English archbishop in 1281, "precipitates the people into the ditch of error." A French bishop addressed the Council of Vienne in 1311 with his own complaints about the "contemptible persons of abject life, utterly unworthy in learning and morals," who populated the priesthood. From their "execrable lives and pernicious ignorance," he insisted, "infinite scandals arise."

Indeed, the clergy were so contemptible, according to the French bishop, that "the lay folk hold the priests as viler and more despicable than Jews."[10]

If the common clergy were as sinful as their bishops believed them to be, then we should not be surprised at the impiety of their parishioners. "With Sunday," complained one medieval chronicler, "reigneth more lechery, gluttony, manslaughter, robbery, backbiting, perjury, and other sins, more than reigned all the week before."[11] The theological illiteracy of ordinary men and women, in fact, was the stuff of pointed joke-telling even in the Middle Ages. According to one disapproving Dominican friar, a pious traveler in the English countryside, encountering a shepherd in service to the lord of the local manor, asked the shepherd whether he "knew the Faith," to which the shepherd quickly and stoutly assented.

"Do you know the Father, the Son, and the Holy Ghost?" the traveler persisted.

"The father and the son I know well, for I tend their sheep, but I know not that third fellow," the shepherd answered. "There is none of that name in our village."[12]

Although a Dominican cleric might tell jokes about an unschooled shepherd, the fact is that the common folk of Christendom led far richer spiritual lives than their confessors suspected. As practiced in Europe during the High Middle Ages, in fact, Christianity can be seen as a thin veneer over the far older folkways still cherished by ordinary men and women, who might go through the motions at the parish church and then seek other comforts when the priest was not watching. Joan of Arc, among the most famous victims of the Inquisition, boasted to her interrogators that "I learned my Pater and Ave and Creed from my mother," but she also conceded that the women of her village sought the intervention of the "Fairy Ladies" who were thought to haunt an ancient and gnarled tree in the nearby countryside. The water from a spring near the tree, she allowed, was believed to cure those who were sick with fever. "I have seen girls hanging garlands on the boughs of that tree," she confessed, "and I have sometimes done so with them."[13]

Indeed, the medieval Church, as the self-appointed guardian of theological law and order, was constantly at war with the imaginings and desires of its own congregants. Consider, for example, the delights and distractions offered by the wandering poets and singers known as troubadours, a commonplace of countless romance novels and adventure movies set in the Middle Ages. Like entertainers in every age, they sought to amuse rather than instruct their audiences, and the songs they composed and performed were regarded by the Church as scandalous and sinful. Famously, the troubadours celebrated the love of a knight in shining armor for his "lady fair"—but the lady was not necessarily his wife and might even be somebody else's wife, as in the tale of Lancelot's love affair with Guinevere in the Arthurian legend. For that reason, the Church condemned the chivalric traditions of feudal Europe—and the whole notion of "courtly love," which had seized the imagination of both lords and ladies and the general populace—as "a form of wanton paganism."[14]

To counter the unwholesome influence of the troubadours, and to divert the ardor of their audiences into safer channels, the Church was perfectly willing to invent new traditions of its own. The medieval Church had not yet signed off on the final draft of its own dogma, and its theologians continued to debate the fine points of its rituals, sacraments, and theology. Thus, for example, the Church introduced a newfangled cult in the eleventh century: the Virgin Mary was offered as an object of adoration in place of the sexually desirable and available woman who figured in the songs of the troubadours. Only in 1050 or so did the familiar and beloved Ave Maria—"Hail Mary, full of grace . . ."—begin to appear in the breviaries of pious Catholics as a specific antidote to the "lady fair" and her knight-suitors.

The shifting ground on which the Roman Catholic church was built would embarrass the efforts of the Inquisition to draw the line between orthodoxy and heresy. "There were important questions which had not yet been definitively answered," explains historian W. L. Wakefield, "areas of uncertainty in which were encountered religious ideas of which it was not possible to say: 'To be a Christian, you must hold this belief'; or 'If you believe that, you are not a Christian.'" Yet, as we shall see, the Church was never reluctant to define the outer limits of correct belief, and the question of whether an otherwise pious man or woman stood on the right or wrong side of the line would turn out to be, quite literally, a matter of life and death.

The unsettled state of Christendom in the years leading up to the Inquisition only encouraged an upwelling of exotic beliefs and practices. At Le Mans in 1116, a charismatic preacher known to us as Henry the Monk succeeded in attracting spirited crowds (and in scandalizing both the clergy and the gentry) by calling on wealthy women to throw off their jewelry and by inviting young men to take prostitutes as wives. At about the same time in Antwerp, a man called Tanchelm endeared himself to his followers by distributing wine and entertaining them with a theatrical style of preaching. Tanchelm liked to dress up in a golden robe, for example, and participate in a wedding ceremony with a statue of the Virgin Mary.

Even the ravings of an apparent lunatic might succeed in attracting a few credulous disciples. Sometime around the year 1000, a peasant named Leutard from the village of Vertus in Châlons-sur-Marne, awakened one morning from a shattering nightmare in which he had been tormented by bees that entered his body through his genitals and exited through his mouth, buzzing and stinging all the way and "bidding him to do things impossible to men." He interpreted the dream as a command to send away his wife and destroy the crucifix hanging in the local church, and he was inspired to preach to the villagers before drowning himself in a well.

Among the teachings that the local bishop found to be heretical was Leutard's insistence that good Christians need not pay tithes, a reminder that heresy was often perceived by the Church as a financial or political threat rather than merely a theological one. Modern scholars have debated whether Leutard's wild ideas were the result of a psychiatric disturbance called ergotism—a form of psychosis caused by ingesting a fungus that grows on rotting rye bread—but the medieval chroniclers blamed Leutard for infecting the populace with the plague of false belief, and they did not fail to notice that the diocese of Châlons-sur-Marne was later "struck three times by heresy."[15]

Such eccentrics may strike us as laughable, if not downright pathological, but charismatic preachers like Henry and Tanchelm, and even the village madman of Vertus, were answering the urgent and authentic spiritual needs of contemporaries who felt alienated from the Roman Catholic church. For some pious Christians, the high ceremony of the Roman Catholic mass, the rich vestments of the presiding clergy, and the opulence of the cathedrals in which the rite was conducted all seemed at odds with the ministry of Jesus as plainly depicted in the Bible. Indeed, the point was not lost on certain members of the clergy itself, including men like Francis of Assisi and Domingo de Guzmán, founders of the monastic orders that would come to play a crucial role in the Inquisition. Among the profound ironies of the Inquisition is that the Church itself can be charged with provoking some of the heresies that it punished with such rage and severity.

After all, how could the pope and the princes of the Church reconcile their imperial ways with the words of Jesus as reported in the Gospels? "Foxes have holes, and the birds of the air have nests, but the Son of man has nowhere to lay his head." And how could the bishops, comfortably settled in cities across Europe and living off rents, tithes, and taxes, explain why they did not follow the instructions that Jesus issued to the seventy disciples that he sent out into the world to preach? "Carry no purse, no bag, no sandals," says Jesus. "Whenever you enter a town and they receive you, eat what is set before you."[16]

Some of the most revolutionary ideas in medieval Christendom, in other words, erupted from the pages of the Bible, a fact that helps explain why the Church discouraged the unsupervised reading of the scriptures and the translation of the biblical text into languages that ordinary Christians could understand. The *via apostolica*—"the way of the apostles"—was embraced by Christians who recoiled at the corrupt and decadent spectacle that the Church presented and looked into their own Bibles to answer the question "What would Jesus do?" As it turned out, the provocative question was asked by popes as well as radical priests like Henry the Monk, and the answers brought the kettle of Christianity to a high boil.

The moral squalor that prompted an eccentric like Tanchelm of Antwerp to liken the Church to a brothel, for example, also prompted Pope Gregory VII (1020–1085) to address what he admitted to be a "foul plague of carnal contagion." The so-called Gregorian Reform established the strict rule of chastity for priests, thus putting an abrupt end to the tradition of clerical marriage that dated back to the beginnings of Christianity and reinforcing the biblical notion that human sexuality was not only sinful but demonic. At the same time, Pope Gregory VII sought to discourage the practice of simony, the buying, selling, and bartering of church offices for profit and political advantage. But the Gregorian Reform could not and did not curb the appetites of the clergy, high and low, for sexual pleasure and self-enrichment. Ironically, the stark contrast between the high-minded papal pronouncements and the sorry practices of the clergy only deepened the disappointment of spiritual seekers throughout Christendom and sharpened their appetite for more meaningful spiritual pursuits.[17] "A first cause for the recrudescence of heresy in the West," explains historian Malcolm Lambert, "lay in the expectations roused by Gregorian reform and its failure to fulfill them."[18]

Some of Pope Gregory's well-intended measures created new problems that a renegade priest might take it upon himself to solve. The pope, for example, issued a prohibition against marriage between men and women related by blood, a decree that was meant to curtail the sin of incest. As a practical matter, however, the new rule reduced the number of available marriage partners, especially in smaller towns and villages. And so, when Henry the Monk called on young men of good families to take harlots as wives—but only after he ritually cut their long hair, burned their alluring garments, and thus purified them—he was creating a fresh supply of marriage partners to replace the ones declared off-limits by Pope Gregory.

Sometimes the reformers inside and outside the Church embraced the same aspirations and the same approach to achieving them. Both Francis of Assisi (1181/82–1226) and Domingo de Guzmán (ca. 1170–1221) sought to purify themselves by taking strict vows of poverty and going out into the world as barefoot beggars to preach the Christian faith, all in imitation of Jesus and the disciples. The religious orders that they founded were embraced by the Church, and they were canonized as saints upon their deaths. A man named Peter Valdes (sometimes inaccurately rendered as "Waldo") (1140–ca. 1205) also vowed to pursue the *via apostolica,* but he suffered a very different fate. His followers were among the first targets of the Inquisition, and they remained within its crosshairs for centuries. By a further irony, the Inquisition was staffed by Dominicans and Franciscans, thus turning the imitators of Christ into the persecutors of their fellow Christians.

Valdes was living a privileged life in the town of Lyons in southern France when, like Francis and Dominic, he experienced a life-changing revelation. One day he passed a street minstrel who was singing about Saint Alexius, the son of a rich man who refused the marriage that had been arranged for him and chose instead a life of pious destitution. Thus inspired, Valdes settled a portion of his fortune on his baffled wife, installed his daughters in a convent, took a vow of poverty, and embarked on his own self-appointed ministry. During the famine of 1176, for example, he fed the poor at his own expense while, at the same time, eating only what was offered to him by others. His followers called themselves the Poor Men of Lyons and later, after the death of their founder about 1205, they came to be known as the Waldensians.

"They go about two by two, barefoot, clad in woolen garments, owning nothing, holding all things in common like the apostles," wrote Walter Map (ca. 1140–ca. 1209), an English delegate to the Third Lateran Council in 1179, "naked, following a naked Christ."[19] By yet another irony, the vivid but also unsettling phrase that Map used—"naked, following a naked Christ"—is borrowed from Jerome, the fifth-century church father who translated the Bible from its original Hebrew and Greek into Latin. Jerome himself was canonized for his efforts, but the translation of Holy Writ into vernacular languages soon came to be condemned by the Church as a threat to its monopoly on interpretation and instruction. The Waldensians, who imitated Jerome by preparing and using their own translations of various biblical texts, and who insisted on the right to preach even though they were not ordained as members of the clergy, were defying two of the prerogatives that the Church valued and protected with fierce determination. "If we admit them," concluded Walter Map, "we shall be driven out."[20]

Here we see the tripwire between the kind of Christian rigorism that the Church was willing to sanction and the kind that it insisted on punishing. The Franciscans and the Dominicans were chartered orders of the Roman Catholic church who lived and worked under the authority of the pope, but the Waldensians and others like them were outsiders whose true belief did not permit them to bend to the will of the Church. They all aspired to a reformed and purified Christianity, but Francis and Dominic were raised to sainthood while Peter Valdes and his followers were condemned as heretics.

By the year 1000, the so-called Dark Ages—a term coined by Petrarch to describe the isolation and ignorance of feudal Europe—were already coming to an end. Adventurers, merchants, pilgrims, and crusaders were beginning to explore the eastern reaches of Christendom and even more far-flung places in Africa and Asia. And when they returned to the cities of western Europe, they brought back a treasure trove of new ideas—arts and crafts, food and drink, texts and teachings. The emblematic example, which turns out to be wholly fanciful, is the tale of how a Venetian merchant-adventurer named Marco Polo reached the court of Kublai Khan in China in the thirteenth century and returned to Italy with the recipe for pasta. In fact, the phenomenon began a couple of centuries before Marco Polo, and the things that the travelers brought home were far more explosive than spaghetti.

Perhaps the single most exotic import into western Europe during the High Middle Ages was a variant of Christianity that appears to have originated in the tenth century in Bulgaria, a kind of theological no-man's-land that lay on the frontier between eastern and western Christendom. A Bulgarian village priest, whose adopted name was Bogomil ("worthy of the pity of God"), introduced his congregants, "newly and shakily converted from paganism," to his own peculiar version of Christian belief and practice. According to the medieval chroniclers whose writings have come down to us from the era of the Crusades, a few knights from France and Italy on crusade in the Holy Land encountered the followers of Bogomil in Constantinople or Macedonia and carried their strange new ideas back to western Europe like tainted fruit in their baggage.[21]

At the core of the so-called Bogomils' theology was a simple answer to the perennial question of why evil exists in a world supposedly created by a benign deity. The founder of Bogomilism taught that there were, in fact, two sources of divine power in the cosmos, one good and one evil. It's an idea that historians of religion call dualism, and it can be traced back through the gnostics of the early Christian era to the even older apocalyptic texts of Judaism and Christianity, such as the book of Daniel and the book of Revelation, and from these ancient texts all the way back to the earliest traditions of Zoroastrianism in far-off Persia. But, as often as the idea of dualism had been reworked over the millennia, it found a new and remarkable expression among the Bogomils.

The world as we know it, according to the Bogomils, was created not by God but by the fallen angel called Satan and, as a result, everything on earth is purely and irretrievably evil. Only upon the death of the human body does the soul locked within its fleshly prison rise to the spiritual realm and reunite with God. In the meantime, the Bogomils aspired to distance themselves as much as possible from the things of the world that Satan had made, including the making of babies and the consumption of food derived from animals that engage in sexual procreation. For that reason, not only sex itself but also the consumption of meat, eggs, cheese, and milk were declared taboo.

The Bogomils also understood that only a few devoted men and women were capable of such self-discipline while waiting to be liberated from earthly existence by their own deaths. So they expected the purest asceticism from only a small number of devotees who submitted to a ritual of initiation and then dedicated themselves to lives of rigorous self-denial. The rest of the rank-and-file of the Bogomils were free to live ordinary lives in the carnal world while supporting the initiates in their renunciations and devotions.

Fasting and celibacy, of course, were familiar to the Christian world, and the principal prayer of the Bogomils was the Pater Noster ("Our Father who art in heaven, hallowed be thy name . . ."), a commonplace of Christian practice. Other aspects of Bogomilism, however, pushed them outside the bounds of Christian orthodoxy. For example, they rejected the cross as a religious symbol precisely because it suggested that Jesus of Nazareth was a creature of flesh and blood who had been crucified by the Romans. The Bogomils, by contrast, refused to imagine that God had descended to a world created by Satan, inhabited a human body, and suffered the indignities of torture and death.

The Bogomils were an outgrowth of Christianity, but they rejected the authority of the church under whose jurisdiction they lived, that is, the Eastern Orthodox church. Like its counterpart in the West, the Orthodox Church in eastern Christendom condemned all religious dissidents as heretics, and the Bogomils were accused of various atrocities and outrages by their persecutors. One Christian monk who had secretly embraced Bogomilism was said to have installed (and used) a latrine behind the altar of a church in order to symbolize his contempt for its corruption and carnality. And, like almost every other persecuted faith, the Bogomils were said to engage in the sex orgies and rituals of infanticide and cannibalism that had once been charged by the Romans against the first Christians.[22]

"In the evening, they bring together young girls," wrote one eleventh-century Orthodox propagandist, "extinguish the candles so the light shall not be witness to their abominable deeds, and throw themselves lasciviously on the girls, each one on whomever first falls into his hands, no matter whether she be his sister, his daughter or his mother." Nine months later, "when the time has come for the unnatural children of such unnatural seed to be born," the babies were supposedly seized, drained of their blood, and then burned alive. Finally, the Bogomils were said to mix the blood and ash of the dead babies in basins "and so make an abominable drink."[23]

The Bogomils did no such thing, of course, and their only real offense was their rejection of the official theology of the Orthodox church. Ironically, the Bogomils rejected human sexuality and aspired toward the strictest spiritual purity, and yet they were defamed by their enemies as perverts and predators who indulged in every kind of sexual outrage. Indeed, it reveals something important about the workings of the human imagination that such perversions existed only in the minds of pious prelates obsessed with their own authority. The patriarchs and priests, who regarded themselves as the guardians of Christian morality, were perfectly capable of conjuring up the same sexual fantasies that would later find expression in the writings of the Marquis de Sade.

We cannot know exactly when, where, or how the strange new ideas of the Bogomils rooted themselves in western Europe, but the Church began to notice them as early as the eleventh century, first in Cologne and Liège and later in southern France. Bernard of Clairvaux (1090–1153), a Cistercian monk later canonized as Saint Bernard, was dispatched to admonish the followers of Henry the Monk, but he also came across some even more aberrant Christians. Bernard called them "weavers and Arians," the latter term borrowed from one of the earliest heresies of fourth-century Christianity, but the men and women who caught his attention may have been among the first practitioners of a new kind of Christianity that had been borrowed from the Bogomils.

The resort to antique vocabulary to describe the latest expression of the religious imagination in medieval Europe reminds us that the Church had always been quick to condemn every strain of Christianity that was not regarded as strictly orthodox. Thus, for example, the latest Christian dissidents to emerge in western Europe were also dubbed Manichaeans—a dualist faith from Persia that Augustine had first embraced and then condemned in the late fourth century—and Marcionites, an even older gnostic sect of early Christianity. At other times and places, the newest heretics in Christendom were called Bulgars, in recognition of their kinship with the Bogomils from far-off Bulgaria—the French version of the word is *boulgres* and its English counterpart is the root of the modern word *bugger*. As we shall soon see, the use of "bugger" as a term for anal intercourse is derived from the imagined sexual practices of the Bogomils and their kindred spirits.

The latest innovation in Christian belief was reflexively condemned by the Church as heresy. And once the new heretics came to the attention of the Church, they seemed to show up everywhere. They were called Publicans in northern Europe, *piphles* in Flanders, and *texerants* in France. They were variously known in Italy as *ribaldi, bulgari, insabbatati, paterini, policani, turlupini, speronisti, gassari, pisti,* and *pangenia.* None of these terms were flattering—*ribaldi,* for example, means "riff-raff." The town of Albi in southern France was wrongly thought to be the center of the new heresy, and so its practitioners came to be called Albigensians. But the name by which they are known best is *Cathari,* a Greek word, or its English equivalent, the Cathars.[24]

By whatever name we know them, the Cathars were destined to become the very first victims of another new phenomenon that was seen for the first time in the Middle Ages—the machine for the extermination of heretics known as the Inquisition.

Significantly, none of the names used by the Church to identify the new sect were actually used by the sectarians to describe themselves. Although they were denounced as enemies of Christianity by the medieval clergy—and a modern scholar like Norman Cohn still dismisses them as "exotic and non-Christian"— they insisted on calling themselves "Christians" or even "Good Christians." For convenience, however, and in deference to conventional usage, we will continue to call them by the name that their persecutors coined and used—the Cathars.[25]

The Cathars regarded themselves as "the *only* true Christians" and the guardians of "a stream of pure underground Christianity, often persecuted, but always surviving and reaching back to the days of the apostles." If they placed themselves in opposition to the Roman Catholic church, it was only because they came to believe that Catholicism was a corrupted version of Christianity whose clergy were "servants of Satan's Church." They read and revered the New Testament, although they preferred some scriptures above others: the book of Revelation, with its account of a "war in heaven" between God and Satan, was wholly consistent with their core theology; and the Gospel of John, a text in which the fingerprints of gnosticism have been detected by some modern readers, figured prominently in their ceremonies.[26]

Yet it is also true that the Cathars were apparently influenced by a fantastic variety of sources, ranging from ancient and obscure writings to the sermons of their own charismatic teachers and leaders. A direct linkage between the Cathars and the Bogomils can be seen in the fact that their readings included the *Interrogation of John* (also known as *Secret Supper*), a Bogomil text carried from Bulgaria to western Europe in about 1190. But they also seemed to know the Jewish apocalyptic writings, the mystical speculation and storytelling traditions that had attached themselves to the Bible among both Jews and Christians, and perhaps even more exotic texts that reflected the gnostic and Manichaean elements of their belief system.[27]

The dualist theology of the Cathars was almost surely borrowed from the Bogomils. They imagined the existence of two divinities, a benign one who reigns in heaven and a malign one who reigns on earth. They condemned the carnal world as a place of pure evil, and they longed only to be set free from their bodies so that their souls could return to the celestial paradise. They expressed their theology in the kind of folktales and fairy tales that every religion invents for itself, borrowing freely from Jewish and Christian texts and traditions, and adding a few twists and tweaks of their own. Indeed, we can glimpse a rich and playful religious imagination in the shards of Catharism that remain available to us despite the best efforts of the inquisitors to eradicate them.

The creation story as told in Genesis, for example, was reimagined in a Cathar text that depicts Adam and Eve as a pair of angels, pure and sexless, who are imprisoned by Satan in bodies fashioned of clay. Satan seduces them into the sin of sexual intercourse by creating a serpent out of his own spittle and then teaching Eve how to use her new and unfamiliar body by inserting the serpent's tail into her vagina in the primal act of sexual intercourse. Here we find the best evidence that the Cathars were *not* the sexual adventurers that the Church made them out to be. For the Cathars, then, the sexual anatomy of human beings is the work of the Devil in the most literal possible way.

The notion that the human body is the prison cell of a celestial spirit provided the rationale for the fundamental rite of Catharism, the *consolamentum,* an elaborate initiation ceremony based on the laying on of hands rather than water baptism. A copy of the Gospels was held over the initiate's head, and the person presiding over the ceremony laid his or her hands on the initiate's body. The first seventeen verses from the Gospel of John were read aloud, and the congregation joined in the recitation of the Lord's Prayer, their fundamental credo. The *consolamentum* ended with a ritual exchange of greetings, variously called the kiss of peace or "the Cathar kiss" (*osculum insabbatati*), and the public confession of sins by the congregants.[28]

The soul of a man or woman who received the *consolamentum,* the Cathars believed, would be permitted to cease its restless wandering from body to body and ascend once and for all to heaven. One who had been "consoled" was thereafter known as a *perfectus,* that is, a perfected one. But the liberation and ascension of the soul would take place only upon the death of the human body in which it was imprisoned, and so it was essential for the *perfectus* to refrain from any conduct that would corrupt the body for the rest of his or her mortal life. For that reason, the *perfecti* were called upon to lead lives of heroic asceticism, shunning not only sexual relations but every other occasion for taking pleasure in the things of this world.[29]

The heroic self-discipline practiced by the *perfecti* matched or exceeded the rigors of any other Christian ascetics. They were forbidden to indulge in sexual acts of any kind, and newly consoled *perfecti* who were married were expected to separate from their spouses. Even when they engaged in the ritual of laying-on hands during the *consolamentum,* for example, women touched men only by placing an elbow to a shoulder, and the kiss of peace was "given from man to man and woman to woman."[30]

A *perfectus* was forbidden to own property or to take the life of a living creature, human or animal. Three times a week, the *perfectus* was permitted to consume only bread and water, and three times a year, the fast was to last a full forty days. Even when they were permitted to eat, the *perfecti* were expected to shun any food that was the result of procreation, including meat, eggs, milk, cheese, and other animal products. (An exception was made for seafood because of the belief, held by both Catholics and Cathars in medieval times, that fish were "the product, not of coition, but of water itself.") As a result, one sign that a man or woman among the Cathars had achieved the exalted status of a "perfected one" was the physical appearance that results from near-starvation—pale skin and a gaunt aspect were signs of honor.[31]

By starving themselves into emaciation, the Cathars were making an unspoken claim to a more authentic Christianity than the kind practiced by the princes of the Church. When they renounced all attachments to the material world, including marriage and property, they sought to honor the pious Christian tradition of *via apostolica*—an aspiration that had eluded so many of the priests and prelates of the Roman Catholic church. The worst offense committed by these supposed heretics was their insistence on shaming the Church by setting a better example of Christian piety.

"They continue to be true imitators of the apostolic life, seeking not those things which are of the world, possessing no house, or lands, even as Christ had no property," wrote one alarmed German churchman in 1143. "'You, however,' they say to us, 'add house to house, field to field, and seek the things that are of this world.'" And the Cathars, alluding to the words of Jesus as quoted in the Gospel of Matthew, emphasized their ironic predicament: "We, the poor of Christ, who have no fixed abode and flee from city to city like sheep among the wolves, are persecuted as were the apostles and martyrs."[32]

Only the *perfecti,* however, were burdened with the full weight of lifelong sexual abstinence, fasting, poverty, pacifism, and veganism. The rest of the Cathars, known as "believers," were expected only to refrain as best they could from the worst excesses of their Catholic friends, neighbors, and relations and to cherish the hope that they themselves might find the strength to bear the full burden of the faith. The distinction between the *perfecti* and the believers—and the conviction of the Cathars that they alone were practitioners of authentic Christianity—was embodied in the ritualized greetings exchanged between them. "Pray God for me, a sinner, that he make me a good Christian and lead me to a good end," a believer would say, and the *perfectus* would answer: "May God be prayed that he may make you a good Christian."[33]

Indeed, the single most controversial feature of Catharism resulted from the constant and poignant longing of believers to become *perfecti* before they died. Many Cathar believers apparently delayed the *consolamentum* until illness, injury, or old age threatened to end their lives. By undergoing the ritual of initiation at the last possible moment, they would be required to bear the burdens of a *perfectus* only on their deathbeds, when they were no longer capable of succumbing to the temptations of carnal sin. Some Cathars, it appears, spent their final days and hours on a diet of sugared water; some literally fasted themselves to death. According to the accounts preserved by the Inquisition, one fortunate Cathar named Gentille D'Ascou was dead within six days of being "consoled," but a woman from the town of Coustassa reportedly lingered another three months. For the Cathars, it was the ultimate act of faith, but the critics of Catharism, then and now, have preferred to characterize the last rite of the Cathars, known as the *endura,* as "a form of suicide."[34]

"*Perfectus,*" like so many other terms applied to Catharism by its persecutors, was not used by the Cathars themselves; the title by which they referred to the *perfecti* was the humble phrase "Good Men." And the Good Men resembled nothing so much as the mendicant friars of the Franciscan and Dominican orders; they wore black robes and sandals of a distinctive style, and they traveled in pairs among the cities, towns, and villages to preach and teach the Catharist beliefs and to perform the ceremony of the *consolamentum.* One reason that Cathars were attracted to the craft of weaving as a livelihood—as Bernard of Clairvaux noticed early on—was that medieval weavers were itinerant workers who could move from place to place without attracting undue attention from the authorities.

The Cathar believers tended to be sober, law-abiding, inoffensive people, if only because one of the principles of Catharism, based on a close and literal reading of the Gospels, was that a Christian should not bear arms or take a life. Indeed, the Cathars were regarded as exemplary citizens throughout southern France, where they were tolerated and even admired by the local nobility and gentry. When a Catholic knight was commanded by a stern bishop to drive out the Cathars from his community, the knight courageously affirmed their admirable qualities: "We cannot," demurred the knight. "We have been reared in their midst. We have relatives among them, and we see them living lives of perfection."[35]

Nor was every Cathar the kind of religious fanatic that their enemies made them out to be. "Ardent believers married and begot children," writes historian Walter Wakefield, "no less frequently than their Catholic neighbours." The point is made in a poignant story told about a woman named Sybil whose infant daughter, Jacoba, had fallen ill and appeared to be close to death. The *consolamentum* was administered to the baby, and the *perfectus* cautioned Sybil against feeding her dying daughter now that she had been "consoled." The mother, however, could not bear to hear the cries of the hungry babe.[36] "[W]hen the Perfect and her husband left," we are told, "she gave Jacoba the breast, to the anger of her husband."[37]

The spread of Catharism may have owed something to the exalted stature of Cathar women, who were fully entitled to be "consoled" and thereby achieve the status of a *perfectus*. Here, too, was a point of contrast on which Catharism may have seemed far more appealing than Catholicism to the common folk of medieval Europe. Once elevated to the high rank of a perfected one, a woman was entitled to lead the congregation (but only if no male *perfecti* were present to do so) and to receive the ritual greeting afforded by believers to a *perfectus*. "No position in Catholicism, not even that of abbess," explains historian Malcolm Lambert, "offered the status which accrued to the woman who received the *consolamentum*."[38]

The Cathars may be seen as successful competitors for the hearts and minds of the Christian laity in medieval Europe rather than as polluters of Christianity. By the twelfth century, Catharism amounted to a rival church with its own hierarchy of bishops and priests and its own system of dioceses in southern France and elsewhere around western Europe. A certain highwater mark was reached sometime after 1167, when a mysterious figure from far-off Constantinople called *Papa* Nicetas—*papa* is a Latin term for a pope—convened a gathering of Catharist clergy from all over Europe at the French town of Saint-Félix-de-Caraman, where he persuaded them to accept the more rigorous form of dualism that was practiced in the birthplace of Bogomilism and rebaptized them into their newly invigorated faith.

Politics rather than theology is surely the best explanation for the fear and loathing with which the Church regarded the phenomenon of Catharism. The Supreme Pontiff in Rome was no more comfortable in coexisting with a Cathar pope than with the patriarch of Constantinople, and he resolved to bring the full weight of his authority down on the competitors who had appeared within his own realm and dared to call themselves Good Christians. The first weapon to be deployed, however, was a purely rhetorical one. The Cathars would be denounced and defamed before they would be destroyed, a strategy that represents our first glimpse of the brave new world of the Inquisition.

"Cathar" is most likely derived from the Greek word for cleansing or purification—as used, for example, in the English word *catharsis*—and the term grudgingly acknowledges that a man or woman who had been fully admitted into Catharism was regarded as having been purged of the inevitable corruption of a mortal life. It is also true, however, that the same root word, rendered as *katharoi* or "purified ones," had been used to identify at least two other heresies that afflicted the Church in its first centuries of existence, neither of which is plausibly linked with the Cathars of the twelfth century. Thus, the decision to label the Cathars with a word whose root refers to purity was darkly ironic, and the Church intended to bury rather than praise the Cathars.

So hateful was the Catholic reaction to Catharism, in fact, that one medieval propagandist came up with an even more damning explanation for the root meaning of the word. Perhaps, he proposed, it was derived from *cattus,* a Low Latin term for cat, because the Cathars were falsely accused of offering worship to a black cat, supposedly the incarnation of Satan, by kissing the satanic creature "abominably, under the tail." Thus did "the Cathar kiss" come to be characterized as the imagined practice of kissing the bare bottoms of the *perfecti* who presided over their worship services. And the same slander, as we shall see, was carried forward and applied to every other imaginary heresy that came to the attention of the Inquisition.[39]

Such free-associative sexual libel, as it turns out, is typical of the impulse of religious authoritarians to demonize all heretics by attributing to them every manner of outrage that a perverse human mind could imagine. Indeed, the impulse to equate theological error with sexual adventure starts in the Bible—"I will not punish your daughters when they play the harlot, nor your brides when they commit adultery," complains the cranky

Hebrew prophet Hosea, "for the men themselves go aside with harlots, and sacrifice with cult prostitutes"—and has never really ended. But it was raised to a fine art by the persecutors of heresy in medieval Europe, and the manuals and handbooks that guided the work of the Inquisition are spiced with perversities that existed only in the dirty minds of the priests and friars who were their authors.[40]

We have already seen that those burned as heretics at Orléans were condemned not only for practicing a kind of harmless amateur gnosticism but also for engaging in child murder, cannibalism, and orgiastic sex. Ironically, but also tellingly, the same charges had been laid against the first Christians by their adversaries in ancient Rome, where Christianity was similarly regarded as a secret cult whose members killed and ate babies in the course of the demoniacal sex orgies that served as their worship service. In fact, the sordid accusations appear to have been borrowed directly from the writings of Justin Martyr, a Christian apologist of the second century who recorded and then repudiated the libels of Christianity in pagan Rome. Historian Walter Lambert dismisses the lurid tales told about the Orléans sectarians by a medieval chronicler as nothing more than a "literary digression," but they can also be seen as something far worse—a willful lie and a habit of the persecutorial mind.[41]

Slander, as we shall see, was a powerful weapon in the crusade against religious liberty and diversity in medieval Europe and long after, and it was used by the Church to turn the Cathars' theology against them in clever if bizarre ways. The Catholic theologians who investigated the Cathars understood that they regarded the human body as a cage in which an angelic soul was held captive, and that the *perfecti* refrained from sexual intercourse in order to avoid the imprisonment of yet more souls through the act of procreation. The Cathars themselves aspired only to abstinence from sex, but Catholic persecutors with pornographic imaginations accused them of tolerating and even encouraging every kind of "nasty sexual aberration" that did not result in pregnancy, including anal intercourse, bestiality, and oral sex. Thus did *boulgre* become "bugger," and thus did "bugger" take on the connotation of anal intercourse.

The same twisted logic was applied to the Catharist attitude toward marriage. A *perfectus*, as we have seen, was expected to separate from his or her spouse after the ritual of initiation, or at least to refrain from sexual contact with the spouse. And, because marriage was likely to result in pro-creation, the Cathars did not regard a wedding as a sacred rite to be cel-ebrated within their church. But the enemies of Catharism convinced themselves that the Cathars actually favored extramarital sex, and they were accused of keeping women as concubines rather than sanctified wives and engaging in the sexual free-for-alls that were supposed to take place at the end of the *consolamentum* ceremony.

So, too, was the end-of-life ritual called the *endura* given strange and dire interpretations by the Cathars' enemies. A dying man or woman might be too sick or too weak to eat or drink, of course, and the ravages of a fi-nal illness surely made it easier for the religious true believer to fast until death. But the spiritual self-discipline of a dying Cathar was characterized by Catholic critics as an act of suicide, and it was later suggested that the *perfecti* who gathered around the bed of a dying Cathar would routinely speed the ritual to its desired end by choking or smothering the helpless man or woman, thus turning the *endura* into an act of sanctified murder.

Once set into flight, the imaginations of the inquisitors and the propa-gandists in their service reached ever greater altitudes of speculation and invention. Although the Cathars claimed to renounce the ownership of property, they were said to possess vast hoards of gold, silver, gemstones, and other treasures. They were even thought to have purloined the most sa-cred object in Christian tradition; the legendary Holy Grail was supposedly locked away in the secret treasury at the fortress of Montségur, a remote Cathar sanctuary high in the Pyrenees on the frontier between France and Spain. Here is yet another lie that reflects a certain obsession of persecutors across the ages—the notion that one's enemy has succeeded in amassing a secret fortune by means of deceit and devilry. Indeed, the looting of victims was a favorite technique of the Inquisition and its successors.[42]

All these accusations and speculations are dismissed by modern histori-ans. Principled theologians might even find themselves forced to concede that the Cathars had committed no crime except the one that every person commits in failing to embrace fully every jot and tittle of the dogma pre-scribed by the religious authorities. But the popes and princes who made war on Catharism were less interested in the fine points of theology than in getting and keeping wealth and power, and they were perfectly willing to make use of a willful lie as a lubricant for the consciences of the crusaders who were called upon to exterminate men, women, and children. Then as now, demonization of the victim is the necessary precondition for genocide.

Bernard of Clairvaux, as we have already seen, was sent to save the souls of Christians who had fallen under the influence of the charismatic preacher known as Henry the Monk, and Bernard's mission was expanded to include the newly detected heresy of Catharism, then only vaguely known as a sect of "weavers and Arians." When he arrived in Languedoc in 1145, ready to do battle with the minions of the Catharist church, his arsenal consisted only of his own earnest words of persuasion—Bernard's aim was to win the hearts and minds of errant Christians through preaching and public debate rather than by arrest, torture, and execution. "Heretics are to be caught," he reasoned, "not by force of arms but by arguments through which their errors may be refuted."[43]

Bernard himself was a mystic and an ascetic, and he was as unhappy about the excesses of the Church as any of the heretics who were his declared enemies. Like the *perfecti* of Catharism, Bernard's physical appearance—his spare diet rendered him pallid and emaciated, and he wore only the simplest of clothing—was the best evidence that he practiced what he preached. Moreover, like the gnostics of Orléans who declared that they regarded the scriptures as nothing more than "the fictions of carnal men, scribbled on animal skins," Bernard was willing to entertain the subversive notion that words written on parchment were not the only or even the best resource for achieving spiritual enlightenment. "You will find something much greater in the woods than in books," he wrote. "The woods and stones will teach you what you cannot learn from other masters."[44]

The roots of the Inquisition, in fact, can be traced back to the otherwise benign missionary work of friar-preachers who, with nothing more than their own ardent words, sought to persuade their fellow Christians to correct their errors and return to the Church. Like Bernard himself, other cloistered monks of the Cistercian order were released from their cells and sent into the world to preach against the heretics. By the opening decade of the thirteenth century, the newly chartered Franciscans and Dominicans, too, were charged by the pope to "go humbly in search of heretics and lead them out of error," according to a papal bull of 1206. By way of shining example, Domingo (Dominic) Guzmán himself, founder of the Dominican order, once argued with an errant innkeeper in Toulouse from sundown to sunrise before finally winning him back to the Church, and he later established a safe house for the women and children whom he succeeded in spiriting away from the Cathars.[45]

The willingness of the Church to fight a war of words led to a few scenes that are strange indeed when viewed in the light of what we know now about the Inquisition. Catholic monks engaged in public disputations with the *perfecti* of the Catharist church, including one well-advertised debate at which the audience included such luminaries as the archbishop of Narbonne, the viscount of Béziers, and the countess of Toulouse, who happened to be the sister of the king of France. Remarkably, the defenders of the Roman Catholic church were willing to fight according to rules set by the Catharists; since the Cathars rejected the authority of the Hebrew Bible and regarded only the Gospels (and especially the Gospel of John) as holy writ, the Catholic debaters agreed to confine themselves to the New Testament.

The Catharists were not so deferential, or so we are told by the Catholic chroniclers, and they appeared to be utterly fearless in confronting their adversaries. The Catholic clergy "were not bishops and priests," the Catharists are shown to say in the medieval transcripts of these great debates, "but ravening wolves, hypocrites and seducers, lovers of salutations in the market place, desirous of being called rabbis and masters contrary to the command of Christ, wearers of albs and gleaming raiment, displaying bejeweled gold rings on their fingers, which their Master Jesus did not command." Crossing oneself, according to one Cathar preacher, "was only good for batting away flies." And the notion that bread and wine were changed into the body and blood of Jesus Christ in the rite of Communion—the cherished Catholic doctrine of transubstantiation—struck the Cathars as both impious and ludicrous, since the communicants would "have God in their bowels, a God who would inevitably be expelled from the body on their next visit to the water closet."[46]

The debaters, Catholic and Catharist alike, discovered that words alone are rarely enough to change the mind of a true believer. The Church, in any case, was not willing to suffer such taunts and insults for long. Preachers and propagandists began to escalate their rhetoric against the Catharists, and Pope Innocent III eventually declared open war on the dissident Christians whom he condemned as "filth"—a term of abuse previously reserved only for the Muslims who faced the crusaders on the fighting fronts in the Holy Land. Ominously, the dissidents whom Saint Bernard proposed to take "by force of argument" were now characterized in much harsher and even horrific terms, all designed to inspire fear and panic throughout western Christendom. "The heresy of Catharism gives birth continually to a monstrous brood," declared Pope Innocent III, "by means of which its corruption is vigorously renewed, after that offspring has passed on to others the canker of its own madness and a detestable succession of criminals emerges."[47]

Pope Innocent III resolved to escalate the war on heresy by preaching a new crusade, not against the Muslims in the distant Levant but against the Cathars across the frontier in southern France. On November 17, 1207, the pope sent a letter to the king of France, calling on him to raise an army of crusaders to march into the province of Languedoc to exterminate the Cathars. Significantly, the pope offered the same spiritual rewards available to crusaders who traveled all the way to the Holy Land to take up arms against Islam—the pope's forgiveness for their past sins and the status of a martyr if they fell in battle against the enemy.

In seeking to cut out the cancer of heresy, however, the pope sanctioned the use of a new and even more radical instrument. By contrast with Saint Bernard and Saint Dominic, who armed themselves only with sermons and texts in their struggles against the Cathars, the crusaders sent into southern France were to be soldiers of Christ in the most literal sense. "For the first time in Europe, a pope was calling upon Christians to kill other Christians," explains Karen Armstrong. "Innocent was setting a precedent for a new kind of holy war that would become an incurable disease in Europe."[48]

The crusaders were charged with the solemn task of rooting out heresy throughout Europe but especially in the towns of Toulouse, Agen, and Albi in southern France, where the Cathars were thought to gather in the greatest numbers and where they were sheltered by a defiant local gentry. Albi, as it turns out, was hardly the Vatican of the heretical church, but the name of the town came to be used as a kind of code word for Catharism and served to focus the fears and fantasies of the knights and soldiers who took up the cross. For that reason, the crusade that Pope Innocent III preached in 1207 against the Christian dissenters of France has come to be called the Albigensian Crusade.[49]

The town of Albi lay in the province of Languedoc, a place-name that literally means "the language of yes" and refers to the fact that the word *yes* in the dialect of southern France is *oc* rather than *oui*. It's a bit of word-play that captures the spirit of southern France in the late Middle Ages—easygoing and tolerant, prosperous and independent, a stronghold of the troubadours and the chivalric tradition of courtly love, and a stopping place on the route along which both ideas and merchandise reached Europe from points east. Not surprisingly, the Cathars, too, thrived in the welcoming and open-minded cities of Languedoc.

Other beneficiaries of the spirit of Languedoc were members of the Jewish community, who fared far better in southern France than elsewhere in medieval Europe. They were not granted full citizenship, but they were permitted to own land, engage in business and the professions, and live where they pleased. They were able to delve into the mystical traditions of Kabbalism, and some historians have suggested that Jewish and Cathar ascetics inspired and influenced each other. What we learn from the example of Languedoc on the eve of the Inquisition is that ordinary men and women, when given the opportunity to explore the varieties of religious experience, do not simply shut up and submit to the dogma offered by the religious authorities.

One outspoken farmer in medieval Languedoc, for example, was heard to say in the village square that the Bishop of Pamiers and Jesus himself had been brought into the world "through fucking and shitting, rocking back and forth and fucking, in other words, through the coitus of a man and a woman, just like the rest of us." To which an outraged villager replied: "If you don't stop it, I'll break your head open with my pick-axe." A dying Catholic, when urged by a Cathar *perfectus* and his companions to submit to the *consolamentum,* found enough strength to forcefully turn them away: "Stop harassing me, you devils." But the records of the Inquisition also preserve a similar story told about a dying Catholic who was offered the Eucharist by a Catholic priest: "*Sancta Maria, Sancta Maria,* I can see the Devil."[50] "[W]hether you were a Cathar or a Catholic," observes historian Emmanuel Le Roy Ladurie in his classic sociological study of a medieval French village, "you were always the devil to somebody."[51]

The apparent willingness of the Albigensians to speak bluntly about their doubts and convictions is the first and most important reason that they found themselves targeted by a crusade. But it is not the only reason. The pope found a willing ally in the French king, Philip Augustus, who had motives of his own for sending an army into Languedoc; the king resented the autonomy of the provincial aristocracy of southern France and sought to impose his royal authority on them. And the men who actually crusaded in Languedoc— the great nobles of northern France—were more interested in acquiring new lands and new titles than in crushing the Cathars. The meshing of religion and politics can always be detected in the workings of the Inquisition and explains where and why it operated as it did.

The triggering event of the Albigensian Crusade, for example, was a particularly ugly confrontation between the pope and the minor nobles of southern France who refused to bend to his will. The pope had grown impatient with the efforts of the mendicant orders to defeat Catharism by words alone, and he sought to escalate the war against heresy by actively searching out, arresting, and punishing the Cathars, Waldensians, and others who defied the authority of the Church. The burden fell on the local counts and dukes, including some who were practicing the faith they were now ordered to eradicate and others who regarded the Cathars as good citizens undeserving of persecution. That's why, as we have seen, an otherwise pious Catholic knight might demur when called upon to make war on Cathar men and women who were his friends, neighbors, and close relations.

The flashpoint came when a Cistercian monk named Peter of Castelnau showed up at the court of Count Raymond VI of Toulouse and conveyed the papal order to make war on Catharism. Like other nobles who had received similar decrees, Raymond was resentful and defiant, and he suggested to Peter that he might be at risk if he remained in Toulouse. On his way out of town, in fact, Peter was struck down with a knife blow from an unknown assailant. The pope declared his dead legate to have died a martyr, blamed the murder on Raymond, issued a decree of excommunication against him, and called upon all good Catholics to avenge the legate's death by taking up the cross against Catharism in the province of Languedoc.

The pope's promise of relief from suffering in purgatory was all the more inviting because it was available without the need to make the dangerous, expensive trek to the Holy Land that was required of other crusaders. But the primary motive of the men who answered the call to crusade was a worldly one. The lords of northern France—the Duke of Burgundy, the Count of Nevers, and the Count of Saint-Pol among them—valued the prospect of taking for themselves the wealth and property of Count Raymond and the other unruly aristocrats of southern France. The war on heresy was only a pretext, and, as we shall see, it often slipped from their minds.

"Crusade was a blunt instrument," observes historian Malcolm Lambert. "Innocent was not the master of the spirits he had conjured up."[52]

The first army to take the field in the Albigensian Crusade was commanded by a papal legate called Arnauld Amalric, abbot of the Cistercian monastery at Cîteaux, and his first objective was the walled city of Béziers, which supposedly sheltered a couple of hundred or so Cathars. When the town fell to the crusaders on the feast day of Saint Mary Magdalene in 1209, according to a famous tale told by one medieval chronicler, the men under the abbot's command sought a clarification of their orders. "Lord, what shall we do?" they asked. "We cannot distinguish the good from the wicked." The warrior-monk, later raised by the pope to the rank of archbishop, is said to have pronounced a death sentence on all the residents of Béziers, piously echoing the words of Paul in his letter to Timothy. "Kill them all," said the good abbot. "The Lord knows those who are his own."[53]

At least seven thousand men, women, and children were murdered at Béziers—the abbot himself put the death toll at fifteen thousand in his triumphant report to the pope—and the cathedral was pulled down as a symbolic punishment because the local Catholics had failed to exterminate the Cathars among them on their own initiative. The massacre was intended to strike terror in the other cities and towns of Languedoc, and so it did. Indeed, the fact that the crusaders slaughtered the local populace so indiscriminately, killing Catholics and Catharists alike, reveals how little they cared about the announced goal of the Albigensian Crusade. Like so many other military adventures at so many other times and places, the reason for going to war offered by the pope was starkly at odds with the motives of the men who actually fought the war.

The emblematic example is Simon de Montfort (ca. 1165–1218), a minor noble whose family seat was located near Paris. On the ill-fated Fourth Crusade, which set out to liberate the Holy Land and ended up conquering the Christian city of Constantinople, de Montfort had supposedly refused to join his fellow crusaders in the slaughter of Christians. But his scruples did not prevent him from taking command of the Albigensian Crusade, and he was no less willing than Arnauld Amalric to use terror as a weapon of war. After the town of Bram fell to de Montfort, for example, he assembled one hundred of its defenders and ordered his soldiers to blind them and hack off their noses and upper lips. Only one victim was permitted to keep an eye so he could lead the others to the nearest town, where the ghastly procession of blind men would serve to warn against the consequences of taking up arms in self-defense.

As his reward for such brutality, de Montfort was granted the lands and titles of the nobles whom he had defeated in battle or terrorized into submission, including those of the defiant Count Raymond VI, the man whose role in the murder of the papal legate had set the crusade into motion. At the high water mark of his reign, de Montfort claimed to rule over a vast stretch of southern France as count of Toulouse, viscount of Béziers and Carcassonne, and duke of Narbonne, and he became, if only briefly, one of France's wealthiest landowners. Remission of sin in the afterlife was perhaps less compelling to Simon de Montfort than the riches he managed to accumulate in the here and now, all because of his ruthlessness as a crusader against his fellow Christians.

Of course, the crusaders did not neglect their duty of murdering Cathars when they were able to single out a few of them from the rest of the population. At the town of Minerve, for example, some 140 *perfecti* were arrested, bound, and burned alive in the first of several such spectacles that ornamented the Albigensian Crusade. At Lavaur in 1211, de Montfort ordered that the knights who had defended the walled town be hanged from gibbets, and as many as four hundred Good Men were put to the flames in one of the greatest single atrocities of the crusade. Among the victims was the lord of Lavaur, who was hanged along with his knights, and his sister, who was punished for offering sanctuary to Cathar war refugees by being "thrown down a well and stoned to death."[54]

The persecution of flesh-and-blood Cathars was never more than a side-show in the Albigensian Crusade. "Out of the 37 places de Montfort is known to have besieged," writes historian Sean Martin, "contemporary chroniclers record only three where Perfect were actually known to be." What mattered more to the king of France was extending his royal sovereignty over the southern provinces, and the northern lords who actually went to war were intent on making themselves the owners and rulers of the counties they conquered. Also in play were the ambitions of Peter of Aragón, whose lands lay across the Pyrenees in what would later become the kingdom of Spain, and who tried to claim a slice of southern France, too. And when the defenders of Languedoc took to the field of battle, they were seeking to preserve their own autonomy against the invading armies from the north rather than protecting the Cathars' right to practice their faith.[55]

Surely the realpolitik that was the motive of popes, kings, and counts was not wholly lost on the ordinary men and women of Languedoc, if only because the crusaders took so little care to distinguish Cathars from Catholics in conducting their war on heresy. The invaders engaged in scorched-earth warfare, setting fire to houses and standing crops, poisoning the wells and cutting down the orchards, blackening the skies with smoke from smoldering ruins. Men taken in battle were "mutilated, blinded, dragged at the heels of horses, used for target practice." The same atrocities were practiced by local gentry who were fighting to protect their own prerogatives. The Albigensian Crusade was, after all, a dirty little war among contesting lords rather than the holy war it was advertised to be, and God was wholly absent from the field of the battle.[56]

The Albigensian Crusade sputtered on for a couple of decades. Simon de Montfort did not live to see the so-called Peace of Paris, the treaty by which the fighting in southern France was ended in 1229. He was killed during the siege of Toulouse in 1218 when a shot from a catapult inside the walled city struck his helmet. To the defenders of Toulouse, de Montfort was a foreign invader and conqueror, and they took pleasure in the fact that the battery was operated by a detachment of women—"dames and girls and married women"—who had taken the place of the fallen soldiers. But the death of de Montfort did not spare the city from conquest and carnage, and the medieval chroniclers who composed the *Chanson de la croisade albigeoise* seemed to realize that no one could claim victory.[57] As the nameless poet who composed the second half of the chronicle put it:

In the field of Montoulieu was planted a garden which every day sprouted and put forth shoots. It was sown with lilies, but the white and red which budded and flowered were of flesh and blood, of weapons and of the brains which were spilled there. Thence went spirits and souls, sinners and redeemed, to people hell and paradise anew.[58]

The king of France was pleased with the outcome of the Albigensian Crusade. His sovereignty over southern France was assured, and his family was to inherit the ancestral lands of the rebellious Count Raymond. But the Peace of Paris did not bring an end to the war against the Cathars. Ironically and fatefully, the Albigensian Crusade failed in its stated goal: the Cathars may have been burned alive by the hundreds, but they had not been exterminated. Some of them had gone into hiding; others had scattered across Europe from Italy to Bohemia to Poland, where they established new churches and communities or joined existing Cathar settlements in remote villages and mountain valleys. The "monstrous brood," as Pope Innocent III had phrased it, was still alive and at large.

Only a couple of hundred *perfecti* remained in Languedoc, where they found refuge in the high-walled fortress at Montségur in the Pyrenees. Well supplied with food and water, and protected by the steep slopes of the thousand-foot-high peak on which the fortress stood, they remained beyond the reach of the crusaders for decades. Not until 1244 was Montségur finally besieged and conquered by a Catholic army, but only after a couple of Good Men had managed to escape with the storied Cathar treasure, probably consisting of a few holy books and perhaps what was left of the coins that had been tithed by faithful believers. The rest of the surviving *perfecti,* including the Cathar bishops of Toulouse and Razès, were marched under guard to an open field and burned alive. The place is still known as the *prat dels crematz*—"the field of those who were burned."

The Church never lost sight of the original cause of war. But a new and different campaign would now be undertaken against the Cathars—and, in a larger sense, against every expression of religious liberty and social diversity—and a wholly new weapon would be deployed. Preaching, even by sainted luminaries like Bernard, Dominic, and Francis, had failed to win the hearts and minds of errant Christians. The crusade against Catharism had sent hundreds to the stake in southern France, but thousands more continued to practice their faith in secret all over Europe. Thus did Pope Innocent III conclude that "ceaseless persecution continued to perpetuity" was the only way to achieve a final solution to the problem of heresy.[59]

Pope Innocent resolved to recruit, arm, and deploy an army whose sole mission would be to search out, punish, and, if possible, exterminate men and women whose beliefs and practices were seen as heretical by the Church. No longer, however, would he rely on kings and princes to do his bidding. The new inquisitorial army and its elaborate supply chain fell under a vast papal bureaucracy whose formal title was the Holy Office of Inquisition into Heretical Depravity. Ironically, its frontline troops would be supplied by the mendicant ("begging") orders, the Dominicans and the Franciscans, whose friars had vowed to live the *vita apostolica* ("apostolic life") and whose original mission had been to preach rather than persecute. Starting in the thirteenth century, and continuing for another six hundred years, it came to be known simply as the Inquisition.

3

THE HAMMER OF HERETICS

Innocent may boast of the two most signal tri-
umphs over sense and humanity,
the establishment of transubstantiation and the
origin of the inquisition.

EDWARD GIBBON,
The Decline and Fall of the Roman Empire

The very first inquisitor, according to the apologists of the Inquisition, was God himself. When God interrogates Adam in the Garden of Eden, seeking to extract the truth about the famous case of
the forbidden fruit, he is setting the example that was followed by the flesh-
and-blood inquisitors who entered history in the thirteenth century. Indeed,
the Sicilian inquisitor Luis de Páramo, claimed a lineage that included Moses, King David, John the Baptist, and even Jesus of Nazareth, "in whose
precepts and conduct he finds abundant authority for the tribunal."[1]

But the Inquisition must be seen as, among other things, an audacious
work of the human imagination. The lawyer-popes who presided over the
Roman Catholic church during the Middle Ages were the first to dream
of creating an institution wholly dedicated to the eradication of heresy
throughout Christendom, including a corps of inquisitors drawn from
the ranks of the monastic orders; an army of bailiffs, clerks, constables,

notaries, and scriveners; a network of spies and informers that every good Christian was expected to join and serve; a labyrinth of dungeons, torture chambers, courts, prisons, and places of execution; and a vast archive in which the transcripts of investigation, trial, and judgment would be preserved for the convenience of future inquisitors.

Whether the papal dream came true in all of its Kafkaesque detail is still debated by revisionist historians, but we can glimpse the vision of the Inquisition that danced in the heads of sleeping popes by consulting the papal bulls, episcopal canons, and inquisitor's manuals that prescribed the standard operating procedures for flesh-and-blood inquisitors for more than six hundred years. It was first known by the fearful title of *Holy Office of Inquisition* into Heretical Depravity (*Inquisitio haereticae Pravitatis sanctum Officium*), a phrase that betrays the fear and loathing that the first inquisitors felt for their victims. The same institution, however, has carried other official designations over the centuries, including one that captures the near-delusional arrogance of the Church in undertaking the inquisitorial project: Supreme Sacred Congregation of the Roman and Universal Inquisition. Even today the same office exists under a rather more modest moniker, the Sacred Congregation for the Doctrine of the Faith.

The Inquisition did not spring fully formed from the heads that wore the papal crown, nor was the Holy Office of Inquisition the first or only apparatus for the persecution of heresy in the long history of Christianity. The early Christian church was continually bedeviled by the problem of sorting out which beliefs and practices were orthodox and which were heretical, and the unfortunates who found themselves on the wrong side of the line had always been the victims of arrest, torture, imprisonment, and execution. In that sense, the Inquisition was not an act of pure invention; rather, it was assembled and fine-tuned after centuries of tinkering, "moulded step by step out of the materials which lay nearest at hand."[2]

The history of the Inquisition is classically divided into three periods. The medieval Inquisition began in the aftermath of the Albigensian Crusade in the mid–thirteenth century and continued to operate in France, Italy, and elsewhere in Europe for another couple of hundred years, persecuting first the Cathars and Waldensians and then miscellaneous other victims, including the Knights Templar, renegade Franciscan priests, men accused of alchemy and sorcery, and women accused of witchcraft. The so-called Roman Inquisition, a phenomenon of the Counter-Reformation in the sixteenth century, directed most of its efforts against Protestants and various humanists and freethinkers in Italy. And the Spanish Inquisition, the last-surviving and most famous branch operation of the Inquisition, was created in 1478 to search out Jewish converts to Christianity whose conversions were suspected of being insincere, and remained in formal existence until 1834.

Yet these convenient markers fail to convey the vastness and strangeness of the Inquisition, which took on many other guises and configurations over the centuries and across the globe. So grandiose were the ambitions of the Inquisition that inquisitors were authorized and sometimes even appointed for places where the pope and the Church enjoyed little or no authority, including such distant and exotic locales as Abyssinia, Armenia, Egypt, Georgia, Greece, Nubia, Russia, Syria, Tartary, Tunis, and Wallachia. The papal legate in Jerusalem was instructed to put the Inquisition into operation in the Holy Land in 1290, but the so-called Syrian Inquisition was stillborn when the crusaders were evicted from their little kingdom by a Muslim army in the following year. By 1500, the Spanish Inquisition was burning heretics in Mexico and South America, and the Portuguese version of the Inquisition was doing the same in the colony of Goa on the Indian subcontinent. "An inquisitor," notes Henry Charles Lea, "seems to have been regarded as a necessary portion of the missionary outfit."[3]

Nor did the Vatican invariably serve as the command center of the Inquisition. Again, the Spanish Inquisition is only the most famous example of the commandeering of the machinery of persecution by a secular government. After Ferdinand and Isabella of Spain petitioned the pope for an Inquisition of their own, the king of Portugal decided that he needed one, too. The king of France, when he sought to replenish the royal treasury by looting the Knights Templar, called on the Inquisition to sanctify the destruction of the old crusading order on trumped-up charges of homosexuality and heresy. Even when a municipal or provincial branch of the Inquisition remained under the nominal authority of the pope, it might take on its own style and set its own priorities. An inquisitor in the thriving commercial center of Venice, for example, conducted an auction at which the goods seized from twenty-two convicted heretics were sold and the money added to his own coffers.

Yet it is also true that the men who invented and operated the Inquisition always aspired toward uniformity, continuity, and ubiquity. Nothing else captures the inner meaning of the Inquisition quite like the manuals and handbooks composed by the earliest inquisitors and circulated among those who followed in their footsteps. From the lawyer-popes, to the princes of the Church, to the hooded friar-inquisitor at work in the torture chamber, all of them sought to impose a Mad Hatter's vision of law and order on the bloody enterprise of persecution. Thus, for example, the inquisitors were supplied with lists of questions to ask a suspect under interrogation, scripts to recite when consigning an accused man or woman to prison or to burning at the stake, forms to fill out when requesting the return of an escaped prisoner, and even a writ that could be copied out when an accused heretic was found to be not guilty—a form that was seldom, if ever, actually used.

Precisely because the inquisitors were guided in their work by the canons, decrees, formbooks, and handbooks that were preserved and consulted over the centuries, the Inquisition achieved a remarkable degree of standardization. To be sure, some of the practices and procedures varied from place to place and changed over time. The burning of Cathars in Languedoc by the medieval Inquisition, for example, was a much cruder affair than the great spectacle offered in the public square of Madrid when the Spanish Inquisition mounted an auto-da-fé. Then, too, the very first inquisitors faced open resistance from their outraged victims, a phenomenon that would diminish and then disappear as the Inquisition grew in size, scope, and sheer shelf-confidence. Even so, the workings of the Inquisition did not fundamentally change over its six-hundred-year history. The Inquisition was a machine with interchangeable parts, just as its inventors had intended, and its victims in every venue and every age suffered a similar and terrible fate.

How far back we must look to find the roots of the Inquisition remains an open question. The core idea—and the word itself—was borrowed from the jurisprudence of pagan Rome, the original persecutor of Christianity, and only later imported into the canon law of the Roman Catholic church. Unlike the Roman legal procedures called *accusatio* and *denunciatio,* in which a private citizen or a public prosecutor presented evidence of wrongdoing to a judge, the form of criminal prosecution called *inquisitio* permitted a single man to perform the roles of investigator, prosecutor, and judge—a notion that offends the fundamental notion of fairness in English and American law. Yet, at least one historian insists that the "time-honored system of the grand-jury" in Anglo-Saxon tradition ought to be regarded as "a prototype of the incipient papal Inquisition"—an ironic observation in light of the fact that England was one place in Europe where the Inquisition did *not* operate.[4]

Inquisition into heresy had long been carried out by Catholic bishops on their own initiative and authority. The trial of the gnostic cultists at Orléans in 1022 was conducted by a panel of French bishops, and the so-called episcopal inquisition—a term that is used to refer collectively to the inquisitions conducted by bishops—coexisted (and sometimes competed) with the Inquisition even after the popes arrogated to themselves the leading role in the enterprise of finding and punishing heretics. Thus, for example, the celebrated medieval German mystic Meister Eckhart (1260–ca. 1327) was tried twice for heresy, once by a tribunal of bishops in Germany, which acquitted him, and later by the Inquisition, which convicted him posthumously. Indeed, the episcopal inquisition proved to be insufficiently fierce for the papal war on heresy that began in earnest in the thirteenth century—one reason that the Inquisition was called into existence in the first place.

A tale told about the bishop of Besançon illustrates how benighted an otherwise pious cleric might turn out to be. Troubled by rumors of a small band of wonder-workers said to be capable of performing authentic miracles, the bishop felt obliged to determine whether they had acquired their powers from God or Satan. And so, remarkably, he called on the services of a clerk reputed to be a practitioner of the black arts, apparently overlooking the fact that sorcery, too, was an act of heresy and thus punishable by death. "The cunning clerk deceived the devil into a confidential mood and learned that the strangers were his servants," reports Henry Charles Lea with tongue in cheek. "[T]hey were deprived of the satanic amulets which were their protection, and the populace, which had previously sustained them, cast them pitilessly into the flames."[5]

On other occasions, even the most pious bishops and popes were so flummoxed by the mere sight of flesh-and-blood heretics that they simply did not know what to do with them. When a few Cathars were rounded up in Flanders in 1162, the archbishop of Reims shipped them off to Pope Alexander III (ca. 1105–1181) for punishment, and the pope promptly shipped them back to the archbishop with the admonition that "it was better to pardon the guilty than to take the lives of the innocent." Such bleeding-heart liberalism seems quaint and even poignant when compared with the bloody-mindedness that would soon characterize the Inquisition, and it helps to explain why a corps of inquisitors was later called into existence.[6]

When Pope Innocent III (1160/61–1216) resolved to root out Catharism once and for all in the opening years of the thirteenth century, he was not willing to rely on the bishops scattered across Europe, many of whom he regarded as corrupt, or inept, or too comfortable with their Cathar neighbors, and sometimes all three at once. Instead, he started by recruiting a few churchmen of his own choosing to serve as his personal emissaries (or "legates"). They became a kind of flying squad of heretic hunters, and various popes dispatched them to hotspots all over Europe where the smoke and fire of heresy had been detected. Here begins the so-called legatine inquisition, an early phase of the war on heresy and the first stirrings of *the* Inquisition.

The very first man to carry the official title of *Inquisitor haereticae Pravitatis* (inquisitor into heretical depravity) was Conrad of Marburg (ca. 1180–1233), a legatine inquisitor who was sent first to Languedoc by Pope Innocent III and later to the Rhineland by Pope Gregory IX. A rabid ascetic and an apparent sadist, Conrad is also credited with slapping the label of "Luciferanism" on the Waldensians, whom he wrongly regarded as Devil worshipers rather than Christian rigorists, and tantalizing his superiors with near-pornographic tales of their imagined sexual and theological excesses.

Conrad is a good example of the kind of human being who is temperamentally suited for the career of a professional persecutor. An aristocrat by birth and the beneficiary of a university education at Paris, he cultivated a reputation for piety and self-denial, and he fasted himself into pallor and emaciation. At the height of his fame, he rode from place to place on a donkey in imitation of Jesus, attracting adoring crowds who welcomed him with candles and incense. Once charged by the pope with the task of burning heretics, he allied himself with a couple of "self-appointed inquisitors"—a "one-eyed, one-armed rogue" named Johannes and a Dominican lay friar called Hans Torso—and the three of them set up operations "on papal license." They shaved the heads of the accused to mark them as suspected heretics and questioned them so brutally that the archbishop of Mainz complained to the pope about the false confessions that were being extracted from innocent men and women under the threat of the stake.[7] "We would gladly burn a hundred," boasted an unapologetic Conrad, "if just one among them were guilty."[8]

Conrad sought victims among the gentry as well as among the common folk, perhaps because of his zeal in the pursuit of heresy or perhaps because the wealth of a convicted heretic was subject to confiscation. In 1233 his eye fell on Count Henry II of Seyn, a wealthy nobleman who had demonstrated his own Christian piety by endowing churches and monasteries and even going on crusade. Conrad produced a witness who claimed to have seen Henry riding on a monstrous crab on his way to a sex orgy. But Henry, unlike Conrad's humbler victims, was not cowed into confession. Rather, the count insisted on confronting the inquisitor and putting him to his proof.

Conrad's fate provides a cautionary example of both the excesses of the legatine inquisitors and the defiant response that a papal legate might encounter from local clergy and gentry. Count Henry demanded a trial before a tribunal consisting of the king, the archbishop, and various other clergymen. Questioned in the presence of these judges, Conrad's witnesses revealed that they had given evidence only to spare themselves from the stake, and the tribunal refused to convict Count Henry. When Conrad fled the city of Mainz, frustrated and disgusted, he was tracked by a hit squad whose orders were to put an end to both Conrad and his little crew. Set upon and slain on the road to Marburg five days after the acquittal of their last victim, they thus suffered the same fate as that of another papal legate, Peter of Castelnau, whose confrontation with Count Raymond at Toulouse had sparked the Albigensian Crusade.

Yet another inquisitor was dead, but his ominous title and function survived for another six centuries. When it came to heresy hunting, the weakness of the legatine inquisitors, as far as the papacy was concerned, was their inefficiency rather than their brutality. "Conrad's lack of scruple over evidence may well have brought as many innocent as guilty to the fire," observes historian Malcolm Lambert, "and still let the heretics, Cathar or Waldensian, escape." But Conrad's wild-eyed sexual slanders were wholly plausible to Pope Gregory IX, who imported them into an influential papal bull titled *Vox in rama* (A voice on high) and thus "gave Conrad's poisonous stories a vogue they might not otherwise have had." The inquisitor himself may have suffered a sudden and violent death, but his leering notion that heresy is invariably and inevitably wedded to sorcery and sexual excess enjoyed a much longer life.[9]

Still, a practical lesson had been learned. Neither the episcopal inquisition nor the legatine inquisition was sufficient to the task of achieving a final solution to the problem of religious diversity within the realm of the Roman Catholic church. A kind of perfect storm of zeal, paranoia, and hubris inspired the Church to design a wholly new weapon for deployment in the war on heresy. The ancient Roman legal procedure of *inquisitio* would be entrusted to an army of friar-inquisitors recruited from the ranks of the mendicant orders, and they would be charged by the pope with the task of cleansing Christendom of every kind of heresy. Once called upon to live in imitation of Christ, the friar-inquisitors were recruited to serve in a corps of persecutors whose instruments of torture were identical to those that had been used in pagan Rome.

The irony was apparent to Dostoevsky, whose Grand Inquisitor is ready to burn Jesus Christ himself as a heretic, but it was wholly lost on the flesh-and-blood inquisitors who murdered their victims by the countless thousands. For them, the work of the torturer and the executioner was always for the greater glory of God and the Church, or so they succeeded in convincing themselves.

The creation of the Inquisition as an arm of the Church has been tracked by historians through a series of papal decrees and church councils starting as early as 1184. But the man who is generally credited with (or blamed for) bringing the Inquisition into formal existence is Pope Innocent III, a brilliant and accomplished canon lawyer who ascended to the papal throne in 1198 and remained there for eighteen tumultuous years. Innocent, as we have already seen, is the man who first sent the Dominicans and Franciscans into Languedoc to call the Cathars back into the Church. When preaching failed, he charged the king and nobles of France to go on crusade in their own country against the Cathars who refused to be converted. And when the Albigensian Crusade failed in its mission of exterminating the Cathars, it was Pope Innocent III who resolved to root out heresy once and for all by entrusting the task to a corps of papal inquisitors, the charter members of the Inquisition.

Innocent, the most celebrated of the lawyer-popes of the medieval Church, sought to drape the machinery of persecution with the mantle of law and theology. On November 1, 1215, he convened an assembly of more than four hundred bishops, eight hundred abbots, and various emissaries from the kings and princes of western Europe, all of them gathered in the Lateran Palace in Rome. At the end of their deliberations, the so-called Fourth Lateran Council voted to approve a new set of ecclesiastical laws (or "canons") that were intended to dictate the beliefs and practices of obedient Christians—and to punish the disobedient ones. The document in which the work of the Fourth Lateran Council is recorded has been called "the first sketch of the Inquisition," but it also provided a useful precedent for lawmakers in Spain in the fifteenth century and Nazi Germany in the twentieth century.[10]

Many of the canons appear to be unrelated to the persecution of heresy, but the whole document hums with the urgent concern of the Roman Catholic church to assert its absolute authority over Christendom. The clergy and congregants of the Eastern Orthodox church, for example, were warned to "conform themselves like obedient sons to the holy Roman church, their mother, so that there may be one flock and one shepherd"—or else "be struck with the sword of excommunication." Because it was sometimes impossible to tell Jews and "Saracens" (that is, Muslims) from Christians—and "thus it happens at times that through error Christians have relations with the women of Jews or Saracens, and Jews and Saracens with Christian women"—they were ordered to wear garments of a kind that would set them apart from Christians. And a new crusade "to liberate the Holy Land from the hands of the ungodly" was ordered to depart on June 1, 1217.[11]

Even the canons that do not seem to refer to heresy can be understood as a stern caution against even the slightest innovation or variation in matters of faith. The very first canon of the Fourth Lateran Council, for example, asserts the theological monopoly of the Roman Catholic church, which is declared to be "one Universal Church of the faithful, outside of which there is absolutely no salvation." Dualism of the kind embraced by the Cathars is implicitly condemned—"We believe and openly confess there is only one true God"—although the credo goes on to allow that God actually comprises "three Persons indeed but one essence," that is, "Father, Son and Holy Ghost." The affirmation of baptism in water and the doctrine of transubstantiation—the belief that the bread of the Eucharist is miraculously "changed (*transsubstantio*) by divine power into the body, and the wine into the blood" of Jesus Christ—can be understood as an oblique repudiation of the Cathars, who rejected both items of Catholic dogma.[12]

Only the third canon directly addresses the goal of ridding Christendom of what the clerics called "heretical filth." But it amounts to a declaration of total war on heresy of all kinds and, at the same time, a general conscription of all Christians to serve on the front lines. "We condemn all heretics, whatever names they may go under," the council resolved. "They have different faces indeed but their tails are tied together inasmuch as they are alike in their pride." Any Christians "who receive, defend or support heretics" were themselves to be excommunicated. Anyone in a position of authority was under a solemn obligation to the Church to persecute heresy: "Thus whenever anyone is promoted to spiritual or temporal authority," the third canon states, "he shall be obliged to confirm this article with an oath."[13]

Bishops were sternly reminded of their duty to "force the faithful to denounce any heretics known to them," and any bishop who failed to do so was to forfeit his office in favor of "a suitable person who both wishes and is able to overthrow the evil of heresy"— a pointed reminder of the failings of the episcopal inquisition. The secular lords of Christendom, too, were admonished not to tolerate the presence of heretics within their realms. The goal of the Church, in other words, was to require all officers of Church and state—and, later, the population at large—to serve as spies and informers in the war on heresy. If they failed to turn in a suspected heretic, they were guilty of "fautorship"—that is, the crime of aiding or abetting a heretic—and faced punishment no less severe than that imposed on the heretics themselves.

Some of the well-established penalties for heresy were reaffirmed—confiscation and forfeiture of property, removal from public office, and excommunication for heretics who recanted and then reverted to their old beliefs. New and ominous penalties were added. Once detected and condemned, for example, an unrepentant heretic was to be "abandoned" by the Church and "handed over to the secular rulers to be punished with due justice," a formula that later came to serve as a sanctimonious euphemism for death by burning at the stake.[14] Significantly, the war on heresy in western Europe was declared to be the moral equivalent of the Crusades in the far-off Holy Land. "Catholics who take the cross and gird themselves up for the expulsion of heretics," the third canon affirmed, "shall enjoy the same indulgence, and be strengthened by the same holy privilege, as is granted to those who go to the aid of the holy Land."[15]

Innocent III did not live long enough to see the canons of the Fourth Lateran Council put into full operation. "At his death in 1216," concedes historian Edward Burman, "the Inquisition did not yet exist." But it is also true that Innocent's long, bloody campaign against religious liberty and diversity, culminating in the canons of the Fourth Lateran Council, would "lead irrevocably to the creation of the Inquisition." He was the author of the very idea of a war on heresy, which expressed itself in the Albigensian Crusade as well as in the burning of heretics by the legatine inquisitors. He was the first pope to recognize the usefulness of the Dominicans and Franciscans in the persecution of heretics. And he convened the council whose enactments of church law would serve as the constitution of the Inquisition, thus dignifying what was essentially a program of Church- and state-sponsored terrorism.[16] Once the blueprints of the Inquisition were available, men in power did not hesitate to put them to use.

Still, it was left to Innocent's successors to assemble the various parts into the elaborate contraption that came to be called the Inquisition. The Council of Toulouse in 1229, for example, endorsed the notion of the Inquisition as a permanent fixture of the Church rather than a series of ad hoc tribunals. The papal decree titled *Excommunicamus,* issued in 1231 by Pope Gregory IX, expanded upon the antiheretical canons of the Fourth Lateran Council. By April 20, 1233, when Pope Gregory IX formally charged the friars of the Dominican order with the duty of serving as inquisitors, the Inquisition was fully deployed. Once in place, it would not pause in its work for six hundred years, when the last victim of the Inquisition was put to death as a heretic.[17]

By a certain Orwellian logic, the Inquisition always fancied itself to be the spiritual benefactor of the men and women whom it arrested, tortured, and killed. Pope Innocent III encouraged the inquisitors to regard the persecution of heresy as strong medicine intended to restore the spiritual health of the heretics even if it meant afflicting their bodies or even ending their mortal lives. Pope Gregory IX, too, saw the Inquisition as "an integral part of pastoral care." Thus did the inquisitors come to justify the prosecution of accused heretics as "an act of love" and "profound Christian charity" toward errant Christians who had put their souls at risk by straying from the benign embrace of the Mother Church. The same rationale has been invoked by apologists down through the ages when they piously insist that the Inquisition imposed only "penances" and deferred to the civil authorities when it came to torture and execution.[18]

For that reason, too, it made sense for the Church to recruit inquisitors from the ranks of its own clergy. But the popes who called the Inquisition into existence declined to entrust the task to a motley crew of ordinary priests. Rather, they chose the friars of the newly chartered Dominican and Franciscan orders to serve as the shock troops of the war on heresy. Thus were friars of the so-called mendicant orders called away from their work as wandering preachers and charged with the new mission of finding and punishing heretics of all kinds. And that is why the uniform of the inquisitor—a hooded robe like the one worn by Tomás de Torquemada (1420–1498)—consisted of nothing more than the ordinary habit of his order.[19]

One might be tempted to believe that a man who had taken vows of poverty, chastity, and obedience out of a zealous desire to live in imitation of Christ would be temperamentally unsuited for the role of persecutor, but the opposite turned out to be true. Indeed, the religious zeal that attracted men to the mendicant orders could be readily turned against the victims of the Inquisition once the friar-inquisitors accepted the idea that those dragged into the torture chamber and burned at the stake were "heretical filth" rather than mortal human beings. So fierce and so faithful were the

Dominicans in doing the dirty work of the Inquisition that they came to be described with a fearful pun—*Domini canes,* "the hounds of God."

The friar-inquisitors brought with them certain skills and training that were especially useful in dealing with dissident Christians. The friars' command of church dogma, for example, came in handy when they were called upon to confront the occasional Cathar *perfectus* who had been caught up along with the less sophisticated victims of the Inquisition. "How can the fire that burns the houses of the poor and holy be created by God?" a Cathar is shown to taunt his interrogator in the pages of one inquisitorial tract. "How can the God who sends suffering to good men be good himself?" To hear the inquisitors tell it, the investigation of an accused heretic was sometimes the occasion for disputation rather than interrogation, and a working knowledge of Catholic theology was as important as the interrogator's skill with the techniques of torture.[20]

The friars were regarded as suitable candidates for inquisitors for more practical reasons as well. They were available to serve full-time in that role and, if called upon, for the rest of their lives. Because they had taken a vow of poverty, they were thought to be untempted by the bribes that might be offered by wealthy defendants or their families. Perhaps even more important, as far as the masters of the Inquisition were concerned, the Dominicans and Franciscans were deferential to authority, a crucial quality in light of the fact that the proceedings of the Inquisition were to be conducted in the strictest secrecy. All of them had taken vows of obedience when they joined their orders, and a papal bull of 1260 formally redirected their loyalty from their own Dominican and Franciscan superiors to the pope himself. The intimacy of the relationship between the pope and "the Preaching Friars Inquisitors," as they came to be known, is captured in a canon in which they are addressed as "our cherished and faithful children in Christ."[21]

Among the friars who were available for the work of the Inquisition, "wise and mature men capable of asserting their authority" were preferred. University graduates and especially men with doctorates in law and theology were especially attractive candidates. A church council at Vienna in 1311 set the minimum age of an inquisitor at forty, although the ever-growing manpower demands of the Inquisition eventually forced the Church to accept men as young as thirty. Bernard Gui, perhaps the single most famous medieval inquisitor and the author of the inquisitor's handbook titled *Practica officii inquisitionis heretice pravitatis* (Conduct of the inquisition into heretical depravity), offered his own idealized job description.[22]

The inquisitor, Gui insisted, should be "diligent and fervent in his zeal for the truth of religion, for the salvation of souls, and for the extirpation of heresy," but he should never allow himself "to be inflamed with the fury of wrath and indignation." He is cautioned against slothful habits, "for sloth destroys the vigor of action." He must walk the middle path, "persisting through danger to death" and yet "neither precipitating peril by audacity nor shrinking from it through timidity." He ought to resist "the prayers and blandishments of those who seek to influence him," and yet he must also avoid "hardness of heart." To hear Gui tell it, the inquisitor was a model of priestly piety and judicial restraint.[23] "Let truth and mercy, which should never leave the heart of a judge, shine forth from his countenance," wrote Gui, "that his decisions may be free from all suspicion of covetousness or cruelty."[24]

Few of Bernard Gui's fellow inquisitors, however, actually manifested the fine qualities advertised in his inquisitor's manual. Some were careerists who saw the Inquisition as a way of moving upward in the hierarchy of the Church. (By the sixteenth century, two inquisitors had risen in succession to the rank of Supreme Pontiff as Pope Paul IV and Pope Pius V.) Others, as we have noted, were speculators and profiteers who figured out how to use the inquisitorial system to enrich themselves at the expense of their victims. And the Inquisition surely sheltered more than a few outright sadists for whom the inquisitorial torture chamber was a theater of sick pleasure.

The opportunities for self-aggrandizement were simply too numerous and too inviting for many of the inquisitors to resist. An inquisitor in Padua found it less profitable to persecute accused heretics than to sell them "clandestine absolutions," a practice that resulted in what one historian calls "frauds against the Church and the Inquisition itself," since it robbed the Inquisition of both the victims and their money.[25] Other inquisitors yielded to the temptation to use their power and position against their personal enemies, real or imagined. "Old grudges would be satisfied in safety," writes Lea, who cites the observation of the English jurist Sir John Fortescue, an eyewitness to the operation of the Inquisition in Paris in the fifteenth century: "It placed every man's life or limb at the mercy of any enemy who could suborn two unknown witnesses to swear against him."[26]

Paradoxically, some of the most zealous inquisitors were themselves former members of the persecuted faiths who turned their insider's knowledge against their former coreligionists with special fury. The two "self-appointed inquisitors" who had joined ranks with Conrad of Marburg were said to be former heretics. Indeed, a Cathar *perfectus* who was willing to confess and convert represented a valuable prize for the Inquisition, both as an example to encourage the others and, more concretely, as a willing source of detailed information about unrepentant heretics.

The sobriquet of the Dominican inquisitor known as Robert le Bougre indicates that he had been a Cathar before he joined the Inquisition—*le Bougre* (the Bulgar), as we have already seen, refers to the Bulgarian origins of Catharism. He was so effective at extracting confessions that he was said to possess the power to "infatuate" his victims, which helps explain why he was able to send so many to the stake. On a single occasion in 1239, he presided over the burning of 183 Cathars in a single gruesome spectacle that a contemporary chronicler praised as "a holocaust, very great and pleasing to God." Robert le Bougre is described by Edward Burman as "a homicidal maniac," but he earned a more admiring nickname from his fellow inquisitors: *Malleus Haereticorum,* the Hammer of Heretics.[27]

The first inquisitors were simply recruited from the ranks and dispatched in pairs to the towns and villages that were the fighting front in the war on heresy. Over the centuries, however, the Inquisition grew into an elaborate and highly formal bureaucracy, with the friar-inquisitors on the bottom rung of a chain of command that reached all the way to a kind of chief executive officer who theoretically answered only to the pope himself. Torquemada, for example, was designated as the grand inquisitor of the Spanish Inquisition in the fifteenth century. A couple of centuries later, the Inquisition operated under the nominal authority of the Congregation of the Holy Office at the Vatican, and the Congregation's members were cardinals officially described as "Inquisitors-General throughout the Christian commonwealth against heretical pravity."[28]

The real work of the Inquisition, of course, was always conducted by those humble friars who wore the hooded mantle of the mendicant orders rather than a cardinal's red hat. And the greatest number of them were probably not sadists or homicidal maniacs; rather, they have been described by Malcolm Lambert as nothing more offensive than "zealous, hard-working bureaucrats" who, not unlike the clerks who devised the railroad schedules for Auschwitz, showed up every day and simply did their jobs. No matter where they stood in the hierarchy, all the inquisitors prided themselves on their hard work in ridding Christendom of "heretical filth." That's why Cardinal Robert Bellarmine, the inquisitor-general who persecuted Galileo for believing that the earth revolves around the sun, earned the very same honorific that had been bestowed four hundred years earlier on Robert le Bougre—the cardinal, too, is hailed as "the Hammer of Heretics" in the official records of the Inquisition.[29]

The grim work of the medieval Inquisition always began with a solemn religious ceremony. "When you arrive in a town," Pope Gregory IX formally instructed the friar-inquisitors in 1231, "you will summon the prelates, clergy and people, and you will preach a solemn sermon." Only then were the inquisitors to "begin your enquiry into the beliefs of heretics and suspects with diligent care." Anyone who, after investigation and interrogation by the inquisitors, is "recognized as guilty or suspected of heresy," Gregory continued, "must promise to obey the orders of the Church absolutely." But if they do not, "you should proceed against them, following the statutes that we have recently promulgated against the heretics."[30]

The inquisitor's opening sermon was the occasion for a public display of the terrible power of the Inquisition. To encourage attendance, indulgences were offered to those faithful Christians who assembled to hear the sermon. But the whole populace of a town or village—every male over the age of fourteen and every female over the age of twelve—was required to show up, and anyone who secretly entertained a belief that was forbidden by the Church was expected to come forward and confess to the crime of heresy. One's absence from the so-called *sermo generalis,* which might be readily noticed in a small town or village, was essentially a public admission of guilt.

Clearly, the inquisitor hoped and perhaps even expected that his preachments would move the crowds to acts of spontaneous public confession and thus spare him the work of searching out heretics. Some men and women, in fact, were so inspired—or so terrorized—that they confessed their heretical beliefs then and there, if only because an early and uncoerced confession might persuade the inquisitors to impose only a mild punishment or none at all. But the Inquisition never relied on sermons to induce spontaneous confessions. Indeed, the mission of the Inquisition was to flush out even the most secretive and disciplined dissidents, to break their will to resist, and to turn them into witnesses against their fellow believers. At these tasks, the Inquisition proved to be relentless, merciless, and highly successful.

The monks who carried the title of Inquisitor into Heretical Depravity enjoyed the ultimate authority to condemn and punish the convicted heretic, but they never acted alone. A vast, powerful, wholly secret bureaucracy was put at their disposal, ranging from auxiliaries, attorneys, bailiffs, clerks, notaries, and scriveners to constables, jailors, torturers, and executioners. The inquisitors, who generally traveled and worked in pairs, were accompanied wherever they went by armed servants, generally known as *servientes* or familiars, who acted as bodyguards, henchmen, and enforcers. They were served, too, by a network of spies and informers who supplied the Inquisition with whispered denunciations. The whole mechanism was designed to gather data in secret and in bulk, and then use the data to identify suspects, fill the waiting cells, and ultimately feed the flames of the auto-da-fé with human flesh. "What has survived in folk memory and literature of the medieval Inquisition is not so much the zeal of individual inquisitors," observes Edward Burman, "as the generalized and widespread terror of the Holy Office itself."[31]

The inquisitors and their servitors set up operations in the towns and villages across Europe where heresy was detected or suspected, pressing into use whatever facilities they needed or wanted. Bernard Gui, for example, set up operations in the Dominican convent in Toulouse, a venue he dubbed the "Hôtel de l'Inquisition," and a Franciscan inquisitor might do the same in a monastery belonging to his own order. Other inquisitors availed themselves of a local church or, in a city that boasted a cathedral, the bishop's palace. Or, if the inquisitor preferred, he could always commandeer a town hall since, as Lea writes, "the authorities, both lay and clerical, were bound to afford all assistance demanded." Indeed, any reluctance to cooperate with the inquisitors was treated as evidence of fautorship and might prompt the inquisitors to send the reluctant mayor or abbot into the same dungeon where the other accused heretics were locked away. To emphasize his spiritual authority, the inquisitor was addressed in person as "Most Reverent."[32]

Once established in their working quarters, the inquisitors promptly began to collect the confessions and denunciations that were the raw material of industrial-scale persecution. A medieval version of the secret police was first authorized by the Council of Béziers in 1246—the inquisitors were called upon to select a priest and one or two laymen in each parish "whose duty it should be to search for heretics, examining all houses, inside and out, and especially all secret hiding places." All parish priests were required to serve as informers, reporting to the Inquisition if any of their congregants failed to perform the penances imposed on them by the Inquisition as punishment for acts of heresy. In fact, all good Christians were under a standing order from the Church to come forward and report any evidence of heresy that might come to their attention, and the failure to comply amounted to the crime of fautorship.[33]

A "serving-wench" accused of heresy by the medieval Inquisition, for example, protested her innocence throughout her long interrogation, but when her living quarters were searched, a scorched sliver of bone was supposedly found hidden in a wooden chest—the pitiful remains of a fellow believer who had been burned at the stake, or so it was alleged. To add weight to the fragmentary evidence, the friar-inquisitors secured the testimony of a convicted heretic who swore that she had accompanied the serving-wench when she collected the relic from the ashes of the execution.

Then, too, a self-confessed heretic was required to name names in order to escape the worst punishments available to the inquisitor. It was not enough for the accused to admit their own heretical beliefs; they must also reveal the identities of their fellow believers—"and the hiding-places and conventicles of darkness" where they gathered to pray—or else the confession would be regarded as halfhearted and unacceptable. The betrayal of others was regarded as "the indispensable evidence of true conversion," and the refusal to do so exposed the suspect to the additional charge of fautorship. Here was one of the many traps into which a victim of the Inquisition might fall—the accused heretic might imagine that he was saving his own life by confessing to the charges against him, but he would quickly discover that the failure to denounce friends and relations, no matter how principled or compassionate, rendered the confession incomplete, insincere, and "imperfect." Indeed, a refusal to name the names of other heretics amounted to a crime in itself.[34]

The legal obligation of suspects and witnesses to name names provided the Inquisition with an efficient tool for flushing out additional heretics in great numbers. An accused Cathar named Suarine Rigaud, for example, provided the inquisitors with the names and dwelling places of 169 other men and women during her interrogation in 1254. The naming of names achieved much more than filling the prisons of the Inquisition with more bodies to afflict and burn. Fear of betrayal by an accused heretic under interrogation poisoned relations among friends and within families, shattered the congregations of dissident Christians who worshiped together, and reinforced the reign of terror that was the Inquisition's single most powerful weapon. "A single lucky capture and extorted confession would put the sleuth-hounds on the track of hundreds who deemed themselves secure, and each new victim added his circle of denunciations," writes Henry Charles Lea. "The heretic lived over a volcano which might burst forth at any moment."[35]

Another source of information was the medieval equivalent of the jail-house snitch, whose services were regarded as so valuable by the Inquisition that they outweighed even the vilest crimes on the part of the informer. A Carmelite monk who had been found guilty of "the most infamous sorceries" in 1329, for example, managed to persuade the inquisitors to soften his sentence by going to work on "sundry heretics" among his fellow prisoners, and he dutifully reported to his masters whatever incriminating remarks he extracted by false displays of friendship or perhaps merely invented. When the monk came up for sentencing, his good work as an informant was cited "in extenuation of his black catalogue of guilt."[36] His fate reminds us that the Inquisition apparently regarded the Christian rigorism of Cathars and Waldensians as a greater threat to the Church than the secret practice of sorcery by one of its own monastics.

All reports of "heretical depravity" from the various sources—confessions, denunciations, searches, interrogations—were carefully collected, recorded, organized, and filed away for ready use by the Inquisition. Perhaps the most fearful and enduring feature of the inquisitorial bureaucracy was its relentless collection and preservation of information. The archives of the medieval Inquisition, a vast collection of handwritten and hand-copied documents ranging "from the first summons to the final sentence in every case," provided the inquisitors with what we would today call a database. And the inquisitors put the database to good use in tracking down men and women who imagined that they had escaped detection and then catching them in inconsistencies once they were put under interrogation.[37]

Sometimes a man or woman suspected of heresy came to the attention of the Inquisition in a kind of dragnet operation called an *inquisitio generalis,* and sometimes in an *inquisitio specialis* that focused on a single accused heretic whose name had been given up by a friend or relation. Now and then, a victim might attract the attention of the Inquisition merely because he or she was known to be rich. After all, an important source of funding for the bureaucracy was the wealth confiscated from condemned heretics, both money and property, and the fines levied against them and their heirs. But the appetite of the Inquisition was vast and indiscriminate, and its victims were drawn from both genders, all classes, and every rank.

Once a suspected heretic had been denounced to the Inquisition by an informer, a spy, or a self-confessed heretic trying desperately to save himself at the expense of his fellow believers, the inquisitors brought the entire apparatus to bear on the defendant. A formal citation would be sent to the priest of the parish where the suspect resided, and he was obliged to deliver the bad news to the defendant in person and then to the whole congregation, repeating the accusation in church for three consecutive Sundays or feast days. The public charge was a punishment in itself, of course, because the accused heretic would suddenly find himself alone and friendless. Anyone who sheltered or assisted him in any way risked prosecution for the crime of fautorship.

The accused heretic was expected to surrender himself to the inquisitor who had issued the charge against him, but if he refused—or if it was suspected that he might try to flee—the inquisitor's armed servants would seek him out, place him under arrest, and deliver him to one of the prisons set aside for the confinement of accused and convicted heretics. Either way, the defendant commonly remained in custody while the staff of the Inquisition carried out its long, slow, exacting investigation. Some unfortunate victims might remain in a cell, not yet convicted or even charged, for years or even decades. Meanwhile, confessed heretics, informers, and other witnesses were questioned, transcripts were prepared and signed, evidence was gathered, all in preparation for the secret trial at which guilt or innocence would be decided and punishment handed down.

The inquisitors resorted to old and crude techniques of physical torture to break the will of suspected heretics, a subject that will be explored in detail in the next chapter. They also perfected and used various weapons of what we would call psychological warfare to reduce their victims to a state of isolation, anxiety, and vulnerability. The whole enterprise was styled as the well-ordered workings of canon law based on the ancient Roman legal procedure of *inquisitio,* which empowered the inquisitors to compel testimony from suspects and witnesses alike and to receive as evidence even "a mere *fama,*" that is, a rumor or even a slander uttered in secret against the unwitting suspect.[38]

Here is the point at which *inquisitio* departed from the other forms of criminal prosecution available in medieval Europe. Under the legal procedure called *accusatio,* the prosecution was initiated on the basis of a charge "laid by an accuser at his own peril if it proved false"; that is, the accuser was required to identify himself, post a bond, and pay the expenses of the accused if he or she was acquitted. Another procedure, called *denunciatio,* was initiated by a magistrate on the basis of evidence secured in an official inquiry. The proceedings took place on the record in open court, and the accused was entitled to be represented by an attorney. It is only in the procedure called *inquisitio* that the prosecutor was empowered to rely on a whispered rumor from a nameless informer in placing the suspect under arrest and interrogating him—alone, in secret, and under oath—"his answers making him, in effect, his own accuser," as historian Walter L. Wakefield explains.[39]

Inquisitio had been used by the Church to detect and punish the moral lapses of clergy long before it was deployed in the prosecution of heresy. The right of a prosecutor to rely on rumor and to conduct his investigation in secret was useful in penetrating the conspiracy of silence that might otherwise protect a priest suspected of keeping a concubine or a bishop who was trafficking in titles or indulgences for profit, the besetting sin of the medieval Church. Later, *inquisitio* came to be applied in all church courts, ranging from those of "rural archpriests or deans charging rustics with fornication or adultery" to "trials presided over by cardinals on charges brought against kings and queens," according to Henry Ansgar Kelly, a revisionist historian who insists that the case against the Inquisition has been grossly overstated. Yet it is also true that the Inquisition elevated *inquisitio* into a tool of thought control, used to persecute every manner of religious belief and practice that the inquisitors deemed to be at odds with the Church's dogma.[40]

Thus did the Inquisition seek to create the impression that it was omniscient and omnipresent, a power unto itself that operated in strictest secrecy and yet from which no secret could be kept. Its notion of what constituted admissible evidence was so casual—and its definition of the crime of heresy so sweeping—that the distance between accusation and conviction was almost imperceptible. Between these two fixed points, however, was the ordeal of an interrogation by the friar-inquisitors. Even when the instruments of torture were not used, interrogation was a kind of torture in itself.

The inquisitors were offered much practical advice on the art of interrogation in the inquisitor's handbooks. Bernard Gui, for example, warned that "heretics nowadays try to conceal their errors rather than admit them openly," and he encouraged the inquisitors to arm themselves for theological combat with an artfully clever enemy: "[Heretics] use a screen of deceitful words and clever tricks," Gui wrote. "In this way, they can confound learned men, and this makes these boastful heretics all the stronger, being able to escape by means of tortuous, cunning and crafty evasions."[41]

Interrogation, in fact, was the highest art of the inquisitor. Whatever else a friar-inquisitor brought to his job or acquired over his years of training and practice, the single most important skill was his ability to question an accused heretic. The best of them were possessed of "acute and subtle minds," according to Henry Charles Lea, "practiced to read the thoughts of the accused, skilled to lay pitfalls for the incautious, versed in every art to confuse, prompt to detect ambiguities, and quick to take advantage of hesitation or contradiction." Their victims, by contrast, were generally exhausted, starved, and terrorized after a long stay in the cells and dungeons of the Inquisition. Entirely aside from the special skills and tools of the torturer, the interrogation was an ordeal.[42]

The interrogations were exhaustive, and any recollection might be used to condemn the suspect or someone else as a heretic. "Questions were of the police-court type," explains Malcolm Lambert, "concerned with external acts which revealed complicity with heresy." A ferryman at a river crossing who happened to carry a Cathar *perfectus* as a passenger might himself be convicted on the charge of heresy, for example, and the same fate might befall a servant whose master turned out to be a Waldensian. If a doctor was convicted of heresy, his patients were at risk; the fact that the Waldensians operated clinics and hospitals provided the inquisitors with plenty of new suspects among those who had contacted the Waldensians in search of a cure for illness or the treatment of an injury. Indeed, merely entering a house where a heretic was later proved to be present—or making a polite bow when being introduced to someone who turned out to be a *perfectus*—was enough to place someone under suspicion of heresy in the eyes of the Inquisition.[43] "It is a noteworthy fact that in long series of interrogations," writes Lea, "there will frequently be not a single question as to the belief of the party making confession."[44]

Still, the records of the Inquisition confirm that some victims were, in fact, subjected to close questioning of the "heads-I-win, tails-you-lose" variety that was designed to trap them into a confession of heretical beliefs. He or she might be tricked into a fatal concession with a simple question that assumes the guilt of the accused: "How often have you confessed as a heretic?" Or the inquisitor might pose a trick question that simply could not be answered at all without self-crimination: "Does a woman conceive through the act of God or of man?" an inquisitor asks. If the victim answers "Man," the reply is taken as evidence of heresy because it denies the power of God, but if the same victim answers "God," then the reply is still regarded as heretical—after all, the suspect was suggesting that "God had carnal relations with women."[45]

At moments, an interrogation might begin to sound like an Abbott and Costello routine. According to a line of questioning that appears as an example in Gui's handbook, the inquisitor opens with an article of faith in Roman Catholic dogma: "Do you believe in Christ born of the Virgin, suffered, risen, and ascended to heaven?"

"And you, sir," replies the accused, "do you not believe it?"

"I believe it wholly," says the inquisitor.

"I believe likewise," affirms the accused.

"You believe that I believe it, which is not what I ask, but whether *you* believe it," says the frustrated inquisitor.[46]

Once the inquisitors had rounded up suspects for interrogation in a given town or village, the whole populace was at risk. Starting in 1245, the inquisitor Bernard de Caux carried out an inquisition in two regions of southern France, Lauragais and Lavaur. Almost every adult in these two regions, a total of 5,471 men and women in thirty-nine towns, was summoned and questioned. Interrogation transcripts were compared, and inconsistencies were followed up with a fresh round of questioning. A total of 207 suspects was found guilty and punished—23 were sent to prison, and the rest were sentenced to a variety of lesser punishments, but the otherwise meticulous records do not disclose whether any of the accused heretics in these towns were turned over to the secular authorities for burning at the stake.

Nor did the Inquisition content itself with victims who had reached adulthood. Boys as young as ten and a half, and girls as young as nine and a half, were deemed to be culpable, according to some church councils, and the strictest authorities "reduced the age of responsibility to seven years." Starting at the age of fourteen, a boy or girl could be lawfully subjected to torture during interrogation, although some jurisdictions insisted that a "curator" be appointed for boys and girls accused of heresy. The curator was a curious sort of legal guardian "under whose shade [the child] could be tortured and condemned," according to Lea.[47]

The interrogations yielded a plentiful supply of accusations, most of them compounded of an uncertain blend of truths and half-truths, slander and speculation, and sheer fabrication, all of it extracted from terrified witnesses who were generally anxious to tell their interrogators exactly what they wanted to hear. Since the Inquisition punished not only heresy itself but also the mere suspicion of heresy, whether "light," "vehement," or "violent"—and since "hearsay, vague rumors, general impressions, or idle gossip" were all regarded as equally admissible in the proceedings of the Inquisition—the line between accusation and evidence was virtually nonexistent. What the witnesses were willing to say, or what they could be forced to say under the threat or application of torture, the Inquisition was willing to embrace and use.[48]

Nearly every word spoken by both accuser and accused was taken down by hand by one of the notaries who were present at all proceedings of the Inquisition. Indeed, the notary was fully as important to the workings of the Inquisition as the torturer, the executioner, or the inquisitor himself. If a notary was unavailable—or if he was overburdened by the volume of work—a professional copier of documents, known as a scrivener, would be pressed into service.

At the end of every interrogation, the notary attested to the accuracy of the record, thus "giving at least a color of impartiality."[49] Testimony was supposed to be taken in the presence of two impartial witnesses who would join the notary in signing the transcript to verify its accuracy. But the witnesses were always selected by the inquisitors, who preferred "discreet and religious men" and, whenever possible, Dominicans or other clerics whose loyalties and duty of obedience were directed to the Church. To ensure the absolute control of the Inquisition over its own workings, all witnesses were required to take an oath never to reveal what they had observed during the secret proceedings.[50]

The transcripts may have been voluminous and tedious, but they were not merely filed away and forgotten. Rather, they were copied out and exchanged by inquisitors across Europe in a "fearful multiplication of papers" that served at least a couple of urgent concerns of the Inquisition. First, the inquisitors were careful to create and maintain duplicate records in case the originals were misplaced or destroyed, whether by accidental fire or flood or by the willful act of men and women seeking to hinder the work of the Inquisition. The destruction of records, as we shall see, was a favorite tactic of the courageous individuals who set themselves against the Inquisition in its early years. Second, the records were exchanged and actively consulted by various inquisitors in making cases against accused heretics across vast distances of miles and years.[51]

The notaries and scriveners who assembled and preserved the records of the Inquisition bestowed a useful and terrible tool on the friar-inquisitors. They enjoyed access to the names, whereabouts, friendships, family relations, assets, and business dealings of the accused heretics. "With such data at his disposal," observes Malcolm Lambert, "a medieval inquisitor had resources comparable to that of a modern police officer, ever ready to check and cross-check information." The fact that the Inquisition enjoyed both international jurisdiction and an institutional memory in the form of shared documents checkmated those who dared to hide or flee and guaranteed that the mere passage of time provided no protection for dissident Christians who might have escaped the attention of a particular inquisitor.[52]

An elderly woman in Toulouse was convicted and punished for heresy by the Inquisition on the basis of musty records dating back some fifty years. She had been allowed to rejoin the Church after confessing to heresy in 1268, but when she was charged a second time in 1316, a new generation of inquisitors consulted the archives that had been assembled before they were born and discovered the prior conviction. Relapse into heresy, as we shall see, was regarded as an even more heinous crime than the original act, and a repeat offender was subject to the most severe penalties available to the inquisitor. So the old woman of Toulouse was condemned to "perpetual imprisonment in chains" as a repeat offender, "perhaps even having forgotten the incident of nearly a half-century before."[53]

Entirely apart from their practical utility in tracking down concealed or escaped suspects, the archives can be seen to serve a metaphysical function in the history of the Inquisition. Since the heretical acts and beliefs that so obsessed the inquisitors often existed only in their own overheated imaginations, the scratching of a notary's goose-quill pen on a leaf of laid paper somehow turned fantasy into reality and created what passed for documentary evidence. The alchemy of ink and paper would work the same magic in centuries to come, not only for the Inquisition but for every new generation of persecutors responding to the inquisitorial impulse.

Above all, the Inquisition relied on secrecy and the terror that secrecy inspired. All testimony—whether from the accused, his or her accusers, or others implicated in the accusations and confessions—was taken in examinations conducted by the inquisitors and their various servitors behind closed doors. The names of accusers and witnesses, and the testimony or other evidence they offered, were withheld from the person under investigation. As a result, the victims of the Inquisition were never given an opportunity to confront or cross-examine those who denounced them.

Indeed, the accused would not even know the particulars of the charges against them unless they were able to discern them from the questions put by the inquisitor. When a desperate defendant begged the inquisitor James Fournier (later Pope Benedict XXII) to reveal the supposed offense for which he was being tried, for example, the inquisitor consented to tell him *"de gratia,"* that is, "as a favor." Less fortunate victims were reduced to guessing what particular false belief they were accused of embracing and which nameless accusers—embittered friends or relations, a spiteful neighbor, a rival in business—had slipped their names to the Inquisition.[54]

A man or woman accused of heresy was theoretically entitled to mount a defense to the charges, at least according to the rulings of a few popes and church councils over the centuries. But various papal decrees encouraged the inquisitors to proceed "simply and plainly and without the uproar and form of lawyers," and the bull of 1229 titled *Excommunicamus* formally denied the assistance of legal counsel to defendants in proceedings of the Inquisition. Even at the times and places where attorneys were permitted in theory, the accused heretic who could afford to hire one was hard-pressed to find an advocate who would take his or her case.

When a Franciscan friar named Bernard Délicieux was ordered by his own superior to "defend the memory" of a dead man accused of heresy before the Inquisition in 1300, not a single notary in the city of Carcassonne was willing to assist him in drawing up legal documents to be presented to the inquisitor. The good friar was forced to send to a distant city for a more courageous notary because the local ones remembered how the inquisitor had previously arrested and imprisoned the notary who had foolishly rendered legal services in the appeal that a group of citizens had lodged against the Inquisition with the king of France a few years earlier.[55]

The Inquisition itself, on the other hand, was well supplied with expert legal advice. Starting in 1300, as we have noted, the preferred candidates for the job of inquisitor were men who had earned a doctorate of law at a university. However, most inquisitors were "utterly ignorant of the law," according to the fourteenth-century commentator Zanghino Ugolini, and they "were chosen rather with regard to zeal than learning." As a result, the grand inquisitor Nicholas Eymerich (ca. 1320–1399) recommended in his own manual of instruction that an inquisitor "should always associate himself with some discreet lawyer to save him from mistakes," not only the kind of mistakes that might allow a victim to escape punishment but, even more crucially, the blunders that might cause the inquisitor to be dismissed from his job by his superiors. Eventually, some tribunals of the Inquisition routinely employed an attorney with the official title of Counselor as a member of the paid inquisitorial staff.[56]

Every legal procedure of the Inquisition, in fact, was designed for the convenience of the inquisitors alone. Confessed or convicted heretics, common criminals, and even children—all of whom were ordinarily excluded as witnesses in both church and civil courts—were permitted to give evidence before the Inquisition, but only if they testified against the accused. (If their testimony tended to exculpate an accused heretic, the customary exclusions were applied.) By contrast, the standard legal procedure known as *purgatorio canonica,* which permitted the accused to call on friends and acquaintances to formally support his oath of innocence, was ultimately rendered useless because to do so constituted an admission of one's own guilt as a fautor.

Although a defendant was entitled in theory to discredit the witnesses against him by showing them to be motivated by ill will—the "mortal enmity" of an accuser toward the accused was the *only* grounds for disqualification of a witness who gave testimony before the Inquisition—the legal tactic was rarely available because of the secrecy that applied to the workings of the Inquisition. After all, the defendant did not know the identity of the accuser or the witnesses, the nature of the evidence against him, or even the specific charge on which he was being tried. On rare occasions, an alert and canny defendant might be able to discern a few helpful details about the case against him from the questions put to him by the interrogator, and only then would he be able to come up with the name of an ill-willed accuser in a desperate act of self-defense.*

A rare and colorful example of an accused heretic who guessed the identity of his accuser is found in the records of the Inquisition at Carcassonne. A man named Bernard Pons, charged as a heretic in 1254, discerned that his

---

*One victim of the Spanish Inquisition, a professor on the faculty of the University of Salamanca, managed to identify his secret accusers by simply naming all his fellow faculty members as personal enemies on the assumption that academic politics might have moved them to denounce him. He guessed correctly.

own wife had denounced him to the Inquisition and persuaded three of his friends to testify that she held a grudge against him. All three attested that she was "a woman of loose character." One testified that Pons had caught her in an act of adultery; another testified that Pons had given his wife a beating; and the third testified that "she wished her husband dead that she might marry a certain Pug Oler, and that she would willingly become a leper if that would bring it about." Yet the weight of evidence against the accuser did not persuade the inquisitor that the unfaithful wife had acted out of ill will, and the cuckolded husband was convicted on her disputed testimony.[57]

So the man or woman who faced the Inquisition did so utterly alone. The inquisitors were armed with information extracted under torture from other suspects, or provided by spies and informers, friendly witnesses and confessed heretics—all of them nameless—or culled from the archives of the Inquisition, and they were attended and supported by clerks, notaries, scriveners, attorneys, and other servitors. By contrast, the defendant was frightened, disoriented, usually deprived of food and rest after a long stay in a cell, bereft of advice or assistance, and wholly ignorant of the charges, evidence, and witnesses arrayed against him.

The inquisitorial apparatus in its entirety can be understood, then, as a machine designed to extract a confession from the accused heretic. The use of torture represented the last desperate effort of the friar-inquisitors to terrorize their victims into confessing their supposed crimes and sparing the inquisitors the burden of actually weighing the evidence, such as it was. Only if an accused heretic refused to confess during interrogation was the inquisitor compelled to conduct a hearing at which the evidence was presented, the guilt or innocence of the victim considered, and a verdict rendered.

The trial, too, was conducted in absolute secrecy. Before the proceeding began, the defendant was "required to swear that he would never divulge the details of his 'trial.'" Afterward, he was compelled to acknowledge that he had been offered an opportunity to present a defense and "had not availed himself of it." The trial itself was a mere formality, an opportunity for the inquisitors to reprise the evidence of heresy, formally interrogate the suspect one last time, and afford him a final opportunity to confess before they passed sentence. By that point, no real question remained in anyone's mind about the verdict. Indeed, a trial before the Inquisition anticipates the imaginary tribunal that sits in judgment in Franz Kafka's *The Trial*. "You can't defend yourself against this court, all you can do is confess," observes one of his fictional characters.[58]

Such was the quality of "legal justice" afforded to the victims of the Inquisition. "When the Inquisition once laid hands upon a man it never released its hold," insists Henry Charles Lea. "No verdict of acquittal was ever issued." Yet the elaborate framework of rules and regulations erected around the machinery of persecution was one of the great innovations of the Inquisition, often invoked by its defenders and much copied by its imitators in future years.[59]

At last, the friar-inquisitors were ready to announce the sentence—or, as the Inquisition preferred to put it, the "penance"—that the Inquisition would impose on the convicted heretic. Bernard Gui's handbook includes a formula for pardoning a convicted heretic, but Gui himself cautions his readers that "it is never, or most rarely, to be used." If pardoned, the heretic was formally admonished that "the slightest cause of suspicion would lead him to be punished without mercy," and the Inquisition reserved the right "to incarcerate him again without the formality of a fresh trial or sentence if the interest of the faith required." Once the trial was concluded and the guilt of the accused heretic was confirmed, the Inquisition now proceeded to its single most important function, the one for which it was designed and the one in which the inquisitors took the greatest pride and pleasure— the punishment of the convicted heretic.[60]

Apologists for the Inquisition have argued that it was based on sound legal procedure, and they point to the voluminous body of canon law that accumulated over the centuries in the library of the Vatican. "No one could be legally convicted of a crime without adequate proof," insists Henry Ansgar Kelly. If a man or woman was falsely accused of heresy by the Inquisition, or terrorized into a confession, or punished without cause, he argues, it was only because some renegade inquisitor had violated the body of law that governed its operations. "The abusive practices that came to prevail in the special heresy tribunals do not merit the name of inquisition," insists Kelly, "but rather should be identified as a perversion of the inquisitorial process caused by overzealous and underscrupulous judges."[61]

The defenders of the Inquisition, like Kelly, point out that, strictly speaking, an inquisitor was powerless to impose a sentence on a convicted heretic on his own authority. Rather, each proposed sentence was supposedly submitted for review by a committee of "assessors"—that is, jurists and monastics—and then for ratification by a local bishop. But these legal niceties, when they were observed at all, "were perfunctory to the last degree," according to Lea, "and placed no real check upon the discretion of the inquisitor." The assessors were chosen by the inquisitor and "sworn on the Gospels to secrecy," and any bishop who threatened to withhold his approval of a sentence proposed by the inquisitor could be circumvented by an appeal to the pope or pressured into submission with the threat of one.[62]

The convicted heretic, by contrast, enjoyed little or no opportunity to appeal from an act of the Inquisition, no matter how grossly it may have violated the formal rules and regulations. Some bulls and canons appear flatly to rule out the right of appeal by heretics. In those places and periods of history when an appeal was available in theory, it was to be addressed to the pope in Rome—a long, cumbersome, expensive process—and it could be lodged only before sentence was pronounced. As a practical matter, only a few men and women possessed the opportunity, the means, and the sheer courage to challenge the authority of the Inquisition.

Even then, the innocence of the appellant or the legal defects in the proceedings against him or her were ultimately less important than the quid pro quo offered to the Holy See in exchange for papal intervention. When six confessed heretics were ordered to be released from the Inquisition in 1248, for example, the papal legate who conveyed the order piously noted by way of explanation that they had made "liberal contributions to the cause of the Holy Land."[63]

Then, too, the proceedings of the Inquisition were rendered sacrosanct by a sweeping escape clause provided by the Vatican. Pope Innocent IV in 1245 authorized the inquisitors to absolve their servitors for any acts of violence committed in the discharge of their duties, and Pope Alexander IV in 1256 empowered any inquisitor to absolve any other inquisitor from "canonical irregularities occurring in the performance of their duties." The Inquisition was further insulated from the moral consequences of its work by a rule that protected an inquisitor from excommunication during his lifetime and granted him absolution from sin upon death, at which point he was deemed to be entitled to an indulgence from the period of suffering in purgatory equal to his length of service.[64]

So the Inquisition was always a closed circle within which the inquisitor might do as he pleased and the victim was at his mercy. The inquisitors were so contemptuous of the rights of their victims that the inquisitor's manuals frankly discuss the various "devices and deceits" by which they could be frustrated. "They enjoyed the widest latitude of arbitrary procedure with little danger that anyone would dare to complain," writes Lea. "The inquisitors were a law unto themselves, and disregarded at pleasure the very slender restrictions imposed on them." Even an apologist like Kelly is forced to concede that "[t]hings had come to a sorry pass when the very substance of the inquisitorial procedure was so routinely ignored that violations were no longer recognized as such."[65]

So far, the operations of the Inquisition had taken place behind closed doors and in strict secrecy. Once the inquisitors were ready to impose a punishment on a convicted heretic, however, the doors were thrown open and the public was welcome to watch. Indeed, the sentencing and punishing of heretics was one of the great spectacles of public life over several centuries of European history, ranging from the mass murder of Cathars in medieval Languedoc to the ceremonial incinerations mounted in the *Plaza Mayor* of Madrid with the Spanish king and his court among the enthusiastic spectators. The whole point, of course, was to demonstrate the inevitable fate of any man or woman whose beliefs, whether real or imagined, were deemed heretical by the Inquisition, and thus to strike fear in the hearts of everyone else.

Just as a pious sermon marked the beginning of an *inquisitio generalis,* so too did a sermon serve as the occasion for sentencing heretics who had been detected, captured, tried, and convicted. The Inquisition summoned the citizenry into open court, along with clerics, magistrates, clerks, and lawyers, to hear another sermon before proceeding to the business at hand. Punishment was handed out according to the degree of culpability of the heretic, starting with the mildest punishments and ascending in severity to the death penalty. The ceremony itself was originally called an auto-da-fé (literally, "act of the faith"), a phrase that soon became a euphemism and later a synonym for the cruelest punishment of all, burning at the stake.

The range of punishments available to the Inquisition was limited only by the imagination of the inquisitors, as we shall consider in detail in the next chapter, and some of them showed a genius for improvisation and invention when it came to afflicting the confessed or convicted heretics. The most common "penances" started with the obligation of the convicted heretic to wear a yellow badge as a sign of his or her crime and grew steadily worse—compulsory pilgrimages, expulsion from church and public offices, destruction of houses, confiscation of property, imprisonment under varying degrees of harshness—until the worse offenders were handed to the civil authority to be burned alive.

According to yet another legal fiction embraced by the Inquisition, the inquisitor imposed punishment only on those who confessed to the crime of heresy, recanted their errors, and were welcomed back into the Church. For that reason, the self-confessed heretics were called penitents, and the penalties imposed by the inquisitor were characterized as penance rather than punishment. Those who would not confess and repent—and the ones who had recanted on a previous occasion and later relapsed into heresy—were excommunicated from the Church and turned over to the secular government for the imposition of punishment, whether imprisonment or death. According to the curious euphemism used by the Inquisition, these convicted heretics were said to be "abandoned" or "relaxed" to the civil authority for punishment, as if the Mother Church had loosened its grip and allowed them to fall out of its loving embrace. "With customary verbal dexterity and ambiguity, the Inquisition merely declared the existence of a crime and then handed the victim over to the secular arm," explains Burman. "It is the formula which has enabled apologists of the Inquisition to maintain that the tribunal never actually punished or burned its prisoners."[66]

Over the long history of the Inquisition, the ceremony at which heretics were sentenced grew ever more elaborate, and the burning of heretics en masse achieved its highest expression during the Spanish Inquisition, as we shall see in the next chapter. The public sentencing often took place in the solemn grandeur of a cathedral, but the executions were conducted in the public square, both to accommodate the largest possible audience and to make the point that the Church was not staining its own hands with the blood of the condemned men and women. To encourage attendance, the spectacle was generally mounted on a Sunday, the date was announced in advance from the pulpit at church services, and those in attendance at the auto-da-fé were promised an indulgence by which their souls would be spared forty days of suffering in purgatory.

To heighten the theatrical effect of the ceremony, the cases were allowed to accumulate so that, when the day of judgment finally arrived, the sheer number of victims would demonstrate both the magnitude of the threat to the Church and its power and will to strike back at the "traitors to God." At a single auto-da-fé conducted by the inquisitor Bernard Gui in 1310, for example, twenty penitents were ordered to go on pilgrimages and to wear the yellow cross that marked them as heretics, another sixty-five were sentenced to "perpetual" imprisonment (and three of them were ordered to serve their sentences in chains), and eighteen unrepentant heretics were "relaxed" to the civil authority and burned alive in the public square. The festivities started on a Sunday, and the last heretic was not put to the flames until the following Thursday.

Now and then, however, an inquisitor might dispense with the high ceremonial of the auto-da-fé in order to prevent a man of conscience from cheating the Inquisition of yet another victim. Immediately upon his arrest in 1309, for example, a Cathar teacher named Amiel de Perles commenced the final rite known as the *endura* and refused all food and drink offered by his captors. Rather than permit the prisoner to starve himself to death, Bernard Gui conducted a hasty trial and arranged for a quick execution. At the auto over which Gui presided, Amiel was the one and only victim. More commonly, though, the burning of heretics was the occasion for the kind of theatrical display that reached its highest expression under the Spanish Inquisition.

Not even the grave offered a safe refuge from the Inquisition. A dead man or woman—and even a long-deceased one—could be charged and tried posthumously, and the remains would be disinterred and burned at the stake. The corpse of a certain Alderigo of Verona, for example, was tried in 1287 on charges dating back a quarter-century, when he had supposedly assisted a victim of the Inquisition to escape from the tribunal in Venice. "The inquisitors had waited such a long time," according to historian Mariano da Alatri, "because their power of action was then limited by the large number of heretics in the area." A grisly record for the punishment of "defunct" heretics may have been set by a wealthy burgher of Carcassonne named Castel Faure, who was charged and convicted of heresy some forty-one years after his death in 1278. Faure's bones were left in the ground, but his wife's body was exhumed and burned, and his heirs were dispossessed of their inheritance.[67]

The disinterment and display of rotting bodies by the friar-inquisitors was deeply offensive to the first townspeople who were forced to witness the spectacle, and the earliest efforts of the Inquisition to punish "defunct" heretics prompted protest in the town of Albi. But the burning of dead bodies, like the wearing of yellow crosses or the public scourging of convicted heretics on feast days, was intended to make a point about the reach and power of the Inquisition, its long memory and strong will, and the terrible consequences of daring to entertain any belief that the Church regarded as heretical. If it turned the stomachs of the townsfolk, so much the better. Indeed, the Inquisition was never content to merely punish those whom it regarded as guilty of heresy; rather, it sought to terrify every man, woman, and child in Christendom into obedience by making an example of what would happen to "heretical filth."[68]

"Their bones and stinking bodies were dragged through the town," goes the account of one such posthumous punishment by the medieval inquisitor William of Pelhisson (d. 1268), "their names were proclaimed through the streets by the herald, crying, 'Who behaves thus shall perish thus,' and finally they were burned in the count's meadow, to the honour of God and the Blessed Virgin, His mother, and the Blessed Dominic."[69]

William of Pelhisson, as it turns out, allows us to see for ourselves what happened when the first agents of the Inquisition arrived in Languedoc in 1233, the old killing ground of the Albigensian Crusade, and set up their tribunals in the cities and towns of southern France. The Inquisition represented something unfamiliar and untested, and the inquisitors quickly discovered that the spirit of Languedoc was not yet broken. There and elsewhere across Europe, they were met with defiance and even armed resistance from a populace that had not yet taken the measure of the Inquisition.

In light of the ubiquitous and unchallengeable authority that it would shortly come to represent, the early resistance offered to the Inquisition is an astonishment.

The very first inquisitor to arrive in Toulouse was a Dominican friar-inquisitor called William Arnold. According to the eyewitness testimony of William of Pelhisson, the town fathers marched the inquisitor out of town, "manhandling as they did so," although they allowed that he could stay "if he would give up the Inquisition." At the same time, they issued a proclamation by means of the town herald that "no one was to give, sell, or lend anything whatever or to give assistance in any form to the Friars Preachers," as the Dominicans were called. As it turned out, however, the inquisitors who remained behind the walls of the Dominican convent were determined to stay in town and on task, if only under straitened circumstances.[70] As William of Pelhisson wrote in his memoir of the early days of the Inquisition:

> We friars did have the essentials in sufficient supply from friends and Catholics who, despite the danger, handed us bread, cheese, and eggs over the garden walls and by every other possible means. When the consuls of the town learned of this, they set their guards at our gates and also on the garden, watching the house day and night to prevent any necessities being brought in. They even cut us off completely from the water of the Garonne. This was a more serious blow to us, because we were unable to cook our vegetables in water.[71]

Other acts of resistance were far more intimate—and far more violent. When a wine seller named Arnold Dominic was charged with heresy, he was threatened with the death penalty unless he recanted and, as required by the standard operating procedure of the Inquisition, betrayed his fellow heretics. He was perfectly willing to save his life by naming names, and he gave the inquisitors eleven of them. Unfortunately for Arnold, however, only seven were captured, and the others managed to escape with the assistance of sympathetic peasants. The inquisitor was satisfied, but at least a few of the men whom Arnold had betrayed were intent on revenge. "The aforesaid Arnold Dominic made his confession and was released," wrote William of Pelhisson, "but afterward he was murdered one night in his bed."[72]

PLATE 1. Pope Innocent III excommunicates the Cathars, the very first victims of the Inquisition; Catharism was one of the few heresies to be wholly eradicated by the Church.

PLATE 2. A fanciful view of the mountain stronghold at Montségur, where the last Cathar holdouts were finally seized and burned alive in 1244.

PLATE 3. From the inquisitor's manuals of the Middle Ages to a "letter of apology" published in 1789—and even today—the Inquisition has always found its pious defenders.

PLATE 4. The torture chambers of the Inquisition, like the medieval version depicted here, changed little in appearance or equipment over six hundred years of active operation.

DELLA PUNIZIONE
DEGLI ERETICI
E DEL TRIBUNALE
DELLA SANTA
INQUISIZIONE
LETTERE APOLOGETICHE
DIVISE IN DUE TOMI.
TOMO SECONDO.

PLATE 5. Men and women accused of heresy were sometimes silenced with iron masks fitted with spikes or gags, like the "scold's bridle" shown here, a grim example of the torturer's art.

PLATE 6. Torquemada, clad in the cowled robe of the Dominican order and shown here in the company of Pope Sixtus IV, was the iconic grand inquisitor.

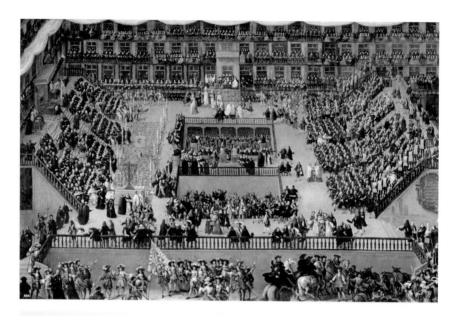

PLATE 7. "As if he were an entrepreneur offering a show," the grand inquisitor did not neglect the production values of an auto da fé like the one in Madrid in 1683.

PLATE 8. Palaces and fortresses, such as the Alcázar at Córdoba, were commonly put at the disposal of the friar-inquisitors by compliant kings.

PLATE 9. The peaked headpiece known as a coroza, shown in a drawing by Goya, was a theatrical touch invented by the Spanish Inquisition to humiliate its victims.

PLATE 10. Critics of the Inquisition delighted in showing the sexual sadism of the friar-inquisitors, but the fact remains that the victims were stripped to facilitate the work of the torturer.

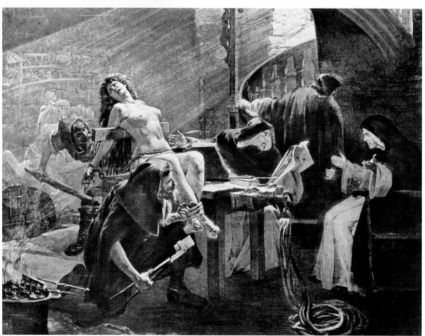

§ 5

(1) Wer dem Verbot des § 1 zuwiderhandelt, wird mit Zuchthaus
bestraft.

(2) Der Mann, der dem Verbot des § 2 zuwiderhandelt, wird mit
Gefängnis oder mit Zuchthaus bestraft.

(3) Wer den Bestimmungen der §§ 3 oder 4 zuwiderhandelt, wird
mit Gefängnis bis zu einem Jahr und mit Geldstrafe oder mit
einer dieser Strafen bestraft.

§ 6

Der Reichsminister des Innern erläßt im Einvernehmen mit
dem Stellvertreter des Führers und dem Reichsminister der Justiz die zur Durchführung und Ergänzung des Gesetzes erforder-
lichen Rechts- und Verwaltungsvorschriften.

§ 7

Das Gesetz tritt am Tage nach der Verkündung, § 3 jedoch
erst am 1.Januar 1936 in Kraft.

Nürnberg, den 15.September 1935,
am Reichsparteitag der Freiheit.

Der Führer und Reichskanzler.

Der Reichsminister des Innern.

Der Reichsminister der Justiz.

Der Stellvertreter des Führers.

PLATE 11. The Spanish
Inquisition turned heresy from
a thought-crime into a blood
crime, a deadly innovation
embraced by Nazi Germany
in the notorious Nuremberg
Laws of 1935.

PLATE 12. The show trials of
Stalinist Russia in the 1930s,
like the Inquisition itself,
demonstrated how innocent
men and women could be reduced to abject confession by
the threat and use of torture.

PLATE 13. Just as the Inquisition compelled its victims to wear cloth crosses, Nazi Germany revived the medieval "Jew badge" to identify and isolate the targets of the Final Solution.

PLATE 14. Like Galileo before the friar-inquisitors of the Roman Inquisition, Bertolt Brecht was subjected to interrogation by the House Un-American Activities Committee in 1947.

PLATE 15. By 1981 the Inquisition had entered Western popular culture as a harmless subject of ridicule in *Mel Brooks' History of the World: Part 1*.

PLATE 16. The coroza, the dungeon cell, and the ordeal by water—now known as waterboarding—were borrowed from the Inquisition and put to use at the Abu Ghraib prison in Iraq.

A special target of the early resisters was the meticulous records that the Inquisition began to accumulate from the outset of its operations. These archives, as we have seen, constituted the institutional memory of the Inquisition and, as such, were a terrible threat to every dissident. At Narbonne in 1235, for example, the citizens who participated in an uprising against the Inquisition seized and destroyed its books and records, and in 1248 a pair of officials who were carrying a set of records were slain and the records burned. So threatening were these attacks on the archives of the Inquisition that a church council in Albi in 1254 ordered that all its records be duplicated and the copies placed in a secure location so that future attacks would not slow down or stop the inquisitors' work.

One incident in particular prompted an especially punishing response with far-reaching effects. The triggering event took place when a man called Peter of Verona (ca. 1205–1252)—a child of Cathar parents who grew up to join the Dominican order and then the Inquisition—was sent to Florence to serve as inquisitor. He recruited Catholic noblemen to join a newly created militia whose members were sworn to protect the Inquisition in its work, and so the war against heresy was literally taken to the streets as "Catholic gangs" and their rivals battled each other. During one such skirmish, Peter himself was fatally wounded by an ax blow but lived long enough to leave a final message written in his own blood on the pavement: "I believe in God." Or so goes the hagiography that came to be attached to the dead inquisitor.[73]

Peter was promptly canonized as the patron saint of inquisitors by Pope Innocent IV, and his violent death inspired the pope to issue "perhaps the most terrible of all Bulls in the history of the Inquisition," a papal decree of 1252 known as *Ad extirpanda* (To extirpate). Torture of accused heretics under the authority of the Inquisition was officially sanctioned for the first time, burning at the stake was openly mandated as the punishment for relapsed heretics, and an armed constabulary was created and provided to the Inquisition for its own use. None of these measures was wholly new, but now they were solemnly encoded in canon law and carried the imprimatur of the pope himself. The machinery of repression and persecution would be replicated across Europe and beyond, always in the name of the Inquisition and its war on heresy. "Men armed with these tremendous powers, and animated with this resolute spirit, were not lightly to be meddled with," writes

Lea. "[The inquisitor's] jurisdiction, in fact, was almost unlimited, for the dread of suspicion of heresy brought, with few exceptions, all mankind to a common level."[74]

When viewed in the full light of history, opposition to the Inquisition in its early days seems heartbreakingly naïve. Successive popes bestowed upon the inquisitors such powers and privileges—and equipped them with such vast resources—that the Inquisition eventually overawed even the most courageous of its adversaries. Once the inquisitors had mastered their own arsenal of weapons, the population under their authority came to realize that no one was beyond the reach of the Inquisition. Eventually, the paranoia that the inquisitors sought to inspire acted as a deterrent not only to acts of open resistance but also to any word or deed that might catch the attention of the Inquisition. The war on heresy turned into a long reign of terror in which fear itself was the most effective weapon.

The inquisitorial archives preserve the evidence of a few isolated efforts at evasion, like the man who is reported to have "spirited away the body of his condemned father before it could be burned," and the desperate entreaties of its abject victims, such as a couple of widows who appealed to the pope for mercy after they were ordered to enter a convent, not as punishment for their own heretical beliefs but only because their dead husbands had been Cathars. For eight years, a rich man from Toulouse named Alaman simply ignored an order to go on a pilgrimage to the Holy Land; when the authorities finally got around to excommunicating him in 1237, he managed to stay out of prison for ten more years. But there is another way of looking at the same facts. The Inquisition did not forgive or forget, and a man or woman might face trial and punishment years or even decades after the alleged crime of heresy had taken place.[75]

A few accused heretics managed to save themselves by going into hiding or by fleeing to places beyond the reach of the Inquisition. Some fled before arrest and trial, some while the proceedings were in progress, and a few succeeded in the rare and daring feat of breaking out of prison while in the custody of the Inquisition. A study of the archives of the Inquisition in the diocese of Toulouse for the period 1249–1257 suggests that twenty-six victims were sentenced to death but an even greater number—thirty in all—were listed as fugitives.[76] Indeed, as we have seen, the trial of an accused heretic so commonly resulted in conviction that, as a practical matter, flight was the only way a victim might escape punishment.

The backwaters of Christendom might afford a sanctuary for an accused or convicted heretic in hiding or on the run. Cathars from Milan and Florence, for example, were able to find a safe haven in the distant and isolated stretches of Calabria and Abruzzi. Remarkably, the first Protestant missionaries to reach Italy during the Reformation discovered that a few Waldensian communities—the forerunners of reformed Christianity—had managed to avoid the Inquisition for more than three hundred years in the remote mountain valleys of Lombardy. As late as 1733, the pope deemed it necessary to order the director-general of the Franciscans to station an inquisitor on Corsica permanently because the distant and isolated island was supposedly "infested with heretics."[77]

The Inquisition was eventually so pervasive, so well staffed and well informed, that it became increasingly difficult for a dissident Christian to find any safe place in western Europe. To locate a suspected heretic and gather evidence against him or her, an inquisitor in one locality was able to consult the archives of other inquisitors across Europe. Indeed, the reach of the Inquisition sometimes resulted in two inquisitors seeking to prosecute the same victim, and the Council of Narbonne established the rule of "first come, first served" to ensure that the first inquisitor to lodge formal charges against a suspected heretic enjoyed the right to claim him or her. For this reason the Inquisition has been called "the first international law-keeping force," a phrase that sums up its vast reach even as it obscures the fact that the Inquisition enforced only the law that criminalized an act of conscience.[78]

One measure of the police power of the Inquisition was its right to maintain its own armed constabulary. At a time when Bologna permitted only knights and doctors to bear arms—and Paris forbade all citizens from carrying "pointed knives, swords, bucklers, or other similar weapons"—an inquisitor was permitted to "arm anyone he pleased, and invest him with the privileges and immunities of the Holy Office." Indeed, some inquisitors found it profitable to license the right to bear arms to anyone willing to pay a fee, thus creating a source of revenue to fund the Inquisition's operations; the inquisitor at Florence, for example, enjoyed an annual income of a thousand gold florins from the arms trade. Pope John XXII himself characterized some of the inquisitorial henchmen as "armed familiars of depraved character and perverse habits, who committed murders and other outrages." But if a troublesome lord or magistrate sought to disarm them, the inquisitor had a ready response.[79] "[A]ny secular ruler who endeavors to prevent the familiars of the Holy Office from bearing arms," decreed the inquisitor Nicholas Eymerich, "is impeding the Inquisition and is a fautor of heresy."[80]

The same sanctimony was invoked to justify every atrocity and excess of the Inquisition. The inquisitor's handbooks, as we have noted, prescribe the precise formula to be used by one inquisitor in addressing a request to another inquisitor for the return of a person who has managed to escape from an inquisitorial prison, and the escapee is described as "one insanely led to reject the salutary medicine offered for his cure, and to spurn the wine and oil which were soothing his wounds." Thus we are reminded that the Church insisted on presenting itself not as a persecutor and a punisher but as "a loving mother unwillingly inflicting wholesome chastisement on her unruly children."[81]

While popes and grand inquisitors continued to utter their pious words of self-justification, however, the real work of the Inquisition was being carried out in the dungeons where the victims were questioned under the threat and application of torture. Here, of course, is the enduring legacy of the Inquisition. Its rituals and protocols, the legalisms and euphemisms, are now preserved only in archives and libraries, but the day-to-day skills and tools of the inquisitors are still in use. Like the remarkable machine for torture and execution imagined by Franz Kafka, the history of the Inquisition was carved into human flesh.

4·

CRIME AND PUNISHMENT

The keys would jangle again; and the first scream
of the next victim often came even before they
had touched him, at the mere sight of the men in
the doorway.

ARTHUR KOESTLER,
Darkness at Noon

"The third degree" is a commonplace of hardboiled detective fiction,
and nowadays the phrase calls to mind a ham-fisted cop at work on
a suspect under a swinging lamp in the backroom of a police station. In truth, however, the third degree is yet another distant but distinct
echo of the Inquisition. Like so much else in the lore of the Inquisition, the
phrase itself allows us to glimpse the obsessive concern with order that governed the imaginations of the inquisitors.

The inquisitor, according to the meticulous rules that governed the work
of the Inquisition, was empowered to subject an accused heretic to questioning under torture according to a scale that measured five degrees of severity. The first degree consisted of stripping off the victim's clothing and
then displaying the instruments of torture to the naked victim, which was
sometimes enough to bring "weak and timorous persons" to confession.
The second degree called for the application of torture to be sustained for a

period no longer than it took for the inquisitor to recite a single Ave Maria or Paternoster, that is, less than a minute. The notorious third degree permitted the torturer to torment his victim in earnest and without the shorter if also prayerful time limits. The fourth degree permitted the torturer to increase the agony of the victim by, for example, jerking the rope from which he or she was hanging. By the fifth degree, the stubborn victim was likely to be suffering from shattered bones, severe loss of blood, and perhaps even a limb torn from his or her body.[1]

The Inquisition, of course, did not invent torture. Ironically, the tools found in a well-equipped inquisitorial dungeon were identical to those that pagan magistrates had used on the bodies of the first Christians during the ten periods of persecution in ancient Rome. But it is also true that the carnage of the torture chamber—a scene that resembled a nightmarish conflation of the abattoir, the blacksmith's shop, and the operating room—was a commonplace of the Inquisition and an emblem of its terrible power. From 1252, as we have noted, the use of torture in the "extirpation of heresy" was officially sanctioned by the pope. Indeed, the inquisitorial reign of terror depended as much on the torture chamber as it did on the hooded inquisitor or the stake at which unrepentant heretics were burned alive.[2]

"The official should obtain from all heretics he has captured a confession by torture without injuring the body or causing the danger of death," Pope Innocent IV decreed in *Ad extirpanda*. "They should confess to their own errors and accuse other heretics whom they know, as well as their accomplices, fellow-believers, receivers, and defenders."[3]

As with everything else, of course, the Inquisition elevated the use of torture to a lofty theological plane, draping the torturer with pieties and legalisms that were meant to sanctify the burning, cutting, tearing, and pounding of human flesh and bone. The affliction of heretics was regarded by their persecutors as "delectable to the Holy Trinity and the Virgin"—a phrase that allows us to imagine the inquisitor literally licking his lips in anticipation of the next torture session—and the elaborate formulas that the handbooks recommended for consigning a victim to the torture chamber always began with the phrase: "By the grace of God . . ."[4]

Torture can be understood as a thoroughly human impulse rather than a godly one, although some torturers might have made the task more agreeable by invoking the authority of a higher power. For others, of course, no such rationale was or is necessary; the job of torturer has always attracted men who plainly take pleasure in their work. But the resort to torture by the Inquisition was motivated by a different and highly ironic motive. The inquisitors were never quite comfortable in convicting an accused heretic on circumstantial evidence or even the direct testimony of a friendly witness. Rather, they always preferred to extract an abject confession of guilt from the accused heretic.

To make a man or woman confess to the crime of false belief—and especially when it is a crime that he or she did not commit—torture is sometimes a practical necessity. Or so the Inquisition discovered, not only to the sorrow of its victims but also as an object lesson to authoritarian regimes down through the ages.

To be sure, the inquisitor was perfectly willing to condemn a suspected heretic on whatever meager evidence might be available, even a whispered denunciation or a mere rumor. As we have seen, suspicion of heresy was itself a crime for which the inquisitor might impose punishment when no evidence of actual heresy was available. But the sweetest victory in the war on heresy was always based on what the Inquisition regarded as a sincere and spontaneous admission of wrongdoing by the accused heretic, one who confessed to the crime, repudiated (or "abjured") his or her former beliefs, and humbly returned to the Church as a convert and a penitent.

Every aspect of the Inquisition, in fact, was designed to secure a confession. When an inquisitor arrived to set up the operations of the Holy Office in a particular town, as we have seen, he preached a sermon in which all heretics were called upon to come forward and confess their errors of belief, denounce any other heretics known to them, and accept whatever penance the inquisitor deemed appropriate. A week-long period of grace was announced, during which heretics were promised that they would be spared the harsher "penances" that the inquisitor was empowered to inflict upon them. All they had to do was confess their own thought-crimes and condemn any other thought-criminals they could think of. If they failed to do so, they were automatically excommunicated.

Confession was the "queen of proofs" in the eyes of the Inquisition, according to a medieval legal aphorism. Indeed, the peculiar nature of heresy—

a crime "whose locus was in the human brain"—meant that it was "virtually unprovable without confession," as historian and journalist Malise Ruthven points out. The inquisitors used every method of persuasion that they could devise to extract an admission of guilt, ranging from the promise of a mild penance to a prolonged session in the torture chamber. Here we come upon a kind of Catch-22 in the inner workings of the Inquisition. Confession may have been the ultimate goal of the Inquisition, but confession alone was never enough. The self-confessed heretic was required to convince the inquisitor that his or her confession was earnest, complete, and free of coercion.[5]

For that reason, if a confession was thought to be motivated by fear of torture or death, it was deemed "imperfect" and the confessed heretic remained at risk of the worst punishments the Inquisition could inflict. Moreover, the confessions of heretics who were quick to condemn themselves but unwilling to betray the names and whereabouts of their fellow heretics were regarded as even more deeply flawed; indeed, such self-confessed heretics were guilty of fautorship as well as heresy, and the Inquisition deemed it necessary to punish them for both crimes.[6]

More than one accused heretic offered the confession that his or her inquisitors wanted only to find that the confession was flawed in some unspecified detail and thus unacceptable. A man named Guillem Salavert, for example, was arrested by the Inquisition on charges on heresy in 1299 and promptly confessed to the crime. But the inquisitor rejected the confession as "unsatisfactory," and so the man remained in a prison cell, untried and unsentenced, until he made a second and apparently satisfactory confession in 1316. But he was still not formally found guilty of heresy and sentenced for his crime for another three years, fully two decades after his first confession. Only after he had already spent twenty years in prison did his formal "penance" begin.[7]

The official records of the Spanish Inquisition capture the heartbreaking dilemma of accused heretics who sought desperately to confess, if only to spare themselves from torture, but found their offers of a confession rejected. One woman who was being interrogated under torture begged the inquisitors to allow her to confess, but they insisted that she recite the particulars of her wrongdoing in order to corroborate the testimony of the witnesses against her. Since testimony was always given in secret and withheld from the accused, she could only guess what accusations had been lodged against her. So the woman was reduced to pleading with the inquisitors to reveal what might amount to an acceptable confession—and the notary dutifully took down every word of her plea.

"*Señores,* why will you not tell me what I have to say?" the woman cried. "Have I not said that I did it all? I have said that I did all that the witnesses say. *Señores,* as I have told you, I do not know for certain. I have admitted that what I have done has brought me to this suffering. Release me, for I do not remember it."[8]

Apologists for the Inquisition insist that the emphasis on confession was actually a measure of the high ideals and good faith of the inquisitors. Bernard Gui, for example, piously insisted that "the mind of the inquisitor was torn with anxious cares" when he was forced to rely on accusation rather than confession, and "his conscience pained him if he punished one who was neither confessed nor convicted." Yet Gui was honest enough to concede that "he suffered still more, knowing by constant experience the falsity and cunning and malice of these men, if he allowed them to escape to the damage of the faith." So Gui, like other inquisitors, put aside his scruples and resorted to the instruments of torture when confronted with a person who denied that he or she was a heretic.[9]

High ideals, in fact, never prevented the Inquisition from using coercion of all kinds to extract confession from the accused and testimony from unwilling witnesses. Nor was coercion limited to the wheel and the rack, the red-hot iron and the strappado, or the other crude tools of the torturer. The machinery of persecution in its entirety amounted to one vast instrument of torture, and its cutting edge was terror. This is not merely a metaphor; the protocols of the Inquisition, as we have seen, required that victims be *shown* the instruments of torture before those instruments were used in the hope that fear alone would be effective in bringing them to confession. But it is also true that every aspect of the Inquisition—the locked doors of its proceedings, the nameless accusers and witnesses sworn to silence, even the hood that obscured the human face of the inquisitor—was intended to strike fear into the heart of anyone entertaining any idea that the Church regarded as wrong.

The Inquisition adopted yet more of its characteristic euphemisms and fictions to resolve the obvious contradiction between extracting a confession under torture and then embracing the confession as having been given without coercion. The use of torture was as obsessively regulated as any other aspect of the Inquisition. The inquisitors insisted, for example, that they decided how many of the five degrees of torture victims would be forced to endure—and what instruments of torture would be used to inflict them—according to their degree of apparent guilt, a Kafkaesque calculation that conveniently overlooks the fact that torture was supposedly applied to confirm whether or not the victims were guilty in the first place.

The inquisitors were untroubled by such ironies and contradictions. According to the Alice-in-Wonderland rationale of the Inquisition, no one was charged with the crime of heresy in the absence of some evidence of guilt, whether a rumor from a nameless accuser or a guilty look on the face of the accused. Every accused heretic was generously afforded the opportunity to confess to the crime, repudiate his or her false beliefs, serve the penance imposed by the Inquisition, and rejoin the Church. Only when the accused heretic stubbornly refused to offer a confession was the Inquisition forced to resort to torture. By the reasoning of the Inquisition, in other words, the victims of torture were the only ones to blame for the necessity of putting them to torture.

Above all, the Inquisition relied on what it regarded as the extraordinary nature of the crime of heresy to justify every excess and atrocity. The heretics, as we have seen, were "thieves and murderers of souls," and the war on heresy justified the deployment of every weapon in the inquisitorial arsenal. To accuse someone of heresy and then allow him or her to go unpunished was simply unacceptable, a threat to the authority of the Inquisition and an embarrassment to the power and glory of the Church. After all, the acquittal of even a single accused heretic would surely bleed away some of the dread and terror that were regarded as crucial in deterring others from false belief. Far worse, as the Church saw it, was the spectacle of a true believer in a forbidden faith who was perfectly willing to suffer bravely and die heroically for that faith. This was the real reason that the Inquisition sought to avoid making martyrs of the accused heretics by torturing them into abject confession.

Like the Grand Inquisitor in *Crime and Punishment*—"I shall burn Thee for coming to hinder us," he tells Jesus, "for if any one has ever deserved our fires, it is Thou"—the medieval inquisitor felt himself not only empowered but obliged to use any and all means to vindicate the authority of the Inquisition. Guilt or innocence was wholly beside the point.[10]

———————————————

Confinement was the first step in extracting a confession from the accused heretic, and sometimes it was sufficient. The cells in an inquisitorial dungeon were cold, dark, and narrow, and the worst of them amounted to nothing more than a tomblike enclosure of stone or brick into which no ray of light ever penetrated and no other human being ever set foot. If bedding was provided at all, it might consist of nothing more than rags or straw, and the rations were restricted to the proverbial bread and water, or—as Bernard Gui put it—"the bread of suffering and the water of tribulation." Pope Clement V, after consulting an official report on the work of the Inquisition in Carcassonne in 1306, concluded that "prisoners were habitually constrained to confession by the harshness of prison, the lack of beds, and the deficiency of food, as well as by torture."[11]

Then, too, prisoners of the Inquisition were forced to endure "the slow torture of delay." Once arrested and imprisoned, the suspects did not know when, if ever, they might again see the light of day; suspects remained in custody until the inquisitor decided (or remembered) that they should be tried and sentenced. Only then did their formal punishment begin. But a suspected heretic might sit in a cell far longer than a convicted one. An attorney named Guillem Garric, accused of participating in a conspiracy to destroy the records of the Inquisition, was arrested in 1285 and locked away in an inquisitorial prison until he was formally sentenced some thirty years later.[12]

While a suspect was in custody, the inquisitors resorted to every manner of coercion, both hard and soft, to induce the prisoner to confess his crimes. After a few weeks or months of confinement, during which a man's family was likely reduced to poverty or even starvation, the inquisitor might allow a brief visit from his distraught wife and terrified children "in hopes that their tears and pleadings might work on his feelings and overcome his convictions." Because the property of a heretic was subject to confiscation at the time of arrest, the family might have already found itself homeless and penniless. And because it was a crime in itself to aid or comfort a heretic, the family of the accused heretic would likely be wholly friendless, too.

The knowledge that his family was reduced to penury might be enough to provoke a confession.[13]

Or the accused—lonely and anxious, fatigued and half-starved—might find himself suddenly called upon by an apparently well-meaning visitor, whether an acquaintance or a sympathetic stranger. The caller would be permitted to spend a few quiet moments with the prisoner, uttering words of comfort and compassion. Unbeknownst to the prisoner, however, a notary would be stationed at the door of the cell, out of sight but within earshot, in the hope of recording some unguarded remark that could be useful to the inquisitors. Heretics who had already confessed and converted, of course, were especially willing and effective as agents of the Inquisition, and they were instructed to use every tool of guile and deceit to lead the prisoner into making a jailhouse confession. For example, an *agent provocateur* might tell his cellmate that he had only faked a conversion to Catholicism in order to fool the inquisitors, thus encouraging the cellmate to regard the agent as a secret heretic in whom the prisoner might safely confide.

Sometimes the suspect would be suddenly and inexplicably removed from his or her tomblike cell and placed in a larger one. The rations of bread and water would be supplemented with more generous and nourishing foodstuffs. A cruel jailor would be replaced by a kinder, gentler one who spoke words of comfort and encouragement. If the suspect was not moved to confession by the display of generosity, he or she was thrown back into the dungeon. Toying with the prisoner amounted to a form of psychological torture—an experiment "to see if his resolution would be weakened by alternations of hope and despair," according to Lea. Its use demonstrates that the good-cop, bad-cop routine, like the third degree, was hardly a modern innovation in the techniques of interrogation.[14]

If these approaches were unavailing, however, the inquisitor was always ready to use the other tools at hand, including the time-tested techniques of the torturer. In fact, torture was so routine in inquisitorial practice that the handbooks provided a formula for use in consigning victims to the torture chamber: "In order that the truth may be had from your mouth and that you should cease to offend the ears of the judges," the inquisitor was instructed to say, "we declare, judge and sentence you to undergo torment and torture." Here the form leaves a blank where the inquisitor is instructed to insert the precise date and place that the torturer's tools would be un-packed and put to use on the naked body of the prisoner. Thus did the in-quisitor, in solemnly reciting the formula from the inquisitor's manuals, unwittingly confirm that the Inquisition was perfectly willing to forgo the ideal of a pure and spontaneous confession and satisfy itself with one that had been extracted from a prisoner by the use of "torment and torture." [15]

A distinction was made during the early years of the Inquisition between common torture—that is, the infliction of pain to extract confession or tes-timony—and the so-called ordeal, which was the medieval equivalent of the modern lie-detector test. As used in the Middle Ages, the ordeal was re-garded as an objective test for truth or falsity, guilt or innocence, and it was used in both civil and criminal jurisprudence as a fact-finding tool. Only later did the Inquisition come to abandon the magical thinking embodied in the ordeal and frankly embrace torture for what it is, the use of fear and pain to make some wretched victim do what the inquisitor wanted him or her to do.

The ordeal by combat, in its original form, pitted two armed litigants against each other, and it was believed that the man who was in the right and deserved to win the case would inevitably prevail in combat. Ordeal by fire called for the application of hot irons to the flesh of an accused crim-inal; it was supposed that the iron would burn the guilty defendant but leave the innocent one unscarred. Ordeal by water was based on the pi-ous belief that water, as the medium of baptism, would accept the inno-cent and reject the guilty when the accused was tossed into the drink. To be sure, anyone who was compelled to undergo an ordeal would suffer terribly in the process, but the suffering of the victim was wholly beside the point. According to the beliefs and values of the High Middle Ages—"irrational, primitive, barbarian," as modern commentators put it—the truth would be miraculously revealed by the invisible of hand of God. [16]

Torture, by contrast, is the intentional infliction of pain in an effort to compel testimony from an unwilling witness or defendant. "By torture," wrote the Roman jurist Ulpian in a classic legal definition that dates back to the third century, "we are to understand the torment and suffering of the body in order to elicit the truth."[17] The efficacy of torture was not understood to be based on divine intervention; quite to the contrary, it was founded on the primal fact that human beings are averse to pain and will generally do anything they can to make it stop. For the sober and meticulous legal commentators, both pagan and Christian, however, torture was not a subject of moral outrage; rather, it was a commonplace tool of criminal jurisprudence, ancient and honorable.

The archives of the medieval Inquisition preserve an incident that demonstrates the original and authentic use of the ordeal. A woman charged with the crime of Catharism was "abandoned to die of hunger" in one of the inquisitorial prisons. She insisted that she had always been an observant Catholic, however, and she continued to participate in the rite of confession, during the course of which she piteously insisted to her confessor that she was innocent of the charge of heresy. The priest advised her "to offer the hot-iron ordeal in proof," that is, to volunteer to subject herself to the application of red-hot irons as proof of her innocence. The fact that she readily agreed to do so is surely the best evidence that she was not a Cathar, but the resulting burns were taken as proof that she was, in fact, guilty as charged. Relying on the results of the ordeal, the Inquisition sent her to the secular authority to be put to death, "with the result of being burned first by the iron," as Lea puts it, "and then by stake."[18]

Belief in the efficacy of the ordeal, however, could not survive the unavoidable fact that the flesh of a human being, whether guilty or innocent, will be burned when exposed to heat. The use of the ordeal as a fact-finding mechanism was eventually banned by Pope Innocent III, but the use of torture was promptly approved by Pope Innocent IV, and so the resort to fire and water took on a subtly different meaning and function as the Inquisition refined its techniques of interrogation. "What followed was," writes Malise Ruthven, "not so much the introduction of torture as the continuation of the ordeals under a new mode of procedure."[19]

So if a suspect accused of heresy refused to confess, or if the confession was deemed "imperfect," or if a witness was reluctant to betray a friend or relation, he or she might be encouraged by the inquisitors with what was still called the ordeal by water or the ordeal by fire. But these were not ordeals in the old sense. Rather, they were simply and plainly examples of physical torture, designed to inflict so much agony that the suspect or witness would finally consent to say what the inquisitor wanted to hear.

Rooted in the crude beliefs of the Dark Ages, the ordeals of fire and water turned out to be durable and effective instruments of torture. They were used throughout the Inquisition by its master torturers and long afterward by those who followed in their footsteps.

The inquisitor's handbook composed by Nicholas Eymerich, the inquisitor at Aragón in the fourteenth century, was an influential source of instruction on the proper use of torture, one that was reprinted in various annotated editions and consulted throughout the existence of the Inquisition. Torture was supposedly a measure of last resort, not to be used "till other means of discovering the truth have been exhausted," according to Eymerich. "Good manners, subtlety, the exhortations of well-intentioned persons, even frequent meditation and the discomforts of prison," Eymerich advised, "are often sufficient to induce the guilty ones to confess."[20]

Still, Eymerich provided a helpful and accommodating list of suspects who could and should be tortured, including anyone "with a general reputation for heresy" and anyone whose answers under interrogation struck the inquisitor as "vacillating." Torture was also mandated for any suspected heretic against whom circumstantial evidence (or "indicia") of heresy could be found; and since the Inquisition recognized three grades of indicia—"remote," "vehement," and "violent"—the inquisitor enjoyed ample discretion to find or fabricate such proofs. Testimony by a witness who claimed to have seen the suspect in a house where a dying Cathar was being given the ritual of *consolamentum,* for example, was a sufficient indicium to justify a session in the torture chamber, but so was the simple gesture of offering a friendly greeting to a man or woman who turned out to be a Cathar *perfectus.* Indeed, the inquisitor was fully empowered to consider "facial expressions, behaviour, apparent nervousness, and so on" as indicia of guilt.[21]

Terror is the essence of torture, as the Inquisition knew so well, and it began with the inquisitor's pronouncement of the formulaic order to the victim to "expose you to torture and torment." From that moment onward, the man or woman condemned to torture was subjected to an unrelenting and steadily escalating series of threats, humiliations, and abuses. The victim was led in solemn procession from cell to dungeon, accompanied by the inquisitors, the armed guards, the notaries who "faithfully recorded every shout, cry and complaint," sometimes a doctor to revive a victim if he or she passed out, and the man whose job it was to apply the tools of torture—ominously, the task was usually assigned to the public executioner. The long, slow walk to the torture chamber, of course, was an act of torture in itself.[22]

Still more theatrical touches can be detected in the formalities that attended a torture session, especially as they were conducted by the Spanish Inquisition starting in the fifteenth century. The processional to the torture chamber was conducted by candlelight or torchlight, according to some accounts. At every step along the way, the inquisitor was at the victim's side, whispering threats and promises to encourage the victim to confess and thus spare himself or herself the ordeal to come. The torturers concealed their heads and faces under high-peaked hoods of the kind later associated with the Ku Klux Klan, revealing only their eyes through holes in the fabric of the hoods. Even the glowing braziers on the dungeon walls "would take on their own terrifying significance," as victims would discover when they saw the torturers at work on other accused heretics.[23]

Once inside the torture chamber, the victim was first stripped of his or her clothing, both to facilitate the work of the torturer and his assistants and to further abase, disorient, and terrorize the victim. Then the various instruments would be ritually displayed to the victim, who was warned that he or she "must pass through all of them unless he told the truth." To the last moment, the inquisitor continued to utter words of enticement and encouragement to the victim; it was not yet too late for the accused heretic to save his or her life by offering the confession that the inquisitor so ardently desired. If no confession was forthcoming, the torturer picked up his tools and set to work.[24]

The most common instruments of torture, as we have noted, required only the fundamental elements of water and fire. The so-called ordeal by water consisted of binding the victim in a horizontal position and forcing water down his or her throat, sometimes by pouring the fluid through a funnel and sometimes by dripping it slowly through a water-soaked linen or silk rag, thus creating the sensation of drowning. As the torturers gained experience, they learned that holding the nose of the victim greatly enhanced the effect. Once the belly was filled with water and fully distended, the victim would be forced into a head-down position in order to put agonizing pressure on the heart and lungs. Then, to sharpen and prolong the pain, the torturer might beat on the victim's belly with fists or a bludgeon.

The water ordeal was especially popular with the Inquisition—and would remain a favorite tool of torturers down to our own time—because, unlike other forms of torture, it required no elaborate equipment, created no messes of blood and pulped flesh to clean up, and left no obvious wounds or scars on the victim. Thanks to the detailed records of the Inquisition, we know that an "ordinary" ordeal called for the application of five liters of water, and an "extraordinary" one consisted of ten liters—yet another example of how the inquisitorial enterprise regulated and standardized every particular of its operations so that even the torture of suspected heretics was turned into a kind of industrial activity.[25]

The ordeal of fire consisted of binding the victim with ropes or manacles in front of a well-stoked fire and placing his or her feet in close proximity to the flames. Again, the torturers devised various techniques for controlling the severity of pain to be inflicted on the victim. Smearing the victim's feet with fat always intensified the pain, but they could fine-tune the process by applying the fat to the whole foot or only on the soles. A firescreen, too, could be used to interrupt the ordeal "for fresh questioning and to provide a respite in case of fainting." But the torturer no longer pretended that the presence or absence of burned flesh was an indication of guilt or innocence; he merely sought to inflict as much pain as the inquisitor deemed appropriate in the course of an interrogation. "A man might leave the Inquisition without being burned," according to one witticism, "but he was certain to be singed."[26]

Fire and water were all a torturer really needed, but the inquisitors also resorted to ever more elaborate mechanical devices to terrorize and brutalize their victims. The strappado, for example, was a rope-and-pulley mechanism affixed to the ceiling of the torture chamber. The ankles and hands of the victim were bound with ropes or shackles, and iron or stone weights were attached to the feet. The rope dangling from the roof was attached to the victim's wrists, which were fixed behind his or her back, and the torturer positioned himself at the other end of the rope. Then the inquisitor put his questions to the victim, and if satisfactory answers were not forthcoming, the torturer assisted the interrogator by lifting, dangling, and dropping the victim, a process that resulted in intense pain and injury.

An expert torturer was able to use the strappado to vary the severity of pain at will. If hanging from the ceiling was not enough to bring the victim to confession, he might apply a whip at the same time. Or he might resort to what was called "full strappado," that is, lifting the victim to the ceiling and then suddenly dropping the victim—sometimes only a few feet and sometimes all the way to the stone floor—thus dislocating joints and breaking bones. The dangling victim was said to "jump" or "dance," according to the parlance of the professional torturer. "Only a confession or unconsciousness," writes Edward Burman, "would halt the process." The strappado was so popular among the inquisitors, in fact, that it came to be "universally recognized as the first torture of the Inquisition"—the "queen of torments," according to the medieval aphorism.[27]

Degrees of torture took on specific meanings when calibrated to a particular tool or machine. When the strappado was being used, for example, the third degree called for merely dangling the victim for an extended period of time. If instructed by the inquisitor to apply the fourth degree, however, the torturer would begin to jerk the hanging body of the victim by raising and releasing the ropes that held the body aloft. And in the fifth degree, "weights were attached to the culprit's feet to increase the agony of the jerking rope," and the torture was sustained for "the space of one or two Misereres," which lasted much longer than a simple Ave Maria or Paternoster. Similar specifications were available to the torturer for each chosen instrument of torture.[28]

Other ancient and familiar instruments of torture were the wheel—a simple wooden wagon wheel to which the accused heretic was bound and then beaten with clubs or hammers as the wheel was turned—and the rack, a rather more elaborate device consisting of a wooden frame with rollers at each end. The victim was laid on the rack, and hands and feet were fixed to the rollers by ropes. As the interrogation proceeded, the torturer turned the handles on the rollers to loosen or tighten the ropes according to signals from the inquisitor. The mounting pressure on the victim's joints resulted in painful dislocations and, if the victim refused to give the answer that the inquisitor sought, his or her limbs were eventually torn from their sockets.

The last of the standard methods of torture was the *stivaletto*. The victim's legs were splinted between wooden boards with tight topes, two boards on each leg. Then the torturer inserted wedges fashioned of wood or iron between the leg and the board. By pounding on the wedges with a hammer, the torturer increased the pressure of the ropes and boards against the victim's flesh and bones, which resulted in ever-mounting pain and eventually the shattering of joints and bones. Later, as the technology of torture improved, the same device was fashioned of metal, and pressure was brought to bear on the victim by tightening a screw that closed the jaws of a metal brace or vice. If the victim persisted in silence or offered only evasive answers, he or she would suffer not only the agony of the torture itself but a lifelong injury that would render the victim unable to walk.

The parade of horribles, however, does not end there. Compelling the suspect to remain awake for a specified period of time was used as a method of torture, then as now: "Forty hours was the common length." Women and children were singled out for a form of torture that was regarded as suitably mild: cords were tied around their hands and wrists, then tightened and loosened as they were interrogated. Yet an expert torturer was capable of inflicting sustained and excruciating pain with only a simple rope, as a priest accused of heresy in Vienna in the fifteenth century was made to understand. After a tag team of "eminent theologians" failed to persuade him to renounce his beliefs, the priest was tightly bound to a pillar with ropes. "The cords eating into the swelling flesh caused such exquisite torture," reports Lea, "that when they visited him the next day, he begged piteously to be taken out and burned."[29]

Such were the instruments of torture that might be found in any well-equipped inquisitorial dungeon at any time over the six centuries of the Inquisition's active operations. The simplest of them, as we have seen, required only a supply of water or a well-stoked fire, and the rest of them could be contrived with a few ropes and boards. All of them were effective in inflicting pain and injury on their victims. Yet they did not exhaust the undeniable human genius for devising ever more imaginative ways of terrorizing and punishing another human being. Once granted the liberty and opportunity to do so, the agents of the Inquisition raised the practice of torture to a high art.

Some of the inquisitors—and the torturers who assisted them—were sadists for whom the opportunity to brutalize a fellow human being was the single best reason to join the ranks of the Inquisition. The victims, as we have seen, were stripped down to undergarments or were wholly naked during torture; the display of bare flesh was essential to the work of the torturers while, at the same time, degrading and humiliating the victims, but it is also true that the sight of naked flesh titillated at least some inquisitors and their henchmen as they watched the torturer at work. Indeed, the torture chamber was never a purely functional space like an operating room or a blacksmith's shop, although it resembled both in its equipage. Rather, it was a theater of pain in which the victim was put on display for the entertainment of his or her persecutors.

Unfortunately, the human genius for both art and invention can be found even in the inquisitorial torture chamber. Of course, the basic tools of the torturer—buckets and funnels, bars and blades, hammers and tongs—required no special skill to make or use. The wheel was something scavenged from a broken-down wagon, and a ladder could be readily used as a rack; the victim's wrists were tied to the top rung, and weights were tied to the ankles to produce the same effect as a more elaborately constructed version of the same device. Some methods of torture required nothing more than a kitchen pantry: victims might be made to inhale the fumes of onions and sulphur until they retched, or eggs heated in boiling water might be thrust under their armpits. But some inquisitors and their servitors seemed to take real pleasure in devising ever more elaborate instruments of torture or ornamenting the commonplace ones in new and imaginative ways.

"The heretic's fork," for example, was a simple but diabolically clever device consisting of a slender iron bar with sharp prongs at both ends; the device was strapped around the neck of the victim in a way that planted one set of prongs deep into the flesh under the chin and the other set of prongs against the sternum. When a victim was thus impaled, "the fork prevented all movement of the head and allowed the victim only to murmur, in a barely audible voice, '*abiuro*' ('I recant')." To drive home the point of the device, so to speak, the phrase was inscribed into the metalwork as a reminder of exactly what the inquisitor wanted to hear from the victim thus afflicted.[30]

Tongs were a commonplace of torture, and they were variously employed to handle hot coals, to pinch the flesh, to close the nose of a victim undergoing the water ordeal, or even to amputate a finger or a tongue, a woman's nipple or a man's genitals. But the ironmonger whose client was the Inquisition, whether on his own initiative or at the special request of his employer, might fashion a pair of tongs so that the hinge resembled the grinning head of a monstrous alligator and the jaws were lined with sharp teeth. The result was an implement that was even handier for inflicting pain and, at the same time, pleased the torturer's twisted sense of humor and struck even greater terror into a victim watching the gaping jaws approach and then close.

Some tinkerers came up with new and ever more nightmarish instruments of torture that served no other purpose than the infliction of pain. One such device, which we briefly glimpsed in the opening pages of this book, was a segmented object of bronze and iron in the shape of a pear that was designed to be inserted into various orifices of the human body. A screw-driven mechanism on the interior of the "pear" allowed it to be slowly expanded as the torturer turned the handle, thus stretching and tearing the tender flesh of the victim from the inside. As a final touch, the artisan who fabricated the pear added an elaborate figure of a leering Satan to please the torturer and taunt the victim in the moments before it disappeared into the interior cavity where it did its work.

Why would an inquisitor go to such lengths when buckets of water and hot irons were so cheap, handy, and effective? "For only one reason," answers Robert Held, referring not merely to the fanciful hardware but to the "universal and eternal institution" of torture itself. "Because it gives pleasure to the torturer."[31]

The same insight, of course, explains why the victim was often stripped naked during torture. Entirely aside from functional considerations—it is easier to torture a naked human being than a clothed one—the undressing of torture victims gratified the twisted appetites of the sexual sadists among the inquisitors and their staff of torturers. The point is made in a vintage engraving of a woman undergoing the ordeal by water at the hands of the Inquisition, an example of the atrocity propaganda favored by the critics of the Inquisition. The illustrator has carefully depicted the victim's pretty face and wholly naked torso, the torturer bent over her body in apparent pleasure, and the audience of inquisitors and their familiars watching the whole ordeal with the fixed stare of dirty old men at a peep show.

Such scenes were favored in art and letters over several centuries, ranging from the pious tracts of early Protestant reformers to the lurid gothic novels of the nineteenth century to the histories and commentaries of the secular humanists of the twentieth century. Indeed, much of what we think we know about the Inquisition derives from the images and narratives created by propagandists for whom "the cruelty and eroticism of inquisitors" is the emblematic sin of organized religion in general and the Roman Catholic church in particular. And we might suspect that the artist who makes a drawing of a naked woman undergoing torture—as well as those who view his work from a safe distance and perhaps in private—may be secretly sharing some of the darker desires of the torturer himself. Putting such mixed motives aside, however, the fact remains that the depictions of inquisitorial excess are based on fact rather than fancy. Not only did the Inquisition embrace the torturer's art in its war on heresy, but it also elevated and dignified the use of torture as a legal and even a pious act.[32]

Jesus of Nazareth, according to the Gospels, was himself the victim of torture. For that reason alone, the Church was always sensitive to the ugly paradox created by the sight of a man in a monk's cowl, who supposedly lived in imitation of Christ, putting questions to a naked man or woman while the public torturer applied a pair of pincers or a hot iron to the victim's bare flesh.

Then, too, the Inquisition soon discovered that false confessions were the inevitable result of torture. If an inquisitor was seeking what modern interrogators call "actionable intelligence"—for example, the names and whereabouts of fellow believers or the sympathetic souls who had sheltered the victim from the Inquisition—a confession extracted under torture might turn out to be worthless. Even a cagey defender of torture like Nicholas Eymerich conceded that the rack and the wheel did not always bring the victim to a satisfactory confession. Some men and women, he observed, were ardent true believers who were perfectly willing to endure pain unto death rather than betray their faith or their fellow believers. Others were so terrified by the torturer that they "confessed to everything without making useful distinctions." And a few of the victims, bloodied and broken and perhaps even comatose, were simply incapable of confessing at all.[33]

For all these reasons, the Church purported to impose various legal and technical restrictions on the use of torture, a fact that is often cited by apologists for the Inquisition. Torture, as we have seen, was authorized only for suspects who gave evasive answers or against whom indicia of heresy had been secured from other sources. Canon law permitted a victim to be tortured only once on any given indicium of heresy, and only a single torture session could be lawfully conducted. If a confession was secured, the victim was required to affirm in a sworn statement that the admission of guilt had not been coerced under the threat or application of torture. If the inquisitor sought to torture a child, he was required to seek the appointment of a legal guardian and make sure the guardian was present in the torture chamber before the carnage began.

Such protocols, of course, are exactly what the defenders of the Inquisition point to when they imagine that the friar-inquisitors succeeded in dispensing "legal" justice if not "moral" justice. But the fact remains that the Inquisition did not even follow its own dubious rules, which were paperthin and easily avoided in practice. Indeed, the inquisitor's handbooks routinely offered tips and techniques for circumventing the limitations on torture, an awkward fact that demonstrates how little the inquisitors themselves respected the regulations that the popes and bishops had sought to impose on them.

Thus, for example, the inquisitors readily evaded the rule against torturing a victim more than once by announcing that a torture session had been "suspended rather than ended," and so a fresh round of torture could be resumed at the pleasure or convenience of the inquisitor. The legal fiction that a torture session had been adjourned rather than concluded was commonly entered into the transcripts of interrogations in the inquisitorial archives. "A second or third day may be fixed to terrify him as a continuation of his torture," explained Eymerich to the readers of his manual.[34]

Then, too, the inquisitor often resorted to outright lies. The records of the Inquisition routinely report that a confession of heresy was "free and spontaneous" when, in fact, the victim had been brought to confession under torture. To justify the mistruth, the inquisitors allowed a decent interval to pass before the confession was formalized in the presence of a notary at a venue other than the place where the victim had been tortured, usually three days after the torture session but sometimes as little as twenty-four hours later. Thus did they succeed in comforting themselves with the notion that the confession was free of coercion on the day and at the place where it was actually put down on paper, even if the victim had been previously tortured, cruelly and at length.[35]

New and ever more ingenious legal ploys were manufactured by the Inquisition to evade even the meager rights afforded to accused heretics by canon law. If a victim dared to withdraw a confession on the grounds that it had been extracted under torture, he or she could be lawfully subjected to torture once again because, as the inquisitors saw it, the recanted confession was a new indicium of a crime. Even worse, the new crime now carried the risk of the death penalty because, according to canon law, an accused heretic who confessed and then recanted could be condemned as a relapsed heretic and burned alive—an effective deterrent to any victim who was inclined to complain that he or she had been tortured into a false confession.

Some inquisitors deemed it unnecessary to engage in such quibbles, making instead the now-familiar argument that torture was wholly justified by the threat posed by their enemies in the war on heresy. When Pope John XII sought to impose some gentle restraints on the Inquisition in a papal decree of 1317 by requiring the joint approval of both the inquisitor and a bishop before an accused heretic or a witness was put to torture, Bernard Gui complained that such formalities would "cripple the efficiency of the Inquisition." At most, Gui suggested, the pope might advise the inquisitors to use torture "with mature and careful deliberation," and then leave them to continue their work without some fussy bishop looking over their shoulders.[36]

The Church, in fact, had already embraced these arguments. In 1256, as we have already noted, Pope Alexander IV had eliminated the need for even the most scrupulous inquisitor to restrain or explain himself by decreeing that any inquisitor was empowered to absolve any other inquisitor for "irregularities" in the conduct of an investigation. The friar-preachers understood the rule to mean that they could freely engage in torturing their victims in plain violation of canon law and then routinely absolve one another. Since everything that they did took place behind closed doors—and since they chose and controlled the notaries and scriveners who witnessed and recorded what happened there—it is unlikely that much concern or conversation was wasted on "irregularities" that may have been taken place in the chaotic and messy confines of the torture chamber.[37]

Given the preference of the Inquisition for confession—and the fact that interrogations were conducted behind locked doors by functionaries who had been sworn to silence—the fact that the inquisitors commonly used torture is hardly surprising and was perhaps even inevitable. Above all, torture was not only tolerated but actively encouraged because the Church regarded the war on heresy as an existential struggle with Satan and his minions on earth; the victims of torture were nothing more than "traitors to God" in the eyes of their persecutors. To the horror and sorrow of countless generations to come, the Inquisition demonstrated that the demonization of one's adversaries makes it legally and morally acceptable to torture and kill them.[38]

Strictly speaking, torture was never regarded by the Inquisition as a punishment for the crime of heresy; it was always and only a tool for extracting testimony from unwilling witnesses and confessions from stubborn suspects. Once the inquisitors were finally satisfied with whatever evidence they had extracted from the victim of torture, they would reassemble to pronounce judgment on the accused heretic and announce the sentence that they had decided to impose. The victim may have already endured years of abuse in the inquisitorial prisons and torture chambers, but the punishment began in earnest only when the torture had ended.

Even then, the Inquisition clung to yet another thin legal fiction when it insisted that the convicted heretic was subject only to "penance" and not to punishment. A heretic who finally confessed his crime, renounced his false beliefs, rejoined the Roman Catholic church, and humbly submitted himself to its authority was now regarded as a penitent rather than a criminal. So it was written in the letter that a convicted heretic might be required to carry while performing a penance: "The bearer sinned by the crime of heretical morbidity, as revealed by confession made in proceedings before us, and of his own will returns humbly to the bosom of Holy Church."[39]

All self-confessed heretics were required to repudiate publicly the false beliefs that had led them into heresy. The inquisitor's handbooks prescribed the phrases to be uttered aloud by the repentant heretic: "I, so-and-so, recognize the true, Catholic and Apostolic faith and detest all heresy," the *forma adjurationis* (form of adjuration) begins, and the confessant proceeds to swear fealty to the pope and the Church, to affirm his or her belief that the wafer and wine of the Eucharist are the literal body and blood of Christ, and to foreswear any further traffic with heretics, all "on pain of eternal damnation."[40] Only then would the inquisitors announce the "penances" that would be imposed on the errant child of the Mother Church.

The severity of the penances handed down by the inquisitor depended on what he regarded as the heretic's degree of culpability and, even more crucially, on the quality of the heretic's confession. A man or woman who came forward and confessed without coercion to some accidental or incidental heresy—for example, an unwitting greeting offered to someone who turned out to be a Cathar *perfectus*—would receive one of the lighter penances. Indeed, some inquisitors were willing to overlook even the most outrageous conduct if it was followed by an earnest confession. Pietro Balsamo, one of the assassins of the inquisitor later dubbed Saint Peter the Martyr, was sufficiently repentant to earn not only a pardon for his crime but also the opportunity to join the Dominican order. But accused heretics who compelled the inquisitor to resort to torture before finally offering up a confession might spend the rest of their lives in prison. And those who refused to confess at all were liable to be burned at the stake as unrepentant heretics.

Accused men and women who refused to confess to the crime of heresy—and, even worse, true believers who openly affirmed their forbidden faith—were the only victims of the Inquisition who were said to suffer punishment rather than penance. According to inquisitorial dogma, however, their punishment was never imposed by the Inquisition itself. Rather, as we have seen, unrepentant heretics passed out of the jurisdiction of the Inquisition and were "abandoned" to the authority of the secular government, which then decided whether to sentence them to prison or death.

 For that reason, the Inquisition itself and the apologists who came later always insisted that the mortal lives of the abandoned heretics were taken by the civil government rather than by the Church, and their blood was on the hands of the public magistrate and the public executioner rather than the friar-inquisitors. The rest of the victims, by contrast, were permitted to remain within the maternal embrace of the Church as long as they performed the acts of contrition imposed on them by the Inquisition.

Perhaps the lightest penance that the inquisitor could impose was the obligation to make a pilgrimage to one or more holy sites. Even so, the cost of making a compelled pilgrimage amounted to the equivalent of a heavy fine, and the difficulty of travel in the Middles Ages meant that a pilgrimage to multiple shrines—or a single distant one—functioned as a kind of exile, sometimes months or even years in duration, during which one's family was left without a provider or a protector. Then, too, pilgrimage might be combined with one or more of the other, even harsher penances available to a stern inquisitor.

The shrine of St. James of Compostela in Spain was a favorite destination chosen by the inquisitors, but a penitent might be sent to Canterbury, Cologne, or Rome, and sometimes to all of them; one unfortunate victim of the Inquisition was ordered to make a total of eight pilgrimages. If convicted of consorting with fellow heretics in a particular place, a penitent might be compelled to return to a church near the scene of the crime, where he or she would be scourged by the local priest in the presence of the congregation on a Sunday or a feast day. The penitent might even be ordered to carry a whip and offer it to good Christians along the way who would do him the favor of beating him. And the compulsory pilgrims were required to bring back signed letters from the local clergy at each destination to prove that they had been there.

Still, a pilgrimage was always preferable to a prison sentence, and a few men sentenced to life imprisonment by the Inquisition were able to bargain for their freedom in exchange for joining one of the Crusades, the longest and most dangerous pilgrimage of all. At least one convicted heretic was sentenced to spend twenty years in the Holy Land as an act of penance, which turned the pilgrimage into the functional equivalent of exile. Given the risks of disease, starvation, and shipwreck—and the danger of going into battle against the armies of the Saracens in the Holy Land—the crusade itself might amount to a death sentence.

Next in severity after pilgrimage was the obligation of a convicted heretic to wear "the cross of infamy"—a yellow cross sewn to one's outer clothing as an unmistakable sign that the wearer had been convicted of the crime of heresy. Sometimes the cross was affixed to the breast only and sometimes to both the front and back of the garment, sometimes for a designated number of years and sometimes for the rest of the penitent's life. Once the wearing of crosses had been decreed by the inquisitor, however, they were to be worn at all times, both at home and on the street, as an indelible mark of one's status as a former heretic. So the wearing of crosses reduced the victim to a pariah, just as it was intended to do, and exposed him or her to abuse, isolation, and ridicule.[41]

Here is yet another example of the attention to detail that characterized all aspects of the Inquisition. Lest the heretic choose a small, obscure cross, the size was specified in the formal sentence pronounced by the inquisitor—"two palms in height and breadth," for example, and sometimes even larger ones. To make sure the crosses were plainly visible, the inquisitor specified that "the clothing on which he wears the cross shall never be yellow in colour." The Inquisition issued a supply of cloth to the convicted heretic at the time of sentencing, "but replacing worn-out crosses was the duty of the penitent." To remove or conceal the cross was regarded as a relapse into heresy, a new and even more heinous crime that was punishable by death.[42]

A certain iconography came to be attached to the heretic's crosses. If worn by a convicted perjurer—or by someone released after a life sentence had been commuted—the cross would have a second transverse arm as a mark of special dishonor. If the wearer had achieved the rank of a *perfectus* prior to conviction, a third cross was added. The image of a hammer sewn to the heretic's clothing indicated that he or she was a prisoner of the Inquisition who had been released on bail. Red tongues were another symbol of perjury, and the addition of a letter to the cross marked the wearer as a forger. Indeed, the heretic's clothing might be adorned with any manner of symbolic marking depending on the mood or imagination of the inquisitor.

While the wearing of crosses was regarded as among the lesser afflictions imposed on the victims of the Inquisition, the sentence amounted to a social and financial catastrophe. A man or woman compelled to wear the heretic's crosses would find it hard to secure work or lodging. Even if the family were not reduced to homelessness and hunger, the sons and daughters of convicted heretics made poor prospects for marriage. The whole family might be ostracized by friends and relations who were fearful of being seen to associate with convicted heretics and then finding themselves accused of the same crime. Indeed, the terrible isolation that resulted from the wearing of crosses was the whole point of the penance.

So it was that convicted heretics sought every opportunity to shed the crosses of infamy. A woman named Raymonde de Got, for example, petitioned Bernard Gui to permit her to shed the crosses in 1309 on a showing of good conduct, but she succeeded only after she had worn them for some forty years. Another convicted heretic, who dared to remove the crosses from his clothing on the assumption that he was no longer required to wear them after agreeing to join the Crusades, was sentenced to an additional penance: until his departure for the Holy Land, he was required to present himself on the first Sunday of every month, barefooted and wearing only his undergarments, a rod in hand, for a public scourging at every church within the city of Carcassonne.

Such sentences allow us to glimpse the ingenuity that the inquisitor was empowered to bring to the sentencing of convicted heretics. Since the Inquisition was a law unto itself, its agents enjoyed the power to invent new and ever more imaginative penances for those in their power. The inquisitor might forbid a convicted heretic from wearing "ostentatious dress or adornments," or he might require the same man or woman to wear a garment that carried scenes and symbols meant to expose the wearer to ridicule and hatred. If sufficiently wealthy, a penitent might be ordered to pay the living expenses of a priest or an impoverished family for a specified time ranging from a year to a lifetime. "His body was at the mercy of the Church," or so the Inquisition asserted, "and if through tribulation of the flesh he could be led to see the error of his ways, there was no hesitation in employing whatever means were readiest to save his soul and advance the faith."[43]

Both the compulsory pilgrimage and the wearing of heretic's crosses, as we have seen, put the victim at risk of financial ruin. But the Inquisition was not always content with such indirect methods, and the property of a man or woman convicted of heresy was at risk, too. The inquisitor might order that a heretic's house be torn down and everything else the heretic possessed be confiscated and sold, thus reducing the family to poverty and disinheriting the children. The inquisitor might impose monetary fines on the convicted heretic or, if the heretic was already dead, on his or her children and grandchildren. Indeed, the profit motive was one of the great engines of the Inquisition, and the opportunity to turn heresy into gold sometimes resulted in a free-for-all among the inquisitors as well as among popes and bishops, kings and princes, all of them scrambling for a share of the loot.

"By confiscation the heretics were forced to furnish the means for their own destruction," writes Lea, whose words apply with equal accuracy to the looting of the victims of later persecutions in Nazi Germany and Stalinist Russia. "Avarice joined hands with fanaticism, and between them they supplied motive power for a hundred years of fierce, unremitting, unrelenting persecution, which in the end accomplished its main purpose."[44]

To be sure, the destruction of a house on the orders of the Inquisition profited no one. Still, the early and more principled inquisitors regarded the house where a *perfectus* lived—or where the last rite of the *consolamentum* had been conducted for a dying Cathar—as something so tainted that it could no longer be used by good Christians. That was why, for example, the inquisitor's decree might prohibit the construction of a new house on the blasted plot of ground where the old house had stood. Even the houses of fautors—those good-hearted souls who did nothing more than shelter a friend or relation who was accused of the crime of heresy—could be reduced to rubble on the orders of the inquisitor. And, according to law, the civil magistrates were commanded by the Church to carry out an order for destruction within ten days after it was handed down by an inquisitor.

When the inquisitors turned to the practical problem of paying the bills, however, it occurred to them that the property of an accused heretic could be put to better use. The materials from a destroyed house, for example, might be retrieved and recycled for the construction of a worthy structure like a hospital or convent. Or the inquisitors themselves might commandeer the house of a convicted heretic for use as a dormitory or prison. Eventually, the Inquisition came to realize that the house of a convicted heretic was not so hateful that it could not be used to turn a profit. Thus began what Lea calls, in a characteristically colorful turn of phrase, the "saturnalia of plunder" that was the highly profitable by-product of the war on heresy.[45]

To increase the cash flow of the Inquisition, some inquisitors offered to commute the harsher sentences in exchange for a cash payment; thus did the inquisitors of Toulouse extract enough money from twelve wealthy heretics to build the cathedral of Lavaur. At other times and places, the inquisitors often behaved more like arbitrageurs and speculators than crusaders against heretical depravity. Lands, houses, money, and other property were seized and inventoried as soon as someone came under suspicion of heresy, to prevent the suspect from hiding or selling the property before a formal order of forfeiture was issued. To protect the interests of Church and state in the plunder, the royal tax collectors in France placed a mortgage against the property of an accused heretic and thus trumped any claims that might be made by his wife and children or a stranger who sought to buy the property from the accused heretic.

Confiscation and forfeiture by order of the Inquisition created a whole new set of uncertainties in business transactions. Sellers of property in the city of Florence, for example, were obliged to post a bond against the risk that the buyer might take up residence in a house and later find out that it was the subject of a new or long-simmering inquisitorial proceeding. The Inquisition was so pervasive and so unsettling that, Henry Charles Lea insists, it literally changed the history of Europe. Commerce and industry languished in the lands where it operated with the greatest authority, such as Italy, Spain, and southern France, argues Lea, and flourished in places like England and the Netherlands, where it was toothless or nonexistent.

To make sure that the possessions of a convicted heretic were thoroughly ransacked, the Inquisition also imposed fines on its victims, sometimes as a form of penance and sometimes as the price for buying the commutation of an even harsher punishment. In some precincts, the obligation to wear the crosses of infamy was accompanied by a fine of five or ten florins of pure gold to "defray the expenses of trial." At first, Pope Innocent IV raised a pious objection to the imposition of fines "to the disgrace of the Holy See and the scandal of the faithful at large," and he later decreed that fines were forbidden in favor of other forms of penance. But the operating expenses of the Inquisition were so considerable that the popes soon found themselves compelled to approve the imposition of fines for "pious uses," which included the payment of the inquisitors themselves.[46]

Whenever the supply of living heretics with available assets ran low, the Inquisition turned to the prosecution of dead ones. Since a "defunct" defendant was unable to protest—and the passage of time since his death meant that witnesses and evidence were sparse or wholly unavailable—the proceedings "against the memory" of dead heretics required even less evidence and less effort than the trial of a live one. The real motive was plainly the confiscation of the dead heretic's fortune, and the grisly practice of exhuming and prosecuting corpses, however offensive it might have been to the general populace, presented an opportunity for the Inquisition to turn a risk-free and effortless profit.[47]

As we have seen, the Inquisition was permitted to accuse and condemn dead heretics for crimes dating back at least forty years and, in some places, a full century. The period ran not from the date on which the alleged crime was committed but when it was detected, which further extended the inquisitor's long reach. As a result, anyone who had done business with someone later accused of heresy—and anyone who had inherited property from the dead heretic—was always at risk that the inquisitor would claim money or property that had passed out of the hands of the dead heretic long ago.

Thus, for example, Fra Grimaldo, the inquisitor of Florence, prosecuted the "memory" of a wealthy and influential Florentine nobleman more than sixty years after the latter's death, belatedly charging the deceased with having submitted to the *consolamentum* on his deathbed and then proceeding against his surviving grandchildren. None of the descendants of the dead heretic was actually accused of heresy; indeed, one of his grandchildren was a friar and another served as the prior of a church. But the property that had once belonged to the dead man was seized by the Inquisition, and the grandchildren who served the Church were defrocked on the grounds that the descendants of a heretic down to the second generation were ineligible to hold clerical rank.

Now and then, some high-minded churchman might address the plain injustice of confiscation and seizure of property. Suppose, for example, that the wife of a condemned heretic was herself a good Catholic; should she be reduced to poverty, too? Under canon law, the dower—a portion of the husband's property set aside for the support of his widow in the event of his death—was held to be exempt from confiscation, but only if the wife could prove to the satisfaction of the Inquisition that she did not know that her husband was a heretic when they were married. Moreover, if she later learned that her husband held heretical beliefs, she would forfeit the exemption if she had failed to report her spouse to the Inquisition within forty days. Even if the wife was entitled to draw on the dower for her livelihood, the right ended on her own death. The children of a heretic were disinherited, and so the dower was confiscated by the Inquisition on the death of their mother.

Any concern for widows and orphans that might stir the conscience of a principled inquisitor was usually outweighed by more practical considerations. The Inquisition was a high-overhead operation, and money was always needed for the support of the inquisitors and their servitors, for the building and running of prisons, and even for such incidentals as the yellow cloth for the crosses worn by repentant heretics and the kindling for the fires on which unrepentant heretics were burned alive. As the war on heresy ran out of Cathars and Waldensians, the Inquisition's restless search for fresh victims came to be driven by sheer greed. "But for the gains to be made out of fines and confiscations, its work would have been much less thorough," observes Lea. "It would have sunk into comparative insignificance as soon as the first frantic zeal of bigotry had exhausted itself."[48]

The plunder prompted a whole new conflict between Church and state. In theory, the income from fines, commutations, and the sale of confiscated property was to be divided in equal shares: one-third to the municipal government of the town where the inquisitors had set up their tribunal, one-third to defray the expenses of the inquisitors who had issued the order of confiscation or imposed the fine, and the rest to the Church for the use of the local bishop and to defray the general operating expenses of the Inquisition. But the actual division of the spoils varied from place to place. In France, the forfeited property of convicted heretics belonged to the king, although he was expected to apportion some of the proceeds to the inquisitors at work in France and to the operating expenses of the inquisitorial prisons in his territories, including rations for the prisoners and wages for their guards. In Italy, by contrast, the Inquisition managed to keep its hands on so many of the spoils that it was self-supporting.

All these practices were wholly legal under the laws of Church and state. But the opportunity to make money off the workings of the Inquisition was hardly limited to fines and confiscations. An inquisitor might profit by selling the licenses to bear arms that were granted to agents of the Inquisition, as we have already seen, or by embezzling the money and property entrusted to his care. Jacques de Polignac, warden of the inquisitorial prison at Carcassonne, was found to have conspired with other officials to take possession of "a castle, several farms and other lands, vineyards, orchards and movables," all of which had been seized from the convicted heretics in his custody. Once his crime was discovered, the crooked jailor and his co-conspirators were ordered to return the plunder—not to the victims from whom it had been taken, of course, but to the Inquisition.[49]

The mendicant orders had been founded on the principle of poverty, but the high ideals of Saint Dominic and Saint Francis did not prevent the friar-inquisitors from turning the prosecution of heresy into a paying business. The inquisitors in the mercantile center of Venice showed a special genius for commerce that was quite at odds with their original vows; they speculated in real estate and lent out the money in their coffers at interest to produce yet more profits. A few engaged in even more cynical abuses: the Franciscan inquisitor known as Brother Mascar of Padua, for example, succeeded in extorting a fortune over his four decades of service in what can only be called a protection scheme—a payoff to the inquisitor would ensure that the Inquisition looked elsewhere for its victims.

By far the most common punishment for convicted heretics and their defenders was a term of confinement behind walls and bars. Accused heretics taken from a holding cell to be tried by the Inquisition were likely to be returned to the same place, sometimes for years and sometimes for life under a sentence of "perpetual imprisonment in chains." Defenders of the Inquisition have pointed out that the inquisitorial jail was no worse than any other medieval prison, both of which were "frightful abodes of misery." But we should not overlook a basic distinction between the two: the population of an ordinary prison consisted of actual criminals whereas the Inquisition concerned itself with men and women who were guilty only of thinking the wrong thought at the wrong time and place.[50]

In service to the legal fiction that the Inquisition imposed only penance and not punishment, the prisons were operated by the civil authorities rather than by the Inquisition. The inquisitor's formula for sentencing a condemned heretic to prison consisted of yet another elaborate circumlocution. The heretic is "to take himself to the prison prepared for him," and if he refuses to do so, the secular authorities are ordered to arrest the noncompliant convict and convey him to the place of incarceration. The passive voice in which the sentence was formulated, and the pious relinquishment of the heretic to the secular government, allowed the inquisitor to wash his hands of his victim's fate.[51]

Inquisitorial prisons were of two kinds, the *murus largus* (wide walls) for suspects and ordinary prisoners, and the *murus strictus* (narrow walls) reserved for men and women whose confessions had been deemed unsatisfactory by the Inquisition or who had attempted to escape from an ordinary prison. In its architecture the *murus largus* was patterned after a monastery, with a series of cells along a common passage. The inmates were able to see and speak with others, spouses were allowed to visit on occasion, and a prisoner might be permitted other callers as well, sometimes a courageous friend and sometimes a spy sent into the cell by the Inquisition. We are told that a disguised *perfectus* might even succeed in calling on a dying Cathar behind bars and administering the *consolamentum* in secret, although the bribery of a guard was surely necessary to achieve such a daring exploit.

The *murus strictus,* by contrast, was essentially a dungeon, and the lost soul who ended up there might not see another human face throughout his confinement. The cells were just large enough for a single prisoner. Even so, the inmate's hands and feet were chained, and sometimes the chains were affixed to the wall to ensure complete immobility. Here were imprisoned the men and women who had confessed only under torture or threat of burning at the stake; the inquisitors convinced themselves that such heretics were likely to "backslide" into the false beliefs that they had repudiated. For that reason alone, in fact, convicted heretics whose confessions were "imperfect" were generally sent into solitary confinement so that they would be "prevented from corrupting others" after the inevitable relapse into their bad old ways.[52]

A third kind of confinement, the *murus strictissimus,* was maintained for those whom the Inquisition regarded as the worst offenders, including men and women who had been members of Catholic religious orders at the time of their crime or conviction. When a nun called Jeanne de la Tour was convicted on charges of holding both Cathar and Waldensian beliefs, for example, she was placed in a sealed cell with only a single narrow opening through which a meager allotment of food and water, and nothing else, was provided. Confinement in the tomblike cell was the functional equivalent of a death sentence.

The inmates of all inquisitorial prisons were fed on bread and water only, a practice that was meant not only to punish but also to reduce the prison's operating expenses. The short rations conferred a secondary benefit: men and women who lived on meager portions of bread and water did not live very long. "[I]f they perished through neglect and starvation," the jailers calculated, "it was a saving of expense." Prisoners might improve their lot if they could afford to bribe the jailors and bring in decent rations from outside the prison, or if they could call on someone who was both brave enough and wealthy enough to pay for such amenities. But even the richest convicts were generally impoverished by fines and confiscations before they ended up in prison, and their friends and relations on the outside were seldom willing to risk the charge of fautorship by sending money or provisions to the gates of the inquisitorial prison.[53]

The cost of keeping convicted heretics in "perpetual" confinement, even under such mean circumstances, turned out to be a considerable burden. As the Inquisition grew in size and scope—and as its jails filled up with accused and convicted heretics—the real price of persecution began to set the various players at odds with one another. Inquisitors, bishops, lords, and town councilors bickered among themselves over who ought to pay for the building of prisons, the salaries of jailors, and the cost of bread, water, and straw for the inmates. As a general rule, whoever seized the property of an accused heretic was supposed to pay for the costs of his or her imprisonment. As a practical matter, though, some inquisitors found it necessary to threaten prosecution on charges of fautorship against bishops or magistrates who were quick to seize the property of condemned individuals but slow to feed them.[54]

Now and then, the Inquisition was capable of an act of genuine mercy. A man named Sabbatier, who had been convicted of heresy and sentenced to prison on the basis of his own belief in Catharism, pointed out to the inquisitor that he was the sole support of his elderly father, "a Catholic and a poor man." The inquisitor deigned to postpone Sabbatier's punishment "as long as his father shall live; and meanwhile he shall wear a black mantle and on each garment a cross with two transverse branches, and he shall provide for his father as best he can." But the quality of mercy was somewhat strained. On the death of his father, the original sentence was to be carried out.[55]

A few intrepid inmates managed to escape the custody of the Inquisition, as evidenced by the inclusion in the inquisitor's handbooks of a form to be used in requesting the return of a fugitive. A man named Giuseppe Pignata, serving a sentence in the inquisitorial prison at Rome in 1693, demonstrated the skill, guile, and patience necessary to achieve such a feat. A gifted artist, he sketched a charming portrait of a guard's lover and traded it for a penknife. Then he persuaded the prison doctor to provide him with a small brazier, pointing out that he had been badly injured during torture and needed a source of heat in his cold cell. He used the brazier as a forge, and turned the penknife into a boring tool that enabled him slowly to dig his way out of the cell. Finally, he resorted to the classic tool of the prison escape—a rope of knotted sheets—to put himself beyond the reach of the Inquisition.

Such exploits were rare. Far more often, victims remained in their cells, shackled and starved, until the inquisitor who put them there finally consented to release them. If convicted heretics seldom served life sentences, they might nevertheless wait years or even decades before the Inquisition bestirred itself to let them go. Even then, the release from prison might be conditioned on the wearing of crosses, the making of a pilgrimage, or some other lingering penance. And, once released, the man or woman who had once been convicted was now broken, impoverished, and disgraced.

The ultimate penalty for the crime of heresy—and the iconic scene of the Inquisition—was burning at the stake. The death penalty was reserved for convicted heretics who had refused to confess or who, having offered a confession, then dared to disavow their guilt. Strictly speaking, as we have seen, the inquisitor never sentenced a convicted heretic to death; rather, the victim was excommunicated from the Church and then "abandoned"

THE GRAND INQUISITOR'S MANUAL

to the public executioner. Yet again, the formbooks consulted by working inquisitors provided a script for the solemn occasion, a formula that first addressed the victim himself and then the public magistrates into whose custody he was now consigned.

"We relinquish him now to secular judgment and, by the authority which we wield, we not only condemn him as a heretic," recited the inquisitor, "but also we bind him with the chain of excommunication as fautors, receivers, and defenders of heretics all persons who knowingly henceforth either harbour or defend him or lend him counsel, aid or favour."[56]

The threat against "defenders of heretics" was directed at any public official who might hesitate to carry out the unspoken death sentence. Since the friar-inquisitor, as an ordained cleric, was forbidden by canon law to shed blood, the formula is pointedly silent on what will actually happen to the victim after he or she is abandoned by the Church. Indeed, the inquisitor was supposed to "pray that no death might ensue," according to historian G. G. Coulton, "even while the utterer of that prayer would have been bound to excommunicate any secular judge who should neglect to inflict death."[57]

The execution of a convicted heretic, like every other aspect of the Inquisition, was designed to inspire terror and horror in the general populace and, especially, in anyone who might be tempted to embrace a forbidden faith, but the grand inquisitor did not neglect the production values, "as if he were an entrepreneur offering a show." Burnings were scheduled for feast days, both to emphasize the sanctity of the Inquisition and to build the crowd; after all, it was a day off from work for the whole populace, and the spectacle amounted to a highly theatrical if also grisly form of entertainment. To accommodate the greatest number of eager spectators, the preferred venue was the public square outside the cathedral where the formal ceremony of sentencing the heretics would take place.[58]

Cardinals and bishops in full regalia, richly dressed nobles and their ladies, even the king and queen were encouraged to attend the burning of condemned heretics as guests of honor. The square would be decorated with flags and banners, and the inquisitorial ranks swelled with priests and soldiers, drummers and trumpeters, heralds and flag bearers. Surely the presence of a crowd would have also attracted food vendors, street musicians, and perhaps more than a few pickpockets. As sheer entertainment, nothing could rival the Inquisition at the moment when its terrible power was on display.

By contrast, the victims presented a less festive sight. According to a pious tradition, a condemned woman would wash her face and remove any cosmetics "so as not to go painted before God." If the victims had been recently questioned under torture, their hair would still be cut short or burned off and their wounds would be fresh; one victim, for example, was carried to the stake in a chair because his feet had been burned to the bone during an ordeal by fire. Even if the victim had spent months or years in an inquisitorial prison, he or she might be crippled by the instruments of torture that had been applied to joints and bones. At dawn on the day of judgment, they would be offered a meager last meal, if they still had any appetite as the last hour of their lives approached.[59]

Other preparations were made in the days before the spectacle. The pyre was made ready by erecting upright stakes in the public square—one for each victim—and then piling straw, kindling, and faggots of wood around the base of each stake. Some burnings were conducted at ground level or even in pits, especially in the earlier, more primitive years of the Inquisition, but a platform of wood and masonry was more often erected in the square to improve the sightlines for the audience. If royalty, aristocracy, or high clergy were in attendance, they would be provided seats on or near the platform so that they could see and be seen by the crowd. The victims were kept offstage to heighten the suspense in advance of the grand moment when they were presented to the crowd.

First, the inquisitors and the visiting dignitaries gathered in a church or cathedral, where a mass was conducted and a sermon preached. The self-confessed heretics who had recanted their false beliefs were welcomed back into the Church and then told what penances, light or harsh, they would be required to make as a condition for forgiveness of their sins. At last, the inquisitors and their distinguished guests exited the sacred precincts of the church or cathedral, which were thought to be unsuitable for the pronouncement of the death sentence, and entered the public square in a formal procession.

Then the condemned men and women, shackled and closely guarded, were escorted to the stake. On hand at all times were friars whose task was not to comfort the victims in the moments leading up to their death but to extract an eleventh-hour confession. Right up to the moment when the straw was set aflame, the friars urged the condemned heretics to save their souls—and possibly their lives, too—by admitting their guilt, recanting their false beliefs, and embracing the Catholic faith. Heretics who confessed in time were likely to spend the rest of their lives in prison, but at least they would not die then and there. By contrast, those who had already confessed to heresy on a previous occasion and had been sentenced to die as relapsed heretics would still be burned alive even if they confessed a second time, but at least—the friars told them—they would save their souls by dying as Catholics.

An admission of guilt, as we have seen, was always an urgent concern of the Inquisition, and never more so than when it came to capital punishment. Burning an unrepentant heretic posed the risk of presenting his fellow believers with a martyr; if we are to believe the evidence of the Inquisition itself, the bones of a dead heretic might be collected and preserved as relics. A display of courage in the face of death by a true believer in a dissident faith might make the wrong impression on the good Catholics in the crowd. For that reason, too, the condemned heretic was not permitted to speak and, in some cases, he was gagged to prevent him from addressing the crowd with some affirmation of faith before going up in flames.

One such gagging device, known as the mute's bridle, consisted of an iron box that was inserted into the victim's mouth and held in place by a collar around the neck. The gag itself might be used to inflict yet more pain and humiliation on the victim; when the Renaissance scholar and scientist Giordano Bruno was sent to the stake in Rome in 1600, he was wearing an elaborate contraption "so constructed that one long spike pierced his tongue and the floor of his mouth and came out underneath his chin, while another penetrated up through his palate." Thus was the victim pointedly punished for his previous false utterings and prevented from making any new ones while, at the same time, he was prevented from uttering any screams that might have "interfered with the sacred music," as Robert Held describes the scene.[60]

Still, despite such elaborate precautions, not every public execution was free of bungling. According to an eyewitness to the burning of the proto-Protestant reformer John Huss at Constance in 1415, the victim was bound to the stake with ropes tied tightly at his ankles, knees, groin, waist, and arms, and with a chain around his neck. After Huss had been thus fixed in place and made ready for burning, however, someone noticed that he was facing east, the direction of Jerusalem, and so the solemn moment was delayed while he was unbound, turned away from the sacred city, and tied up again. The scene might strike us as ludicrous and even laughable if it were not so appalling.[61]

Once the victim was properly bound to the stake, additional straw and wood were added to the pyre, sometimes piled up to the prisoner's neck. The priests ceased their preaching to the condemned man or woman and hastily withdrew to a safe distance, although even then, a cross was sometimes fixed to a long staff and held in front of the victim's face until the moment of death. By that point, of course, the gesture was intended only to taunt and admonish the victim because it was plainly too late to achieve a conversion. At last, the inquisitor clapped his hands as a signal to the executioner to set a lighted torch to the kindling and thus send the heretic to hell.

Some victims of the Inquisition went courageously to their deaths as true believers and willing martyrs. The most intrepid of them, according to one eyewitness account, "laughed as they were bound to the pyre." Another contemporary observer reported that some of the condemned men and women "thrust their hands and feet into the flames with the most dauntless fortitude," as if to make the point that they welcomed martyrdom in the name of their forbidden faith, "and all of them yielded to their fate with such resolution that many of the amazed spectators lamented that such heroic souls had not been more enlightened." Indeed, the public display of true belief by a dying heretic was the worst fear of the Inquisition and one that the monks sought to avoid at all costs.[62]

Modern medical writers have speculated that some victims of the Inquisition, both under torture and at the stake, may have been blessed with "a strange state of exaltation" that resulted from the sudden release of hormones by bodies subjected to stress, shock, and trauma. Yet the fact remains that most of the victims suffered terribly in the flames, and the sound of groans and screams rose above the roar of the fire and the taunts or guffaws of those in the crowd who took pleasure in this horror show. Of course, that is why the Church took such pains to convince its congregants that the victims of the Inquisition were nothing more than "heretical filth" whose disposal was a sacred duty. On the day when the machinery of persecution finally spat out the broken bodies of its victims, they were to be seen as "traitors to God" whose deaths were a victory rather than a tragedy.[63]

A well-fueled pyre might burn for hours, roasting the flesh long after the victims were dead. But the human body is not easily burned to ash, and it was always necessary to remove and dispose of the charred remains. The bones were broken up, the viscera and body parts were gathered, and the whole ghastly mess was tossed on a newly kindled fire for the purpose of reducing it still further. When the second fire burned out, the ashes and fragments of bone were collected and dumped on the waste ground along with the dung and garbage. Or, if the inquisitor feared that someone would try to retrieve a splinter of bone or a stray tooth, he might order the remains to be tossed into a river or stream to defeat the relic hunters. Such were the precautions taken for such famous heretics as John Huss and Savonarola, the radical priest of Florence who was burned alive in 1498 in the same square where he had once organized the famous Bonfire of the Vanities.[64]

So dutiful were the record keepers of the medieval Inquisition that we are able to inspect a kind of expense report for the execution of four heretics at Carcassonne on April 24, 1323. The greatest single expense, at slightly more than 55 *sols,* was for "large wood," and another 23 *sols* were spent on vine-branches and straw. Four stakes cost nearly 11 *sols,* and the ropes cost another 4 *sols* and 7 *deniers.* The executioner was paid 20 *sols* for each victim. The whole job priced out at exactly 8 *livres,* 14 *sols,* and 7 *deniers.** The aroma of burning human flesh may have been regarded by the inquisitors as pleasing to God, but even at such sublime moments, the inquisitors kept one eye on the bottom line. Such was the real price of true belief and the victory of God over the Devil and his minions.

---

*The modern value of medieval currency is difficult to calculate. By custom if not in actual practice, a medieval livre was equal in value to a pound of silver. Twelve deniers were equal to one sou (also called a sol), and twenty sous equaled one livre. To give a rough idea of the purchasing power of medieval currency, a chicken could be purchased in Paris at the end of the fourteenth century for 12 deniers and a pig cost 4 sous. However, the actual value of the currency varied greatly from place to place and over time.

How many men, women, and children were victims of the Inquisition? Despite the inquisitorial obsession for record keeping, the answer is mostly a matter of surmise. As it turns out, historians have recovered documents that describe in obsessive detail the work of some inquisitors at certain times and places, but none at all for many other agents of the Inquisition who operated at other times and places during its long history.

Then, too, the master plan as it appears in papal decrees, canon law, and the inquisitor's manuals is not always corroborated by the notarial transcripts and ledger books that survived the final destruction of the Inquisition in the nineteenth century. To put it another way, we know how the vast machinery of persecution was designed to operate, but we do not know how well it worked in practice—an accident of history that the defenders of the Inquisition have always used to their advantage in arguing that the Inquisition never fulfilled the grandiose dreams of its creators and operators.

Bernard Gui, for example, maintained a register of 930 sentences that he imposed as an inquisitor at Carcassonne from 1308 to 1323. We cannot know with certainty whether the register is accurate or complete, but he reports that he sent only 42 men and women to the stake, and he notes that 3 escaped heretics were to be put to death if captured. By contrast, he sentenced 307 convicted heretics to prison, 143 to the wearing of crosses, and 9 to go on compulsory pilgrimages. A total of 86 "defunct" heretics were sentenced posthumously to burning or imprisonment. The rest suffered penalties that included exile, a spell in the pillory, destruction of houses, and "degradation" of clerical rank. In a few cases, Gui recorded a reduction of sentence; someone sentenced to prison might be permitted to wear crosses instead, and a few were released from the obligation to wear crosses.

Gui might strike the modern reader as a moderate fellow. After all, he apparently sent fewer than fifty men and women to their deaths over a span of fifteen years, and he imposed the death sentence on far more "defunct" heretics than living ones. But even if Gui was wholly accurate in his record keeping, he may not have been a typical inquisitor. Robert le Bougre, for example, put 183 Cathars to the flames at a single auto-da-fé attended by the king of Navarre in 1239 and described by one pleased spectator as a "holocaust, very great and pleasing to God." Some two hundred Cathars were burned alive when the fortress of Montségur was finally besieged and conquered in 1244. As we shall see, the burning of women accused of witch-craft during the late Middle Ages and the operations of the Spanish Inqui-sition after 1492 brought the death toll into the tens of thousands.[65]

Even so, the crimes of the Inquisition cannot be accurately measured by a body count. By both its decrees and its example, the Inquisition was re-sponsible for the erosion of what meager liberties were available to men and women across Europe, the steady expansion of torture and arbitrary imprisonment and the death penalty, the restriction of what was permis-sible to think and read and know, and the establishment of a reign of terror that endured in one form or another for six centuries. Above all, the In-quisition perfected and preserved a model of authoritarianism that contin-ued to operate long after the ashes of the last nameless heretic to be burned alive were scattered to the winds.

5

THE INQUISITOR'S MANUAL

POPE (*Exhausted*): It is clearly understood: he is
not to be tortured. (*Pause.*) At the very most, he
may be shown the instruments.

INQUISITOR: That will be adequate, Your Holiness. Mr. Galilei understands machinery.

BERTOLT BRECHT,
Galileo

The Inquisition achieved a victory of genocidal proportions against
its first victims, but not before driving the Cathars underground
and turning them into fugitives. Instead of wearing the distinctive
black robe that indicated their high rank, the *perfecti* now donned blue or
dark green mantles and contented themselves with a black girdle worn under their clothing or just a symbolic black thread next to the skin. Male and
female *perfecti* traveled in pairs, passing themselves off as married couples
and pretending to be peddlers. Sometimes they resorted to deliberately eating meat in roadhouses and taverns to throw off inquisitorial agents on the
prowl for people whose pale skin and thin torsos suggested that they were
practicing the rigorous self-denial of Catharism.

The *perfecti* sought refuge in a network of safe houses that were maintained here and there across Europe by their fellow Cathars; the hiding place

might be an attic or cellar, a dovecote or sometimes just a shallow hole in the ground concealed by a chest. So the ritual of the *consolamentum* was still available to the ever-diminishing number of dedicated Cathars who managed to avoid arrest, torture, imprisonment, and execution. But they were always at risk of detection by spies in service to the Inquisition or betrayal by self-professed Cathars who had agreed to serve as double agents in order to spare their own lives. By 1330, the last Cathar had been burned alive by the Inquisition, and Catharism was extinct.*

No such victory could be claimed against the other target of the Inquisition in its early years, the Christian rigorists known as the Waldensians. Although they had been lumped with the Cathars and slandered as Devil worshippers, baby killers, and sexual orgiasts—and many of them were, in fact, burned alive by the Inquisition—one group of Waldensians was actually permitted to rejoin the Church under the new name of Poor Catholics, an acknowledgment that the Waldensian beliefs and practices were not quite as diabolical as advertised by their persecutors. A few other Waldensians managed to find sanctuary in remote villages in Italy, where they succeeded in preserving the old faith while the Inquisition busied itself with heretics who were closer at hand. In 1526, when the Protestant Reformation had reached a critical mass, a delegation of surviving Waldensians emerged from hiding to make contact with their kindred spirits in Germany and Switzerland.

"We are in agreement with you in everything," a Waldensian minister (or *barba*) named George Morel wrote to the Christian reformers who had unwittingly followed in the footsteps of the Waldensians. "From the time of the apostles we have had in essentials an understanding of the faith which is yours."[1]

So the medieval Inquisition's original raison d'être—"the most spectacular kinds of heresy," as historian Edward Peters insists on calling the Cathars and Waldensians—disappeared from sight within a century or so after it was first deployed. But the Church refused to declare victory in its war on heresy. Quite to the contrary, the Inquisition continued to search for

---

* The Cathars are gone but not forgotten. The self-invented "neo-Cathar" movement styles itself after the medieval sect, and sightseers in the Pyrenees are encouraged to visit the ruins of Montségur and other castles where the real-life Cathars took refuge in their final days.

new heretics to torture and burn for another five hundred years, and the inquisitors never failed to find them. Indeed, as we shall see, the Inquisition was perfectly capable of conjuring up a new heresy on its own initiative to provide itself with victims.[2]

The sheer staying power of the Inquisition may have been its most horrific feature. Like any bureaucracy, the Inquisition did what was necessary to preserve itself. And the men on its payroll—not just the inquisitors but the familiars, notaries, scriveners, attorneys, doctors, bookkeepers, guards, torturers, and executioners—were not its only constituency. Emperors, kings, and popes, too, found the inquisitorial apparatus so useful in acquiring and maintaining their own wealth and power that they were always reluctant to shut it down merely because the friar-inquisitors had been successful against their first victims. Once the machinery of persecution had been assembled, perfected, and put into operation, the temptation to use it was irresistible and perhaps inevitable.

As the last of the Cathars and Waldensians went up in smoke or went into hiding, the Inquisition had already found a new supply of heretics. Remarkably, the next victims of the friar-inquisitors came from within their own ranks.

The so-called *spirituali* (Spirituals) were Franciscan monks who sought to preserve the ideals of Saint Francis even as the pope commanded that members of their order leave the monastery and enter the world as professional persecutors. The inquisitors, as we have seen, were intent on separating heretics from their money, and using the confiscated wealth to build the infrastructure of the Inquisition. The *spirituali,* as their name implies, preferred to engage in purely spiritual pursuits, including the study of apocalyptic texts that prompted them to expect the end of days, and they insisted on wearing the poorest of clothing to symbolize their vows of poverty. Their patched robes marked them as easy targets of the Inquisition.

Four of the Spirituals, for example, were arrested and tried by the Inquisition at Marseilles in 1318. Under interrogation, they were asked if they recognized the power of the pope to authorize their superiors to decide "what was poverty in clothing," but the apparently innocuous question was a theological trap; if the friars answered yes, they would have been called upon to give up the threadbare habits that they insisted on wearing and put themselves under the authority of what they regarded as the corrupted Franciscan order. By answering no, they condemned themselves as heretics, and the four of them were burned alive. The Spirituals continued to provide the Inquisition with "occasional small batches for the pyre," and their ashes were reportedly gathered by their followers and preserved as relics: "If you are the bones of the saints, help me" was the prayer of a woman named Gagliardi Fardi, or so she confessed when she, too, was tried on charges of heresy.[3]

The spectacle of poor friars being burned alive by a rich and powerful Church only served to stoke the passions of men and women whose religious imagination—as well as their sense of right and wrong—disposed them toward what they regarded as a purer Christianity. Paradoxically, the workings of the Inquisition seemed to encourage an even greater flowering of religious diversity in Christendom, an upwelling of "mystics, prophets and visionaries" and the yearnful and zealous Christians who embraced their teachings. By comparison with the plump and bejeweled princes of the Church, the "poverty fanatics" who were so often the target of the Inquisition may have seemed to be far more sympathetic figures. The burning of accused heretics, according to Malcolm Lambert, "could and did have the effect sometimes of actually spreading heresy."[4]

A whole new vocabulary was coined to identify the apparent proliferation of heresies—the Poor of Lyons, the Poor Lombards, and the Poor Brothers of Penitence of the Third Order of St. Francis, the Humiliati and the Fraticelli, the Beghards and the Beguines, the Arnoldists and the Speronists, the Concorezzenses and the Drugunthians, and many more besides. Some of the labels were used interchangeably to describe the same sect, some were used broadly to describe members of wholly unrelated sects, and some were used to identify heresies that existed only in the fervid minds of the inquisitors themselves. The inquisitors, as it turned out, were so bedazzled and befuddled that they saw heresies where none existed.

The so-called heresy of the Free Spirit, for example, was condemned as "an abominable sect" by the Council of Vienne in 1312. Its members supposedly believed that they had achieved a state of mystical perfection that rendered them incapable of sin and thus free to engage in orgies and other "aberrant sexual practices." One accused heretic named Johann Hartmann, answering the leading questions of an inquisitor during his interrogation in 1367, affirmed that "the free in spirit could have intercourse with sister or mother, even on the altar." But Malcolm Lambert insists that Hartmann himself was "probably a verbal exhibitionist," and the other evidence "sprang from envious gossip, inquisitorial imagination, or distortion of the paradoxical statements of true mystics." Indeed, the sect of the Free Spirit never really existed at all, although more than one eccentric was burned at the stake on charges that he or she belonged to the imaginary cult.[5] "What appeared to have happened," explains author Edward Burman, "is that papal fears, coupled with inquisitorial zeal, created heresies to satisfy a need for new heresies."[6]

Other dissident religious communities were quite real, but they were not the "heretical filth" that the Inquisition imagined them to be. The Beguines, for example, consisted of unmarried or widowed women in the cities of northern Europe who took vows of chastity and lived communally in convent houses, occupied themselves with manual labor and acts of charity, and sought their own spiritual self-improvement through meditation. A Beguine named Marguerite Porete, for example, authored a book titled *The Mirror of Simple Souls* in which she instructed her pious readers on "the progress of the soul through seven states of grace." Like the Spirituals, the Beguines studied the more arcane apocalyptic texts in urgent anticipation of the end-times. The Beghards were their male counterparts, thus named because— just like the original Franciscans and Dominicans—they lived as mendicants and relied on charity for their sustenance.

As self-inspired monastics with no formal allegiance to the Church, the Beguines and the Beghards soon fell afoul of the Inquisition. The hot-eyed inquisitors accused them of engaging in both theological and sexual outrages—the old and inevitable charge of the heresy hunters—and Bernard Gui convinced himself that the Beguines were actually the female auxiliary of the heretical sect known as the Fraticelli. Marguerite Porete was arrested and tried on charges of heresy by the grand inquisitor of Paris in 1310, and both the woman and the books she had written were put to the flames by the Inquisition. A great many other Beguines followed her to the stake even though Pope John XXII cautioned the archbishops in France "to enquire into the beliefs of the Beguines, and distinguish between the 'good' ones and the 'bad' ones."[7]

The inquisitors, though, seem to have been more concerned about the autonomy of the Beguines, who did not answer to fathers, husbands, or priests, than about their supposed carnal or diabolical practices. Bernard Gui, for example, complains in his manual that "they often gather on holy days and Sundays with others who live independently" and read aloud from various texts, including the same ones used by the Church. "Like monkeys, they act in imitation," rants Gui, "although the teaching and preaching of God's commandments and the articles of faith must be exercised within holy Church by her rectors and pastors." Among the questions to be put to suspected Beghards and Beguines, according to Gui's manual, is one that tests their obedience to the pope: "Did he believe that the pope could become a heretic and lose his papal authority if he approved the condemnation of these Beguins as heretics?"[8]

The Inquisition had its own complicated motives for finding more bodies to torture and burn. A final victory in the war on heresy, of course, would have promptly rendered the Inquisition obsolete and put the inquisitors and their servitors out of work. Then, too, the inquisitors sought to enforce the theological monopoly of the Church as a matter of realpolitik, and the Inquisition objected to the Beguines and the Beghards less because they were dangerous heretics than because they submitted themselves to "no Rule and no authority from the Holy See." Indeed, *The Mirror of Simple Souls* continued to circulate as a work of inspirational literature in monasteries and convents long after its author was burned at the stake. "So little obvious was the heresy in it," observes Lambert, "that hardly any of its readers over the centuries questioned its orthodoxy."[9]

Above all, the contraption that had been invented to exterminate the Cathars and the Waldensians achieved a certain forward momentum, and it would have taken a scrupulous and forceful decision by a king or pope to slow it down or stop it. No such order was issued for another five hundred years. Men in power in both Church and state, as we shall see, found the Inquisition to be a practical and powerful tool, one that they preferred to maintain in good working order against the day when they might have occasion to use it for purposes of their own and not merely for the greater glory of God.

King Philip IV of France, known by the fawning title of Philip the Fair, was so distressed by the excesses of the Inquisition on his own soil that he was moved to issue a decree in 1292 by which the royal officer at Carcassonne was ordered to stop arresting and imprisoning citizens of France at the request of the inquisitors unless the suspect had actually confessed to the crime or could be proved a heretic by "the testimony of several trustworthy men." The decree, as it turns out, did not accomplish much—in fact, the inquisitorial outrages at Carcassonne were so egregious that even Pope Clement V was moved to order a formal investigation.[10]

Only a few years later, however, King Philip decided that the Inquisition was not so bad after all. The royal treasury was depleted, and the king resolved to enrich himself at the expense of the Knights Templar, an order of pious warrior-monks dating back to the First Crusade. To accomplish the goal of looting the Templars, he invoked all the powers and prerogatives of the inquisitorial apparatus—arrest, imprisonment, torture, and, above all, confiscation—and claimed to be acting "in the name of the Inquisition." To justify the dispossession and destruction of the Templars, Philip the Fair found it appropriate to slander them as heretics who had committed "a detestable crime, an abominable act, a fearful infamy, a thing altogether inhuman." On October 13, 1307, every Templar in France was placed under arrest in a single sweep, and the property of the order was confiscated.[11]

The charge of heresy against the Templars was especially shocking in light of their long and distinguished history. The founders of the order were knights who had answered the Church's call to go on crusade and take back the Holy Land from its Muslim overlord. After the success of the First Crusade, they remained behind to protect Christian pilgrims en route to Jerusalem from attack by Muslim raiders. By 1120, a handful of these knights had organized themselves into a religious fellowship; no less a celebrity than Bernard of Clairvaux lobbied the pope to sanction them as a new order, and Baldwin II, the crusader-king of Jerusalem, provided them with quarters located on the traditional site of the Temple of Solomon as described in the Bible. Thus did they call themselves the Poor Fellow-Soldiers of Christ and of the Temple of Solomon, and they took the same vows of poverty, chastity, and obedience required of monks under the Benedictine Rule, although their principal duty was to bear arms in service to the Church.

Even after the crusaders were finally driven out of the Holy Land in 1291, the Knights Templar remained a rich, influential, highly visible arm of the Church with estates and enterprises throughout western Europe. Indeed, the prestige of the Templars resulted in the steady accumulation of money and property. According to a much-exploited myth that has inspired medieval poetry such as *Parzival,* Hollywood movies like *National Treasure,* and modern best sellers like *The Da Vinci Code,* the Templars supposedly retrieved the lost treasure of King Solomon and the Holy Grail itself. (Ironically, as we have seen, the Cathars, too, were imagined to possess a secret treasury that included the Grail.) The reality, however, is purely mundane: the Templars started to accumulate wealth by issuing letters of credit for the convenience of pilgrims to the Holy Land and eventually came to function as bankers and financiers.

Indeed, the "Poor Fellow-Soldiers of Christ" showed themselves to be especially gifted at making money. Each knight who joined the Templars was required to surrender his fortune to the order, and wealthy Christian benefactors added to its coffers with charitable donations. Various popes and kings contributed to the treasury by bestowing lands and privileges upon the Templars and relieving them of the obligation to pay taxes. Thus, for example, the headquarters of the Templars was a fortress on the outskirts of Paris—essentially, an "autonomous township" that boasted its own constabulary—and the order functioned as a kind of international banking house.[12]

No one appreciated the resources of the Templars more than the crowned heads of Europe, including the kings of France. They repeatedly borrowed from the Templars to finance both their wars and their opulent lifestyles; when the daughter of King Philip was betrothed to the heir of the English throne, for example, the Templars advanced the money for her dowry. So trusted were the Templars that the French and English kings even deposited the crown jewels with them for safekeeping, and when a monarch left his own palace, he preferred the comfort and safety of a Templar house. As recently as 1304, King Philip had issued a proclamation in which he praised the Templars "for their piety, their charity, their liberality, their valour," and he even asked the grand master of the Knights Templar, Jacques de Molay, to serve as godfather to his newborn son.[13]

Two years later, however, the Templars attracted the unfriendly attention of Philip the Fair, perhaps because of the wealth and influence they enjoyed in France and elsewhere in Europe. Philip was "a bit of a religious megalo-maniac," according to Norman Cohn, and he may have succeeded in per-suading himself that the Templars were, in fact, secret heretics of the worst kind. But it is just as likely that he resented their privileges, feared their power, and coveted their property. Whatever the reasons, Philip vowed to mount a crusade of his own against the Templars, and he sought an ally in the Inquisition, whose Dominican and Franciscan monks had long re-sented the warrior-monks of the rival order. The result was a frenzied spasm of greed, violence, and slander that ended only with the utter destruction of the ancient order.[14]

Guillame Imbert, the Dominican friar who served as inquisitor-general of Paris (and, as it happens, the man who sent Marguerite Porete to the stake), served as confessor to the French king. Philip claimed to have heard the charges against the Knights Templar from his confessor, and he insisted that he was "following the just request of Guillame de Paris" in moving against the order. Within a week of the first arrests, the grand inquisitor himself undertook to interrogate the leading figures in the Knights Tem-plar, including its grand master, and the Inquisition continued to oblige the king by providing friar-inquisitors to conduct interrogations and trials of Knights Templar throughout France and elsewhere in Europe.[15]

The confessions extracted from the first victims were scandalous, but they are hardly surprising in light of what we know about the common in-quisitorial practice of slandering men and women accused of heresy. The confessions are suspiciously consistent with the accusations that had been made against medieval heretics ever since the trial of the gnostic cultists at Orléans three centuries earlier. Given the preference of the inquisitors for leading questions—and for both the threat and the use of torture—it is not surprising that the warrior-monks were willing to validate even the most outrageous fantasies of their interrogators. Modern historians dismiss the case against the Templars in its entirety as an "extraordinary farrago of non-sense" and "absolutely without foundation," but it was enough to send the Templars to the stake.[16]

Once recruited into the order, according to the scenario imagined by their persecutors, the novices submitted to a secret ritual of initiation that required them to "thrice" deny Christ and "thrice" spit on the cross. Then they stripped off their clothing, and the commander of the order kissed each naked novice—first at the base of his spine, then on the navel, and finally on the mouth. The young knights, who had just taken a vow of chastity, were supposedly instructed to submit to any of their fellow Templars who wanted to sodomize them. As the torture of the Templars continued, the victims were prompted by their interrogators to come up with ever more outrageous confessions: the rituals of the Templars supposedly included the worship of an idol, or a black cat, or both; the idol was smeared with "the fat of roasted infants"; the cat was ritually kissed "beneath the tail"; and the novices were required to consume the powdered remains of the burnt bodies of dead Templars "as a magical potion, to make them hold fast to their abominable ways."[17]

The confessions betray a certain confusion, which surely indicates that the victims grasped the main points of the story that their tormentors wanted to hear but got the details wrong. Some of them confirmed that the commander offered three "indecent" kisses to the novices, but others insisted that it was the novices who kissed the commander. Sometimes they reported spitting on the cross, sometimes urinating on it, sometimes dragging it around the room. Although they were supposedly required to submit to the homoerotic attentions of their fellow knights, some of the Templars also testified that the rituals featured a bevy of "beautiful young girls" with whom they engaged in orgiastic sexual encounters. The cat was sometimes black and sometimes gray, sometimes red and sometimes mixed in color, and the idol was variously described as an actual human skull "encrusted with jewels" and as a carved wooden simulacrum, sometimes with a single face and sometimes with three faces. One imaginative Templar, surely addled by the attentions of the torturer, insisted that the idol was "a goat endowed with women's breast and an erect penis."[18]

"[T]wo things clearly emerge," states Norman Cohn in *Europe's Inner Demons*. "[I]n reality, there was no idol; but in the context of the interrogations and trials it had to exist, as the embodiment of Satanic power."[19]

The persecution of the Templars is the first example of the hijacking of the Inquisition by a secular ruler. Pope Clement at first sought to defend the Templars, but King Philip soon "reduced the pope, by a mixture of bullying, cajolery, and trickery, to the position of a mere accomplice," according to Cohn.* On a single day in 1308, for example, Clement dispatched a total of 483 papal letters to kings, bishops, and inquisitors across Europe, sanctioning the mass arrest of the Templars and authorizing the deployment of the friar-inquisitors. Thus did the Inquisition come to play a crucial role in a kind of dragnet that operated across Europe. The Franciscan and Dominican inquisitors, whose envy and hatred for the Templars was simmering long before Philip the Fair brought it to a high boil, put themselves in service to the French king and assisted in spreading the false accusations across Europe. Authoritarian governments of the near and distant future, as we shall see, were inspired by what the king of France was able to accomplish with the primitive machinery of persecution available to the medieval state.[20]

The ordeal of the Templars is also a case study in how the inquisitorial tools and techniques were capable of overmastering even a rich and powerful adversary. The Templars were taken wholly by surprise—the order's grand master had been invited to serve as a pallbearer at the funeral of the king's sister-in-law on the day before his arrest—and so they were especially vulnerable to their tormentors, both physically and psychologically, when they suddenly found themselves behind bars. The victims were offered their lives if they confessed, threatened with torture and death if they did not, and told that their fellow Templars had already offered abject confessions.

A few of the Templars tried to satisfy the demands of their torturers while avoiding the full moral weight of their confessions. Yes, they conceded, the novices were subjected to all these outrages, but when *they* were initiated, the ritual had been adjourned before the worst of the atrocities took place "because a horde of Saracens had suddenly appeared on the horizon, or simply because it was time for supper"! Only four of the 138 Templars who were taken in the first round of arrests ultimately refused to confess, and when Philip convened a show trial only two weeks later, some three dozen of them, including the grand master himself, stood up and affirmed the

---

* In 2007, the Vatican released copies of documents that recorded the trials of accused Templars conducted in Rome between 1307 and 1312. According to the long-suppressed records, Pope Clement acquitted the Templars of heresy although he convicted some defendants on charges of sexual immorality.

charges against them in public.[21] "The brethren are so struck with fear and terror," wrote one stalwart defender of the Templars, "that it is astonishing not that some have lied, but that any at all have sustained the truth."[22]

Remarkably, a total of 120 Templars later insisted on withdrawing the confessions given under torture in Paris, even though they were warned by the inquisitors that doing so would ensure that they would be burned alive as relapsed heretics. Two high officers of the order, including the grand master, joined them in disavowing their confessions and suffered the same fate. The rest of the brethren, however, were not so courageous. One Templar, for example, declared that he "would swear not only that all the accusations against the order were true but also, if required, that he himself had killed Jesus Christ," if only the inquisitors would spare him from the stake. They were permitted to live out their lives in various monasteries scattered around western Europe, now truly poor for the first time in the glorious history of the order, and both the Knights Templar and their legendary wealth passed into history.[23]

The invention of printing with movable type in the mid–fifteenth century is sometimes said to have marked the beginning of the end of the Inquisition, but the opposite may be true. The printing press only encouraged the circulation of the inquisitor's manuals, and the manuals only encouraged the inquisitors in their work. Indeed, the manuals functioned as self-fulfilling prophecies, providing the inquisitors with a scenario of wrongdoing that their victims were tortured into validating. Perhaps the best example can be found in the countless thousands of women who were sent to the stake as witches under the authority of the Inquisition and the civil magistrates who followed its example during the so-called Witch Craze.

Witchcraft had been among the obsessive concerns of both religious and political authorities since antiquity. "Thou shalt not suffer a witch to live" was the command of ancient Jewish law as preserved in the book of Exodus. The law of pagan Rome, too, criminalized some (if not all) practices that came to be called black magic. As early as 724, a church council convened by Pope Zachary banned the practices of "wizardry and sorcery," which were described as "the very filth of the wicked." But the medieval Church seemed to possess a certain insight into the workings of a disturbed human mind, and thus cautioned against the burning of women as witches. The *Canon episcopi* of 906, for example, suggests that those women who "believe and openly profess" that they have engaged in acts and practices of black magic may be suffering only from delusions and should be spared the stake even if the Devil himself was the source of the madness.[24]

Strictly speaking, the crime of sorcery fell outside the jurisdiction of the Inquisition. Once the ancient fear and loathing of witchcraft was alloyed with the newfangled war on heresy, however, the inquisitors found opportunities to prosecute the occasional accused sorcerer or sorceress along with far greater numbers of Cathars and other dissident Christians. For example, a sixty-year-old woman in Toulouse named Angela de la Barthe, accused of engaging in a sexual dalliance with the Devil in 1275, embroidered on the charge against her by telling the inquisitor that Satan thereby fathered a child with the head of a wolf, the tail of a snake, and an alarming appetite for human flesh, which she satisfied by resorting to child murder and the disinterment of corpses. For telling such tales on herself, she was sent to the stake, possibly the first French woman to suffer the death penalty on charges of witchcraft.

The growing panic over sorcerers and sorceresses eventually reached the highest circles of Church and state. Pope John XXII, convinced that an elderly French bishop was trying to murder him by means of black magic, ordered his arrest in 1317 and personally interrogated him on seven occasions. After confessing under torture, the old bishop was burned alive and his ashes dumped into the Rhône. Three years later, the same pope issued a bull by which inquisitors were charged with the authority to persecute the practitioners of ritual magic, and Nicholas Eymerich, author of an early and influential inquisitor's manual, produced a text titled *Treatise Against the Invokers of Demons* in 1369. (Intriguingly, Eymerich claimed to possess arcane knowledge on the subject because "he had seized and read many books of magic before burning them.") Strictly speaking, however, these early measures were directed against the stray practitioner of sorcery rather than a secret cult of witches; thus, for example, a Carmelite monk named Pierre Recordi was tried by the Inquisition and sentenced to life in prison on charges of engaging in "love-magic."[25]

The Witch Craze did not begin in earnest until 1484, when Pope Innocent VIII issued a new decree, the so-called witch-bull, by which he rescinded the *Canon episcopi* and formally extended the authority of the Inquisition to the "correction, imprisonment and punishment" of witches, that is, men and women who have "abused themselves with devils, incubi and succubi, and by incantations, spells, conjurations and other accursed superstitions and horrid charms, enormities and offences, destroy the offspring of women and the young of cattle." Like the Cathars and the Waldensians, the practitioners of witchcraft were imagined to belong to "a secret, conspiratorial body organized and headed by Satan." Since the witch-bull flatly equated witchcraft with heresy—"They blasphemously renounce that faith which they received by the sacrament of baptism," the pope insisted, "and, at the instigation of the enemy of the human race, they do not shrink from committing and perpetrating the foulest abominations and excesses to the peril of their souls"—those accused of witchcraft now fell within the ungentle writ of the Inquisition.[26]

The new reach of the Inquisition put the men and women accused of witchcraft in far greater peril than they had previously faced in the civil courts. The Inquisition, as we have seen, simply ignored the rules of evidence and procedure that afforded some measure of due process in ordinary judicial proceedings. One man who accused a woman of practicing "weather-magic" in a magistrate's court in the fifteenth century, for example, was called on to substantiate the charge, and when he failed to meet his burden of proof, he was drowned as a punishment for making a false accusation. By contrast, the accuser in an inquisitorial trial was allowed to remain absent and anonymous, and the accusation itself was regarded as admissible evidence.[27]

To assist the Inquisition in its new responsibilities, the pope commissioned a pair of Dominican inquisitors in Germany and Austria, Heinrich Kramer and Johann Sprenger, to compose a manual on the detection and punishment of witches, the notorious *Malleus maleficarum* or *Hammer of Witches,* a work whose title echoed the honorific that was bestowed on heresy hunters ranging from Robert le Bougre to Cardinal Bellarmine. Unlike Bernard Gui, whose advice on sorcery had required only two or three pages of text, Kramer and Sprenger devoted five years of effort and an entire volume to the latest front in the war on heresy. First published in about 1486, *Hammer of Witches* became a bestseller among inquisitor's handbooks, available in eight printed editions by the turn of the century and a total of twenty-eight editions by 1600. As a badge of its authority, *Hammer of Witches* included Pope Innocent's witch-bull as a preface, thus "establish[ing] once and for all that the Inquisition against witches had full papal approval, and thereby open[ing] the door for the bloodbaths of the following century."[28]

Hammer of Witches and the other manuals and treatises on witchcraft—more than two dozen appeared between 1435 and 1486 alone—worked their own powerful magic on the inquisitorial witch-hunters, who now detected abundant evidence of witchcraft where before they had seen none. If diabolical sexual atrocities could be plausibly charged against such pious Christian rigorists as the Waldensians and even the warrior-monks of the Knights Templar, the men and women accused of witchcraft were inevitably suspected of even greater outrages. Sometimes the scenario may have originated with the inquisitor himself, and his questions transmitted both the themes and the details to the victim. Other men and women accused of witchcraft may have been "verbal exhibitionists" or plain lunatics. The availability of formbooks and formularies created a kind of feedback loop in which the inquisitor read out loud a series of leading questions, and the defendant affirmed each one, if only to bring the torture to an end. In that sense, the inquisitor's manuals could also serve as instruction manuals to would-be witches. And so the Witch Craze came to function as a kind of self-fulfilling prophecy on a vast scale.[29]

"There were neither witches nor bewitched," observed one astute Spanish inquisitor, Alonzo Salazar y Frias, who preferred to concentrate on the persecution of Jews and Muslims, "until they were talked about."[30]

Even after the witch-bull, the fact is that witch-hunting was never the exclusive domain of the Inquisition. Kramer and Sprenger, perhaps seeking to lighten the workload of their fellow inquisitors, insisted that the Inquisition needed to concern itself only with those accused witches who were also guilty of heresy. By way of example they pointed out that a witch who cast a communion wafer into the mud "to satisfy the devil, and this by reason of some pact with him," was not guilty of heresy if she truly believed the wafer to be the body of Christ. No better evidence can be found that heresy was always a thought-crime: "The deeds of witches need involve no error in faith, however great the sin may be," argue the authors of *Hammer of Witches,* "in which case they are not liable to the Court of the Inquisition, but are left to their own judges," that is, the ordinary ecclesiastical and civil courts.[31]

Like so many other heresy-hunters, Kramer and Sprenger engaged in hateful and prurient speculation about human sexuality in general and, especially, the sexual excesses of women. "[S]he is more carnal than a man, as is clear from her many carnal abominations," they assert, echoing the biblical distaste for menstruation. "All witchcraft comes from carnal lust, which is in women insatiable," they continue. "Wherefore for the sake of fulfilling their lust, they consort even with devils." Once seduced by the Devil, women are charged by their satanic master to "infect with witchcraft the venereal act" by, among other things, exciting men to sexual passion and then making their genitals disappear or otherwise preventing orgasm and conception, causing infertility in other women, "procuring abortions," and turning babies and children over to the Devil to satisfy his vile appetites.

To understand why *Hammer of Witches* has been called "scholastic pornography" and "an amalgam of Monty Python and *Mein Kampf*," we need only pause and consider its meticulous attention to the function (and malfunction) of the male sexual organ.[32] "[W]hen the member is in no way stirred, and can never perform the act of coition, this is a sign of frigidity of nature," Kramer and Sprenger explain, "but when it is stirred and becomes erect, but yet cannot perform, it is a sign of witchcraft."[33]

Armed with such texts, and newly mandated by the pope to seek out heretics who also happened to be witches, the Inquisition put itself in service to the "hunts and panics" that characterized the Witch Craze over the next three centuries. Yet again, the inquisitors veiled their atrocities under the thin drapery of canon law, and they slandered their victims as agents of the Devil who deserved no sympathy from good Christians. The sheer number of women burned as witches far exceeds the body count of the medieval Inquisition, and the scandalous scenes that were conjured up by the witch-hunters to justify the carnage would not be matched until the Marquis de Sade began to put down on paper the inventions of his own disturbed imagination.[34]

A standard set of outrages came to be ascribed to the women who were persecuted during the Witch Craze, which continued to flare up in fits and starts from the fifteenth through the seventeenth centuries. They were said to have entered into a pact with the Devil by which they put themselves in his service, sexually and otherwise, in exchange for the power to afflict the good Christians among whom they lived. Thus recruited and initiated, they were imagined to be members of a vast conspiracy of Devil worshippers and magic-workers far worse than the original victims of the Inquisition.

The sign of the pact was a mark on the flesh, the so-called Devil's mark, which was supposedly insensitive to pain, and the witch was provided with demonic servants known as familiars, who often took the form of black cats or other black-furred beasts. It was believed that the witches flew by night to some forest clearing or forgotten cemetery or ruined castle where they worshipped the Devil in a ceremony strikingly similar in every detail to the rituals attributed by pagan Rome to the first Christians and by the Inquisition to the Cathars and Waldensians—an "obscene kiss" on the anus or penis, a wild sexual orgy, a feast that featured the tender flesh of murdered babies. From these raw materials emerged the standard iconography of witchcraft that is found today only in Halloween costumes and decorations—and only in an expurgated version that has been rendered safe for children.

Witches were believed to possess both the ability and the desire to work all kinds of deadly mischief on their adversaries and enemies, all with the active assistance of the Devil and his demons—sterility or impotence, miscarriages and stillbirths, illness or madness, or death. They were believed to be able to change the natural order of things, causing rain out of season or no rain at all, the sickening of cattle, and the blighting of crops. Above all, they were thought to seek the flesh of unbaptized babies for use in making their potions and brews, including one that supposedly enabled the witch to fly and another that empowered her to remain silent under torture. The Latin word commonly used for witchcraft—*maleficium*—literally means "wrongdoing" and carried the implication that the power to inflict harm on others was derived from the Devil and achieved by resort to black magic.

The gathering of witches for a worship service—at first called a synagogue, then a sabbat, and only much later a black Sabbath—was portrayed in detail by the inquisitors and their fellow witch-hunters, who seemed to delight to piling atrocity upon atrocity and describing every revolting detail. According to the febrile imaginations of the witch-hunters, the Devil manifested as an outsized monster, black in color and crowned with horns, part man, part goat, part bird. The witches kissed him on the left foot, or the anus, or the penis; if the anus was the site of the "obscene kiss," then the Devil "acknowledged their attentions in a peculiarly noxious manner," that is, he defecated on their faces and into their mouths. He heard their confessions, and he punished them for their sins, which might include going to church or slacking off on their acts of sorcery. He preached a sermon and received offerings of coins and foodstuffs. He presided over a grotesque version of the Communion, passing out the sole of a shoe in place of the wafer and "a nauseous black liquid" in place of the wine.[35]

Then the Devil and his minions turned to feasting. The menu, of course, featured roasted baby flesh, as well as wine "tasting like manure drainings." Then, at the sound of pipes, drums, and trumpets, the witches would gather for the dancing that served, quite literally, as the climax of the sabbat. One woman bent over until her head touched the ground, and a candle was planted in her anus to illuminate the festivities. The witches would dance in a circle around the inverted woman, faster and faster, until they spun into a "frantic and erotic orgy in which all things, including sodomy and incest, were permitted." At the climax of the festivities, the Devil would fornicate in various sexual positions with every man, woman, and child in attendance. Only then would the witches return to their homes to do the Devil's bidding and afflict the good Christians who were their sworn enemies.

More than one reader of such accounts, of course, found them not only ludicrous but downright laughable.[36] "Every night these ill-advised ladies were anointing themselves with 'devil's grease,' made out of the fat of murdered infants, and, thus lubricated, were slipping through cracks and keyholes and up chimneys, mounting on broomsticks or spindles or airborne goats, and flying off on a long and inexpressibly wearisome aerial journey to a diabolical rendezvous, the witches' sabbat," writes historian Hugh Trevor-Roper in a kind of summing-up of the obscene and preposterous fairy tales that constituted evidence against the flesh-and-blood victims of the Witch Craze. "In every country there were hundreds of such sabbats, more numerous and more crowded than race-meetings or fairs."[37]

As the sarcasm in Trevor-Roper's account suggests, the supposed practices of sorcerers and sorceresses were fabricated out of the same whole cloth that was used to tailor the accusations against other victims of the Inquisition. To be sure, a few of the ancient folk traditions still practiced in medieval Europe—herbal remedies, fertility rites, and even some aspects of midwifery—might have been regarded as acts of practical magic, at least as the inquisitors defined it. Ordinary men and women, then as now, were amused by fortune-telling and comforted by amulets and talismans, none of which was officially countenanced by the Church. They told their children folktales and fairy tales whose characters and incidents were fanciful and sometimes magical. Even such luminaries as Roger Bacon, the Franciscan monk who is credited with a crucial role in the early stirring of science in western Europe, did not draw a bright line between magic and scientific inquiry. But the conjurations of the witch-hunters surely owed far more to their own dark fears and secret longings than to the actual deeds of the women whom they singled out for slander and murder.

"Jacob Grimm established that certain folk beliefs, including beliefs about fertility, entered into the picture of the sabbat," explains Norman Cohn, "but that proves nothing about the reality of the sabbat."[38]

Some historians have argued that at least a grain of truth can be found at the root of these horror stories, a survival of the pagan beliefs and practices that had always constituted an "underground religion" and only much later came to be called witchcraft when it caught the attention of the Church at the outset of the Inquisition. "Even so skeptical (and anticlerical) a historian as Henry Charles Lea thought so," observes Cohn, "and today it is still widely assumed that such a cult must have existed." But other scholars, including Hugh Trevor-Roper, insist that Devil worship in general and the cult of witches in particular are purely mythic. "There is in fact no serious evidence for the existence of such a sect of Devil-worshippers anywhere in medieval Europe," insists Cohn. "One can go further: there is serious evidence to the contrary." The best such evidence is to be found in the inquisitor's manuals of Bernard Gui and Nicholas Eymerich, both of whom offer advice only on hunting down the occasional practitioner of black magic—"sorcerers, fortune-tellers and those who summon demons," according to Gui's manual. "In fact, neither Eymerich nor Gui even hint at the existence of a sect of Devil-worshippers," writes Cohn, "and that should settle the question."[39]

By a certain irony, modern feminist historians and polemicists proudly affirm that the Witch Craze was inspired by the existence of an underground community of women in the Middle Ages and the Renaissance, including midwives and folk healers, whose purpose in gathering was "trading herbal lore and passing on the news." Even if these women "were not in fact riding broomsticks or having sex with the devil," according to feminist historian Anne Llewellyn Barstow, they were "healing, both by spells and potions, delivering babies, performing abortions, predicting the future, advising the lovelorn, cursing, removing curses, making peace between neighbors." The availability of such services, however wholesome they may appear to modern eyes, was quite enough to arouse fear and loathing in the Church and to bring down the terrible wrath of the Inquisition.[40]

By another irony, the Witch Craze failed to strike any sparks in Spain, where the Inquisition operated on a vast and terrifying scale but chose an entirely different target, as we shall see. After some eighteen hundred men and women confessed to witchcraft during the period of grace at the opening of an *inquisitio* in Navarre in 1612, the Spanish Inquisition conducted a formal inquiry, calling on chemists to examine the contents of the witches' supposed potions and recruiting doctors to determine whether women who claimed to have engaged in sexual intercourse with Satan were, in fact, still virgins. "I have not found indications from which to infer that a single act of witchcraft has really occurred," wrote the same skeptical Spanish inquisitor quoted above. Even in places where women were burned as witches in appalling numbers, some sober observers were willing to allow only that "witches were persons whose minds had been deranged and imaginations corrupted by demons," and they insisted that such victims of delusion and derangement "were not responsible for their actions and confessions any more than the insane."[41]

Nevertheless, a kind of madness seemed to seize the collective imagination. An act of adultery, a failed marriage, a miscarriage or a stillbirth, an infertile woman or an impotent man, a dispute between neighbors, the failure of a business or a crop, a batch of beer that went bad, a plate of spoiled oysters that resulted in a case of food poisoning—any such commonplace of ordinary life might provoke an accusation of witchcraft. For example, when a midwife named Dichtlin, and her daughter, Anna, were accused of witchcraft by their neighbors in a Swiss village in 1502, one witness complained that when his late mother was also working as a midwife, "women called his mother in more than they did Dichtlin, and in time his mother went down with a long illness, and when she came to die, she swore, as she hoped to be saved, that it was Dichtlin's doing." Another witness reported that he had once seen Anna looking into a stream and splashing water between her legs, "and before he got home, there was a heavy downpour." Such was the *fama*—that is, pure speculation and slander—that served as evidence in the proceedings of the Inquisition.[42]

Although some men were tried and burned during the Witch Craze, the fact is that "80 percent of the accused and 85 percent of those executed were female." And although the victims included adolescents and even children, the risk was especially acute for women of a certain age and circumstance. Married women and widows ranging from fifty to seventy years old represented the greatest number of victims. Various physical defects and personality traits were also likely to draw suspicion and, often enough, a formal charge; a woman was more likely to be accused of witchcraft if she were "solitary, eccentric, or bad-tempered," for example, or "ugly, with red eyes or a squint, or pock-marked skin," or merely crippled or stooped with age. A woman named Barbara Knopf, accused of crippling and killing her victims by means of sorcery and charged with witchcraft in Lucerne in 1549, insisted to the magistrate that "she had done nothing, only she had a nasty tongue and was an odd person."[43]

The victimization of old, lonely, eccentric, and disabled women may help explain why so many confessed to the preposterous charges laid against them by the inquisitors and other witch-hunters. Torture was routinely applied to accused witches: "Because of the great trouble caused by the stubborn silence of witches," as Kramer and Sprenger put it in *Hammer of Witches,* "torture is not to be neglected." If the Knights Templar—warrior-monks trained in the art of combat—were so quick to confess to false charges under torture, a frail old woman was unlikely to fare better when the inquisitor reached the third degree. Still, the inquisitors themselves credited their victims with remarkable courage and stamina, although they reasoned that it was the result of supernatural invention, whether divine or diabolical: "Unless God, through a holy Angel, compels the devil to withhold his help from the witch," they insisted, "she will be so insensible to the pains of torture that she will sooner be torn limb from limb than confess any of the truth."[44]

The Inquisition commonly resorted to "sadistic sexual torture," as we have already seen, but the women accused of witchcraft were subjected to the very worst excesses. All victims of torture were stripped, for example, but a suspected witch might be shaved of her body hair down to the bare skin, if only to facilitate the search for the telltale Devil's mark. A supernumerary teat—or just a skin blemish—was regarded as evidence of guilt and resulted in a death sentence, often by burning, sometimes by hanging or crushing. At the core of the Witch Craze, argues historian Anne Llewellyn Barstow, we find an institutionalized form of "sexual terror and brutality" whose aim and achievement were the "organized mass murder of women." To put it another way, Barstow insists that the "witch-hunting" was actually "woman-hunting."[45]

How many of these women did the inquisitors and the other witch-hunters send to the stake or the gallows? How many died under torture? The death toll has been "reliably" estimated at between 200,000 and one million, according to Edward Burman, while Norman Cohn dismisses such figures as "fantastic exaggerations." A feminist writer, Andrea Dworkin, puts the number of women executed as witches at nine million, with Barstow insisting that Dworkin's estimate "is off by about 8,900,000." Thus Barstow adopts Voltaire's estimate of 100,000 victims, first offered by the famous philosopher not long after the end of the Witch Craze in the eighteenth century, but she suggests that twice that number of women were accused of witchcraft. They, too, were victims whose lives were distorted and sometimes destroyed.[46]

Even if the body count is impossible to fix with certainty, the meticulous records maintained by some witch-hunters confirm that the Witch Craze amounted to mass murder on an appalling scale. According to the archives of a single canton in Switzerland, a total of 3,371 victims were tried on charges on witchcraft during the period 1591–1680, "and all, without exception, were executed." After the witch trials in the bishopric of Trier in southwestern Germany in 1585, "two villages were left with only one female inhabitant each." To be sure, a vast, sinister, and deadly conspiracy was at work, just as the Inquisiton had always insisted, but the malefactors were the inquisitors themselves.[47]

The childhood recollections of a young woman who grew up in the French village of Domrémy in the early fifteenth century provide an intriguing glimpse into the folk traditions that so alarmed the Inquisition. Near the village was an old tree, known by the locals as "The Ladies Tree" and "The Fairies Tree," and a spring that bubbled up from an artesian source. "And I have heard say," she recalled, "that those who are sick of fevers drink of that spring and go and fetch its water for health's sake."[48]

The young woman is known to us as Joan of Arc (ca. 1412–1431), and she spoke these words under interrogation during her trial before the Inquisition on charges of heresy and witchcraft. She conceded that some of the old women in the village—"but not of my own family," she was careful to say—claimed to have seen "Fairy Ladies" in the vicinity of another great tree, a beech, and some boys and girls from the village danced around the beech tree and made garlands from its boughs. As the interrogation continued, Joan struggled desperately to distance herself from these goings-on: "I never saw those fairies at the tree, so far as I know," she declared. "I do not know whether I have danced by the tree since I came to years of discretion, but I may well have danced there with my companions, and I sang there more often than I danced."[49]

Joan of Arc, of course, attracted the attention of powerful men for reasons wholly unrelated to dancing fairies. A farm girl who could neither read nor write, she was also a young woman of extraordinary charisma who presented herself to the French king and persuaded him to put her in command of his army. But it is also true that she provided her enemies with the kind of evidence upon which the Inquisition could and did rely in condemning her as a servant of the Devil. She famously wore the garb of a soldier and carried a sword, both of which were reserved to men alone under biblical law and pious tradition. From the age of thirteen, she claimed to see visions and hear voices; at the age of seventeen, she was serving as a seer in the court of King Charles VII; and by the age of nineteen, she was burned alive at the stake as a witch.

Charles himself was dubious at first, and it was only after the teenager was vetted by the royal theologians that he allowed her to serve in his army. But Joan of Arc's real offense was purely a matter of politics. Charles VII was engaged in a war for the French crown against an invading English army and its French collaborators. At Orléans, where gnostic cultists had been burned as heretics some three centuries earlier, Joan of Arc succeeded in breaking the English siege, and the so-called Maid of Orléans was an honored participant in the coronation of Charles VII as the rightful king of France.

But the English army remained on French soil, Paris remained under English control, and the fighting continued. Joan continued to lead the army of King Charles until she was wounded in battle and taken prisoner by the English and their French allies, who promptly resolved to put an end to their vexing adversary once and for all. She was imprisoned and interrogated behind the locked door of her cell, and then put on public trial at Rouen for six days in 1431. The charges of heresy and witchcraft were set forth in seventy articles of indictment, including such specific accusations as dressing like a man, entering into a pact with the Devil, and submitting to a ritual of initiation into sorcery while still a child. The "Voice from God" that she claimed to have heard since early adolescence, according to the bill of particulars, was diabolical rather than divine. The deputy inquisitor of France was summoned to participate in the proceedings and thereby place the imprimatur of the Inquisition on what was simply and clearly a show trial.[50]

The charges against Joan were trumped up to serve the naked political interests of the English and their French allies. Her personal eccentricities were convenient to her persecutors, but their real motive had nothing to do with Joan herself; rather, they sought to defame and discredit King Charles by demonstrating that his now-legendary champion was a witch and a heretic. An oblique clue to the realpolitik behind the trial of Joan of Arc is found in Shakespeare's *Henry VI, Part I,* in which the Maid of Orléans is addressed as "Thou foul accursed minister of hell!" As seen through English eyes, both in her own lifetime and in Shakespeare's time, Joan was a dangerous enemy who took up arms against an English king claiming the right to sit on the throne of France. To the French, then and now, she was "a heroine of the French resistance" who opposed the English invaders and their collaborators in a war of national liberation. Although the Inquisition never managed to extend its long reach to England, the English were not reluctant to invoke its jurisdiction and put Joan on trial as a heretic and a witch, thereby ensuring both her death and her disgrace.[51]

"The King has ordered me to try you," a French bishop supposedly informed Joan, referring to the English monarch, "and I will do so."[52]

The surviving transcripts of the trial of Joan of Arc by the Inquisition allow us to witness for ourselves some of the intimate moments in an actual witch trial. As in any interrogation or trial conducted by the Inquisition, every word uttered in an unguarded moment, every friendship and relationship, was a potential snare for the victim and a weapon in the hands of a skillful inquisitor. When, for example, the interrogator asked whether Joan's godmother—the woman who claimed to have seen those Fairy Ladies dancing around the old beech tree—"was reputed to be a 'wise woman,'" Joan understood the thrust of the question. In the parlance of the Inquisition, a "wise woman" was a sorceress. And Joan sought to parry the thrust: "She is held and reputed a good and honest woman," she insisted, "and no witch or sorceress."[53]

Joan, not yet twenty years old and on trial for her life, insisted that she was a good Christian. "I learned my Pater and Ave and Creed from my mother," she testified. "I confessed once a year to my own parson and, when he was hindered, to another priest by his leave." When she made garlands from the branches of the beech tree, they were intended not for the Fairy Ladies but "for the image of St. Mary at Domrémy." When the inquisitor, following the standard line of questioning for accused witches, demanded to know whether Joan knew of "those who went riding with the Fairies"—"riding" was a reference to night flights on a broomstick to attend a gathering of witches—she continued to assert her own innocence. "That I never did nor never knew," she declared. "I have indeed heard that there was a ride on Thursdays, but I believe not in that which is witchcraft."[54]

Joan was cross-examined at length by the inquisitors about the source of her visions. Significantly, neither Joan nor the judges entertained the notion that she had experienced only visual and auditory hallucinations, but they debated over whether she had trafficked with angels or devils. "The Voice comes to me from God," insisted Joan, who identified her celestial visitors as the archangel Michael and a pair of saints, Catherine and Margaret. The inquisitors insisted that Joan had actually consorted with Satan himself and a couple of demons, Belial and Behemoth. But at least one question and answer reveal the political subtext of the trial and the real reason for her conviction and execution.[55]

Q: Does not St. Margaret speak English?
A: Why should she speak English when she is not on the English side?[56]

Like so many less famous victims of the Inquisition, Joan was granted a life sentence after she agreed to abjure her supposed heresies. As part of the plea bargain, she assured the inquisitor that she would give up her men's clothing. For four days after she had signed the document of abjuration, she endured various acts of brutality and sexual abuse at the hands of her English guards, and then she suddenly repudiated her promise to dress like a woman. According to the cruel and inflexible logic of the Inquisition, Joan was now a relapsed heretic and thus unworthy of the mercy of a life sentence. At 7:00 a.m. on May 30, 1431, she was formally excommunicated "and burned as quickly as was decently possible on the same morning."[57] A Dominican monk accompanied her to the pyre, yet another inquisitorial commonplace, and she begged him to hold a crucifix where she could see it until the flames finally extinguished her life. Her only regret was that her mortal remains would not be interred in consecrated ground. "Alas! That my body, whole and entire, which has never been corrupted," she cried, referring to her self-imposed vow of chastity, "should today be consumed and burned to ashes!"[58]

The fate of Joan of Arc is only the most notorious example of how the machinery of persecution could be put to political use. The Bogomils of Bulgaria in the tenth century—the early precursors of the Cathars—can also be understood in a political context; the founder of the dissident religious community, according to Malcolm Lambert, "gave a voice to a peasantry oppressed by its Byzantine conquerors, its alien Byzantine priesthood and the Bulgarian aristocracy," all of whose interests were well served by treating the Bogomils as dangerous heretics. King Frederick II (1194–1250), a constant rival and adversary of the popes, agreed to criminalize heresy in the imperial law codes as a "quid pro quo" for his coronation as Holy Roman Emperor by Pope Honorius III in 1220. Even the persecution of the Knights Templar by King Philip IV, rightly seen as "a wild orgy of plunder," also served the strategic goals of a French king who sought to outflank and overmaster the pope and arrogate to himself the useful tool of the Inquisition.[59]

"The dangerous admixture of politics and religion," observes Henry Charles Lea, "rendered the stake a favorite instrument of statecraft."[60]

So we have seen that the Inquisition could be made to serve more than one function. Sometimes it was a fearful weapon by which the Roman Catholic church sought to enforce a religious monopoly. Sometimes it was a tool of fiscal policy, both to supplement the tax revenues of a spendthrift king and to enrich the inquisitors themselves by means of extortion. Sometimes it was a convenient way to strike a blow at an unfaithful spouse or an unfriendly neighbor, a rival in love or commerce, or an adversary in matters of war and diplomacy. And sometimes it served all these functions at once. But, even so, we have not exhausted the potential uses of the Inquisition. All along, and especially toward the end of its long history, the machinery of persecution was a weapon of culture war.

On October 31, 1517, the eve of All Saints' Day, the worst fears of the men who invented the Inquisition were fully realized. For nearly three hundred years, they had crusaded to purge Christendom of every belief and practice that strayed even slightly from the dogma of the "one Universal Church of the faithful." When Martin Luther nailed his Ninety-five Theses on the door of the Castle Church at Wittenberg, however, it was plain that they had failed in their mission. The threat—and the fact—of arrest, confiscation, torture, imprisonment, and even burning at the stake turned out to be insufficient to compel ordinary men and women to conform their religious imaginations to a single faith.[61]

By then, the Inquisition was operating creakily or not at all in most of western Europe. Only on the Iberian Peninsula, as we shall see in the next chapter, were the friar-inquisitors still fully employed. The Reformation, however, provoked the Church into a renewed spasm of violence in its long war on heresy. The so-called Sacred Congregation of the Roman and Universal Inquisition, formally established by Pope Paul III in 1542, was intended to function as a refurbished and reinvigorated version of the medieval Inquisition. Old weapons were deployed once again, and new ones were designed to meet the challenge of a new generation of heretics—not Cathars, not Waldensians, but Protestants.

The old authoritarian impulse was still fully alive. The Inquisition had always been quick to burn heretical books as well as the heretics who wrote them. The "defendant" in one inquisitorial trial in 1317, for example, was a commentary on the book of Revelation by a Franciscan monk named Peter John Olivi; the author himself had died in 1298, but his writings were found to be heretical and were put to the flames along with a few of his readers. Even the most vigilant inquisitor realized, however, that the advent of printing rendered it impossible to put every offending title to the flames. So the Roman Inquisition resorted to the promulgation of the *Index Auctorum et Librorum Prohibitorum,* a list of authors and books that Catholics were obliged not to read on pain of excommunication. Among the banned authors were Savonarola, Machiavelli, and Boccaccio. Every word written by Erasmus was condemned, portions of Dante's writings were censored, and special permission from an inquisitor was required to read a translation of the Bible.

Clearly, the Inquisition was now engaged in what we would call a culture war as well as a war on heresy. For example, Paolo Veronese (1528–1588) was put on trial by the inquisitors in Venice because they objected to the inclusion of "dogs, dwarfs, a fool, a parrot, men with German weapons, and a man with a bleeding nose" as incidental figures in the background of a painting ostensibly depicting a scene from the Bible. The fact that Luther was German—and the fact that the Inquisition no longer operated in Germany and was thus prevented from simply burning him alive—prompted the inquisitors to define heresy in some new and odd ways as evidenced in the transcript of Paolo Veronese's interrogation.

Q: Do you know that in Germany and other places infected with heresy it is customary with various pictures full of scurrilousness and similar inventions to mock, vituperate, and scorn the things of the Holy Catholic Church in order to teach bad doctrines to foolish and ignorant people?

A: Yes, that is wrong; but I return to what I have said, that I am obliged to follow what my superiors have done.

Q: What have your superiors done? Have they perhaps done similar things?

A: Michelangelo in Rome in the Pontifical Chapel painted Our Lord, Jesus Christ, His Mother, St John, St Peter, and the Heavenly Host. These are all represented in the nude—even the Virgin Mary—and in different poses with little reverence.

Q: Do you not know that in painting the Last Judgment in which no garments or similar things are presumed, it was not necessary to paint garments, and that in those figures there is nothing which is not spiritual? There are neither buffoons, dogs, weapons, or similar buffoonery. And does it seem because of this or some other example that you did right to have painted this picture the way you did and do you want to maintain that it is good and decent?[62]

Another new front in the war on heresy can be detected in the 1616 edition of the index of banned authors and books, which now included a work of pure science, *Six Books Concerning the Revolutions of the Heavenly Orbs* by the Polish astronomer Mikolaj Kopernik, better known as Copernicus (1473–1543). The fact that Copernicus expressed no opinion on the troublesome points of theology that had cost the Cathars their lives—"Mathematics are for mathematicians," he observed in the book's dedication—did not spare his scientific propositions from being condemned as equally false and heretical. The same inquisitorial cast of mind that refused to countenance any minor variation in Christian true belief now condemned the scientific fact that the earth revolves around the sun as treason to God.[63]

Copernicus, of course, was already dead when his book was banned, and the inquisitors no longer dug up the corpses of "defunct" heretics for posthumous trials. Still, the Inquisition found its way to a flesh-and-blood victim who had come to embrace the same heretical ideas—the astronomer and mathematician Galileo Galilei (1564–1642). Galileo was already famous across Europe when he attracted the attention of Cardinal Bellarmine, the latest bearer of the old title of "Hammer of Heretics," and the Congregation of the Holy Office, the papal council that oversaw the operations of the Roman Inquisition. For the crime of entertaining the idea that the earth revolves around the sun, Galileo was denounced to the Inquisition in 1616 "for grievous heresy and blasphemy concerning the nature of God."[64]

Galileo was not the first famous scientist to be arrested and tried by the Roman Inquisition. Cardinal Bellarmine had already prosecuted, among others, Giordano Bruno (1548–1600), a celebrated polymath and an early advocate of the Copernican theory of the universe, on charges of holding erroneous opinions about various aspects of Catholic dogma, including the divinity of Jesus Christ, the doctrine of transubstantiation, and the virginity of Mary. Bruno had offered only a halfhearted recantation rather than the abject confession that the Inquisition always demanded, and he was burned alive as an unrepentant heretic. As we have already noted, on the way to the stake Bruno was fitted with an iron gag that painfully pinned his mouth shut, a final symbolic gesture by the Inquisition.

Sixteen years later, when Galileo's work was first scrutinized by the Roman Inquisition, he apparently believed that he could avoid Bruno's fate by making fine distinctions between teaching that the earth revolves around the sun and merely speculating that it does. With an excess of self-confidence and a certain tragic naïveté, Galileo insisted that he could offer "a thousand proofs" to show that the Copernican system and the Bible could be reconciled. In doing so, he clearly underestimated both the will and the guile of his persecutors. Indeed, the argument has been made that Galileo's greatest mistake was to alienate the Jesuit priests whose mission it was to defend the Church against the threat of the Reformation, thus making himself a victim of his own arrogance as well as the Inquisition.[65] "If Galileo had only known how to retain the favour of the Jesuits, he would have stood in renown before the world," observed a Jesuit priest named Christophe Grienberger at the time, "and he could have written what he pleased about everything, even about the motion of the Earth."[66]

Then, too, Galileo was so ardent in his pursuit of scientific knowledge that he did not fully appreciate the perils of thinking and speaking freely while living within the reach of the Holy Office. From our perspective, Galileo was ahead of his time, a figure who anticipated a future era when one might fancy himself both a man of science and a man of faith. But that time had not yet come. "He is all afire on his opinions, and he puts great passion in them, and not enough strength in controlling it," observed the Florentine ambassador to Rome in a private letter, "so that the Roman climate is getting very dangerous for him."[67]

As it turned out, Galileo's offer of "a thousand proofs" did not count as evidence in the eyes of the inquisitors, and they concluded in 1616 that Galileo's proposition was "foolish and absurd, philosophically and formally heretical, inasmuch as it expressly contradicts the doctrine of the Holy Scriptures" and "erroneous in faith." Galileo was admonished to "abstain altogether from teaching or defending this opinion" on the threat of imprisonment. According to the records of the Inquisition, the bad news was personally delivered to Galileo by Cardinal Bellarmine, the Hammer of Heretics and the prosecutor of Giordano Bruno: "The said Galileo was . . . commanded and enjoined, in the name of His Holiness the Pope and the whole Congregation of the Holy Office, to relinquish altogether the said opinion that the Sun is the center of the world and immovable and that the Earth moves, nor further to hold, teach, or defend it in any way whatsoever."[68]

Another sixteen years passed, and Galileo was charged with heresy a second time in 1632 after he published a new work, *Dialogue Concerning the Two World Systems,* in which the same dangerous ideas were considered yet again. The question of what Galileo had been told he could and could not do after his first skirmish with the Inquisition figured crucially in his second trial. Pope Urban VIII himself had assured Galileo that he could write about the subject "provided the treatment were strictly hypothetical." Galileo dutifully submitted the manuscript of the *Dialogue* to the Inquisition in both Rome and Florence, and he published the book with the formal permission of the Florentine censor even though the manuscript had been the subject of much concern and consternation among the Roman censors, some of whom frankly did not understand what they were reading. By styling the book as a dialogue, he argued, he had not actually advocated the forbidden idea that the earth revolves around the sun. Moreover, he had appended a "Preface to the Judicious Reader" in which he explicitly stated that the book was hypothetical.[69]

None of these assertions and accommodations satisfied the Inquisition, however, and he found himself denounced as a heretic for a second time. When he pleaded that his ill health prevented him from traveling to Rome to stand trial, the Inquisition threatened to bring him back in irons, sick or not. Ironically, the Republic of Venice—where Veronese had been put on trial for the heretical act of putting a dwarf and a German weapon in a painting of the *Feast in the House of Levi*—offered Galileo a safe refuge from the Roman Inquisition. But Galileo, old and frail and ailing, was already defeated. Indeed, he was no more able to resist the Inquisition than the terrorized old women accused of witchcraft or the Knights Templar who had been tortured into confession at other times and places. "The pallid specter of fear, a craving for acceptance and forgiveness, and the humiliation of begging," writes one of his biographers, Giorgio de Santillana, "were besieging the man who had hitherto been a joyous and whimsical warrior."[70]

Galileo presented himself at the Palace of the Inquisition in Rome, where he was famously subjected to the same grim ritual that had attended the Inquisition's proceedings since its very beginning. He was not told the precise nature of the charges against him; rather, he was put under oath "and asked whether he knew or conjectured why he had been summoned." No attorney was present to assist the old man, and none of the documents that the inquisitors consulted as they interrogated Galileo were shared with him. Like countless other victims of the Inquisition—but unlike the uncompromising Giordano Bruno—Galileo was reduced to utter self-abasement: "My error, then, has been—and I confess it—one of vainglorious ambition and of pure ignorance and inadvertence," offered Galileo. "I have not held and do not hold as true the opinion which has been condemned."[71]

Contrary to a cherished and oft-repeated legend, Galileo was not shown the instruments of torture by his inquisitors, although he was verbally threatened with torture at the time of his interrogation, all according to the ancient formula as recorded in the inquisitor's manuals. Nor did he mutter under his breath the famous words of protest often attributed to him: *E pur si muove* (And yet it moves). Privately, Galileo may have expressed "cold implacable contempt for his judges" and complained that he was the victim of "a masterly conspiracy of 'hatred, impiety, fraud, and deceit' that would startle the world if he could tell." At the end, and in the presence of the inquisitors, however, Galileo readily denied the scientific facts that he earnestly believed to be true. "I do not hold and have not held this opinion of Copernicus since the command was intimated to me that I must abandon it," he declared. "For the rest, I am here in your hands—do with me what you please."[72]

On the day of his sentencing, again like the countless other victims of the Inquisition, the seventy-year-old Galileo donned the white shirt that marked him as a penitent, knelt in front of the assembly of inquisitor-judges, and recited the ancient and solemn formula of abjuration: "With sincere heart and unfeigned faith, I abjure, curse, and detest the aforesaid errors and heresies and generally every other error, heresy, and sect whatsoever contrary to the Holy Church," he declared. "Should I know any heretic or person suspected of heresy, I will denounce him to this Holy Office or to the Inquisitor or Ordinary of the place where I may be."[73]

Thanks to his confession and abjuration, the penances required of Galileo were among the mildest that the Inquisition was empowered to impose. The old man was ordered to recite seven penitential psalms each day for three years, and he was sentenced to "the formal prison of this Holy Office for as long as we deem necessary," although he was permitted to return to his home in Florence and serve out his life sentence under house arrest. Copies of the inquisitorial decree against Galileo, on the order of the Holy Office, were sent "to all Inquisitors against heretical pravity, and especially the Inquisitor in Florence, who shall read the sentence in full assembly and in the presence of most of those who profess the mathematical art."[74]

The trial of Galileo can be seen as nothing more than a finger in the dike of history. His writings may have remained on the Index until 1822, but even while Galileo was still living he was able to publish his final work, *Two New Sciences,* by sending the manuscript to Amsterdam, which lay far outside the ever-diminishing reach of the Inquisition. Elsewhere in Europe, waves of innovation and intellectual liberty were eroding the walls of true belief and received wisdom in every aspect of the human enterprise—arts and letters, science and technology, commerce and industry. In that sense, the Inquisition was already defunct in much of Europe and heading toward obsolescence on the day in 1634 when Galileo fell to his knees and mouthed the same words that had passed the lips of condemned men and women four hundred years earlier.

Yet the condemnation of Galileo as a heretic was far from the last gasp of the Inquisition. Remarkably, the arrest, torture, and burning of heretics was still a lively enterprise in a few other places around Europe, and nowhere more so than in the kingdom of Spain. The same monarchs who had sent Columbus on the fateful voyages that resulted in the discovery of the New

World had also embraced the Inquisition as a crucial tool of state policy and imperial ambition. That ambition, as we shall see, had less to do with the war on heresy than with the purging of what Ferdinand and Isabella saw as the taint of Jewish and Muslim blood. For nearly two centuries after the day on which Galileo rose to his feet and walked out of the Palace of the Inquisition in Rome, the Spanish Inquisition remained in existence, and its long shadow is not yet gone.

6.

PURITY OF BLOOD

Some people say that you should become Christian, but may God ruin my holiday if I advise it. The reason is that once you have become Christian, they will figure out a way to shove your face in the fire.

Interrogation of Juan de Salzedo by the Spanish Inquisition, 1502

By its own admission, if also to its regret, the Inquisition enjoyed no jurisdiction over professing Jews.[1] Bernard Gui, for example, railed against "treacherous Jews," whom he suspected of seeking to "pervert Christians secretly and lead them into Jewish treachery," but readily conceded that the Inquisition was powerless to prosecute them precisely because they were practicing Jews. While the inquisitors were free to proceed against every kind of Christian heresy, their authority over Jewish victims was limited by canon law. Thus, Gui explained to the readers and users of his handbook, the inquisitors were authorized to arrest and punish only Christians who had converted to Judaism, and Jews who had converted to Christianity but continued to practice their old faith—that is, Jews who "return to the vomit of Judaism," according to Gui's own hateful phrase.[2]

Not every inquisitor, however, was entirely scrupulous in following the rules and regulations. Now and then, a cagey or callous inquisitor succeeded in convincing a Jewish man or woman to undergo the rite of baptism, whether by the use of winning words or under the threat of torture and death, and then promptly charged the newly converted Christian with the crime of heresy. On other occasions, the local Jewish populace was ordered to fund the operations of the Inquisition, and if they failed to pay up, the inquisitors proceeded against them as fautors of heresy. To snare a Jewish victim, some inquisitors insisted that the circumcision of a Christian, or the handling of a communion wafer, or even the building of a new synagogue was a crime within its jurisdiction. "The friars acted first," observes Joshua Trachtenberg in *The Devil and the Jews,* "and debated afterward."[3]

Both kings and popes were occasionally moved to intervene when the inquisitors exceeded their writ. After one bloodthirsty Dominican inquisitor tried and burned thirteen Jewish victims at the stake in France in 1288, Philip the Fair—the same French king who later turned on the Knights Templar—stepped in to restrain the Inquisition from seizing Jewish victims who should have been tried and punished by the royal courts, at least as far as the king was concerned. By 1448, Pope Nicholas V was sufficiently aroused to issue a public reprimand to the inquisitors for such excesses and cautioned them against asserting jurisdiction over Jewish victims "except in cases of manifest heresy or anti-Catholic activity."[4]

Although the inquisitors were restricted in what they could do to Jewish flesh and blood, the Inquisition arrogated to itself the right and duty to proceed against Jewish writings. As early as 1233, the books of the Jewish philosopher Maimonides were burned by the Dominican inquisitors at an auto-da-fé in Montpellier. In 1239, Pope Gregory IX issued a decree that obliged the secular authorities across Europe to seize all available Jewish manuscripts and deliver them to the Inquisition for examination. The inquisitors concluded that the Talmud itself and all Talmudic commentaries were, in fact, "perversely heretical" and thus suitable for burning. By 1248, possession of a copy of the Talmud was a crime, and Jewish books were burned by the wagonload in Paris and Rome.[5]

Still, some inquisitors carved out enough space within the metes and bounds of canon law to persecute the Jews with quite as much aggression and brutality as they directed toward Cathars, Templars, and witches. Ironically, the country in which the Inquisition claimed the greatest number of Jewish victims is the same one that had once served as a unique and remarkable place of refuge for Jews. The so-called Golden Age of Spain, much celebrated in Jewish tradition, was an interlude during the High Middle Ages when Christians, Jews, and Muslims seemed to be able to coexist in harmony and prosperity on the Iberian Peninsula—an accommodation known as *convivencia*. At the very moment in history when the medieval Inquisition was preparing to exterminate the Cathars across the border in Languedoc, for example, a Castilian monarch called Saint Ferdinand proudly called himself "king of the three religions."[6]

Yet it was in Spain that the full weight of the Inquisition fell on Jews and Muslims rather than Christian dissidents. The Spanish inquisitors devised a new and vastly more dangerous principle of persecution, one that sought to ensure purity of blood rather than purity of belief. And the inquisitors continued to maintain and operate the machinery of persecution long after it had fallen into disrepair and disuse everywhere else in Europe. To this day, when the Inquisition is mentioned, our thoughts turn reflexively to the near-mythic phenomenon of the Spanish Inquisition.

The Spanish Inquisition did not come into formal existence until 1478. When it did, however, the inquisitors were able to tap into a vast reservoir of anti-Semitic tradition that bubbled and boiled just beneath the surface of European civilization. Indeed, the law, literature, theology, and culture of Christendom had always been tainted with a fear and hatred of Jews, starting with those passages of the New Testament in which the execution of Jesus of Nazareth by the Roman authorities in Judea is blamed on the Jews—"Pilate said to them, 'Then what shall I do with Jesus who is called Christ?' They all said, 'Let him be crucified'"—and continuing through the altar paintings, miracle plays, minstrels' songs, broadsheets, and even the graffiti of medieval Europe.[7]

The emblematic medieval legend of the Wandering Jew, which appeared around the time that the first inquisitors sallied forth, proposed that a Jewish man who had taunted Jesus of Nazareth on the way to his crucifixion was condemned by God to wander the earth without rest until Jesus returned at the end of days. The figure is ubiquitous in Christian art of the

Middle Ages—variously appearing as *Der Ewige Jude* (the Eternal Jew) in German and *Juan Espera-en-Dios* (John Waiting-for-God) in Spanish—and he came to symbolize the hateful notion that Jews were damned by God and thus ought to be shunned by good Christians.[8]

Jews were slandered not only as rootless wanderers but also as heartless usurers, despoilers of communion wafers, poisoners of wells, and ritual murderers who used the blood of Christian children in their religious observances. Precisely because Jews did not recognize Jesus of Nazareth as divine, Christian true believers were taught by the book of Revelation that they worshipped in "the synagogue of Satan." By a long and especially ugly tradition, the figure of the Antichrist who appears in Christian apocalyptic writing was expected to be the spawn of a Jewish whore and the Devil himself. The supposed theological offenses of Judaism resulted in the forfeiture of legal rights for ordinary Jews: "Because of the crime which once their fathers committed against our Lord Jesus Christ," went the so-called Jewry Law of one German kingdom in 1268, "the Jews are deprived of the protection of their natural rights and condemned to eternal misery for their sins."[9]

Jewish men and women, in fact, were seen by some Christians as not fully human or not human at all. The medieval laws against bestiality and sodomy, for example, were sometimes applied to sexual intercourse between a Christian and a Jew on the reasoning that "coition with a Jewess is precisely the same as if a man should copulate with a dog." Thus, an English deacon was burned alive in Oxford in 1222 on charges of bestiality because he had converted to Judaism and married a Jewish woman, and another man was burned as a sodomist in Paris because he fathered several children with a Jewish mistress. Tragically, his Jewish lover, too, was put to the flames—a horrifying but illuminating example of the dehumanization of victims that has contributed to atrocities ranging from the mass murder of the Cathars to the horrors of the Holocaust.[10]

So it was that Jews were subjected to all manner of misery, both official discrimination and mob violence, throughout the period during which the Inquisition was in active operation. As late as 1581, Pope Gregory XIII forbade Jews to employ Christian wet-nurses because of the slander, first endorsed by Innocent III in 1205, that Jews "make these women pour their milk into the latrines for three days [after taking Communion] before they again give suck to the children." Jewish doctors were denounced by Christian clergy as diabolical sorcerers: "It is better to die with Christ," they urged their parishioners in Swabia, a region in southwestern Germany, in 1657, "than to be healed by a Jew doctor with Satan."[11]

Since credit was essential to the economy of medieval Europe, Jews (but not Christians) were permitted to engage in moneylending under secular law but, at the same time, condemned for the practice by the Church: "Jews shall desist from usury, blasphemy, and magic," according to one inquisitorial decree, which classed moneylending as a crime no less heinous than "sorcery, incendiarism, homicide, sacrilege, and fornication."[12]

Surely the most egregious and enduring offense against Judaism in medieval Europe was the so-called blood libel—the wholly imaginary notion that Christians were kidnapped and killed for their blood, which would supposedly be used in various diabolical rituals. The most common variant of the slander was the charge that blood was needed to make unleavened bread for the Passover meal. As early as 1096, and as late as 1891, such charges were actually brought against Jewish defendants in various places around Christendom. The blood libel was the supposed crime that sent thirteen Jews to the stake in France in 1288, as we have already noted, and provoked Philip the Fair into complaining that they should have been burned by a royal judge rather than an inquisitor. But Philip was only quibbling over the question of jurisdiction; he was perfectly willing to believe that Jews, as the sons of Satan, were capable of the vilest crimes.

"What more authentic reflection of the prevailing opinion can we hope to find," muses rabbi and historian Joshua Trachtenberg, "than Shakespeare's lines from *The Merchant of Venice,* 'Let me say "Amen" betimes lest the devil cross my prayer, for here he comes in the likeness of a Jew.'"[13]

Jews, like convicted heretics, were required to wear badges and distinctive clothing to set them apart from Christians, a law that can be found in the same canons of the Fourth Lateran Council that served as the "first sketch" of the Inquisition. The circular yellow "Jew badge" sometimes also depicted a crude drawing of the devil or a pair of diabolic horns. At various times and places, Jews were denied the right to practice law or medicine, to live outside a designated Jewish quarter, or to own land. On top of these legal disabilities—and sometimes because of them—they were targets of violence offered by casual passersby as well as organized mobs. The

Jewish community in Mainz, a center of Jewish law and learning as early as the tenth century, for example, deemed it necessary to suspend the blowing of the shofar—the ram's horn that is sounded during the observance of the High Holidays—out of fear that it would attract the attention of their Christian neighbors and provoke yet another pogrom.[14]

Violence toward Jews spiked sharply during the Crusades. The Muslim overlords of the Holy Land were the designated enemy, but the Christian soldiers who took up the cross paused to wet their blades with the blood of the Jewish men, women, and children they encountered en route to Jerusalem. Since the Church taught that Jews and Muslims were both infidels, such atrocities made a certain theological sense to the crusaders. Indeed, they were taught by the priests who preached the crusades and the chaplains who accompanied them on the march to the Middle East that anyone who refused to embrace the truth as offered by the Roman Catholic church deserved to die. "Look now, we are going to take vengeance on the Ishmaelites for our Messiah, when here are the Jews who murdered and crucified him," went one such sermon, whose author refers to Muslims by using a biblical term. "Let us first avenge ourselves on them and exterminate them from among the nations so that the name of Israel will no longer be remembered—or let them adopt our faith."[15]

Perhaps the single strangest but also most telling example of the dangers that faced medieval Jewry dates back to the First Crusade at the end of the eleventh century. A crowd gathered on the outskirts of a town in the Rhineland to salute a party of knights riding off to join the army of crusaders whose mission it was to take back Jerusalem from the Muslims. The expeditionary force included a miscellaneous assortment of wives, servants, and other camp followers, and one woman among them was followed down the road by her pet goose, which was apparently distressed that its mistress was leaving it behind.

To the modern observer, the scene is comical—a goose waddling after a woman who is herself hastening to keep up with a mounted knight. To the men and women in that crowd, however, the sight of the goose somehow suggested to them that God himself was expressing his enthusiasm for the whole enterprise; surely, they convinced themselves, the goose was filled with the Holy Spirit. Perhaps feeling guilty that *they* were not following the example of the heroic goose, the men in the crowd were inspired to do their own small part in the crusade. And so they set upon the infidels who were closest at hand—the Jews who lived among them. Nothing more than a glimpse of a goose at the right time and place was sufficient to spark an explosion of murderous anti-Semitic violence in medieval Europe.

Slander, discrimination, and wanton cruelty were facts of life for ordinary Jews throughout Christendom long before the invention of the Inquisition. But the older, cruder expressions of Jew hatred were brought into sharp focus and aimed directly at the Jews of Spain by the grand inquisitor Tomás de Torquemada (1420–1498) and the other agents of the Spanish Inquisition—"the darkest page in the dark record of the Jewish people," as historian Cecil Roth wrote in the years just before the Holocaust, "one of the saddest episodes in the history of human thought."[16]

Jews had been living in Spain since at least the third century of the common era and perhaps even earlier, a fact that prompted some of them to "disclaim on this ground any conceivable responsibility for the Crucifixion." Until the late fourteenth century, and especially during the medieval interlude when three faiths managed to coexist peacefully, the Spanish Jews were no worse off than their brethren elsewhere in medieval Europe, and sometimes they fared much better. Unlike the neighborhood set aside for the Jewish population of Venice, known as the Ghetto, and similar Jewish districts across Europe that came to be called by the same name, the Judería in Spanish cities was often a prosperous place where Jewish goldsmiths, jewelers, and other artisans and craftsmen offered their wares and Jewish poets, scholars, and theologians were able to work in comfort and security.[17]

The principle of *convivencia* did not mean that Jews and Muslims were entitled to the same rights and privileges as Christian citizens of the various monarchies on the Iberian Peninsula. Muslims were generally restricted to manual labor, and Jews were largely confined to crafts, medicine, money-changing, and tax-collecting. But they were generally free to observe the rites and rituals of their respective faiths. During a time of drought in one region of Spain, for example, Christians, Jews, and Muslims were all called upon to offer their prayers for rain, and a Torah was carried to the public square for the convocation. "The good Jew and the good Muslim can, if they act correctly," conceded one Spanish author as late as 1490, "go to heaven just like the good Christian."[18]

The old fear and loathing of Judaism, however, ran like a sewer beneath the feet of such open-minded Spaniards, and the long-simmering tensions erupted now and then into open violence. During the long hot summer of 1391, for example, Jewish communities across the Iberian Peninsula came under open attack by Christian mobs who were called into the streets by the sermons of a rabble-rousing priest named Ferrán Martínez, a man so vicious that even the king and the pope sought to silence him. A firestorm of anti-Semitic violence took some fifty thousand Jewish lives in the Jewish districts of both Spain and Portugal. To spare themselves from further Christian violence, Jews by the thousands decided to convert to the faith of their oppressors, perhaps as many as 200,000 in Aragón and Castile alone and thousands more in other places around the Iberian Peninsula. These newly minted Christians were called *conversos,* and they would shortly provide the raison d'être for the Spanish Inquisition and the greatest number of its victims.[19]

The first *conversos* embraced Christianity only to save their lives, or so goes one version of the history of Spanish Jewry. According to conventional wisdom, they submitted to baptism, but they "hastened to wash off the traces of the operation as soon as they returned home." They celebrated their weddings in church and then repeated the ceremony according to Jewish rites behind locked doors. They married only fellow *conversos* so that their children, too, would continue to be regarded as Jews under Jewish ritual law. "They were Jews in all but name," insists Cecil Roth, "and Christians in nothing but form."[20]

Such was the near-unanimous verdict of history on the *conversos* until very recently, both among scholars and by common consent in Jewish circles. They preferred to see the *conversos* as "crypto-Jews"—that is, heroic men and women who were forced to convert to Christianity under threat of torture and death, secretly practiced their original faith while pretending to be Christians, and tragically ended their lives as Jewish martyrs. Ironically, as we shall see, much the same point of view was embraced by the Spanish Inquisition, which condemned the *conversos* as insincere and opportunistic and contemptuously branded them as Marranos—"a word of obscure origin" that is often translated as "swine." The question of whether the *conversos* were earnest Christians or crypto-Jews turned out to be a matter of life or death in the eyes of the Spanish Inquisition.[21]

Even if the initial conversion to Christianity by a Jewish man or woman was coerced under threat of death, as it may have been in many cases, the ability to enter Christian circles also bestowed certain undeniable advantages on the *conversos* and their descendants. Like Jews elsewhere in Europe, Spanish Jewry often suffered under various indignities and disabilities—at certain times and places, they were required to make their homes within the bounds of the Judería, they were commanded to wear beards and badges and outlandish garments to mark them as Jews, they were forbidden to own land or ride on horseback or use the title *don,* and they were barred from certain professions and public offices. Once they had abandoned their old faith and submitted to baptism, by contrast, the first generation of *conversos* was relieved of these burdens and permitted to participate more fully in Spanish life.

The early *conversos* and their descendants, in fact, achieved rapid and remarkable success in the century following the anti-Semitic riots of 1391. They found new opportunities in the government, the courts, the army, the university, and even the Church; remarkably, Jewish blood ran in the veins of the Torquemada family, which provided the first grand inquisitor of the Spanish Inquisiton. Far from marrying only their fellow *conversos,* the newly converted Christians were able to make favorable matches in the highest circles of the Spanish aristocracy. By 1480, "barely a single aristocratic family in Aragon, from the royal house downwards, was free from some Jewish admixture or alliance," according to Cecil Roth, and both the supreme court and the legislature of the kingdom of Aragón included men who were descended from *conversos.*[22]

The good fortune of the *conversos* was distressing to members of the Christian gentry and aristocracy, who resented the new competition for positions of profit and privilege. A distinction came to be made between converts to Christianity and their descendants, who were called New Christians (*cristianos nuevos*), and Christians who had been born into the faith, now pridefully called Old Christians. The *conversos* of Jewish origin found themselves the victims of Jew hatred that came from both the mob and the gentry. Within a century after the pogroms that had prompted the first wave of conversions, both professing Jews and converted Jews would come under attack by the throne and the Inquisition, too.*

Until then, the Inquisition had operated only fitfully in the Iberian Peninsula. Nicholas Eymerich, author of the famous handbook of the medieval Inquisition, had served as inquisitor in Aragón in the fourteenth century, but he was removed from office after the pope received complaints from the Spanish clergy that Eymerich was rather too zealous in the pursuit of heresy. Still, the Old Christians understood how the machinery of persecution designed to dispose of "heretical filth" like the Cathars and Waldensians could be repurposed for the extermination of *conversos* of Jewish origin. And they found a champion in Tomás de Torquemada, the Dominican friar who served as confessor to Queen Isabella I of Castile (1451–1504) and was perhaps the single most notorious figure in the long history of the Inquisition.

Torquemada worked diligently to poison the minds of Isabella and her husband, King Ferdinand II of Aragón (1452–1516), against the policy of *convivencia* that had once allowed Christians, Jews, and Muslims to live in peace on the same soil. The king and queen were both attended by Jewish doctors, and both were willing to accept money from Jewish financiers. Indeed, Isabella regarded the Jews of Castile as her personal possession and saw herself as their protector: "All the Jews in my realms are mine," she had once decreed, "and it belongs to me to defend and aid them." Now, however, Torquemada urged her to undertake the mission of erasing Jewish presence and influence for all times. When Isabella and Ferdinand ascended to the throne of a newly unified Spanish monarchy in 1479 as *los reyes católicos* (the Catholic monarchs), the cherished goal of a purged and purified Spain was finally within reach.[23]

A pretext for the war on Spanish Jewry was supposedly provided, if one was needed, by the amorous adventures of a young *caballero* who ventured

---

* Strictly speaking, *converso* and *cristiano nuevo* (New Christian) were terms applied to any convert to Christianity, whether from Judaism or Islam, and his or her descendants. Marrano referred specifically to a *converso* of Jewish origin, and Morisco referred to a *converso* of Muslim origin.

into the Judería of Seville by night to woo an alluring Jewish woman whose faith apparently mattered less to her suitor than her beauty. He is said to have slipped into her house, silently and discreetly, and thus surprised the members of the household in a compromising scene. A celebration of some kind, attended by a mixed company of Jews and New Christians, was in progress behind closed doors. Since it was Eastertide, which usually coincides with the observance of Passover, the gathering triggered all the ugly old suspicions about the ritual practices of Judaism. Even if the knight had only stumbled upon an ordinary seder meal, as it surely was, the fact that *conversos* were in attendance at all amounted to proof that they were, in fact, crypto-Jews.

The tale was reported to Isabella, who finally resolved to do the bidding of her confessor by putting the Inquisition to the task of ridding Spain of *conversos* who were guilty of the heresy known as Judaizing, that is, secretly practicing Judaism while professing to be Christians and seeking to convince others to do the same. The Spanish ambassador in Rome was instructed to petition Pope Sixtus IV for a suitable decree, and the pope complied in 1478 by authorizing the establishment of a branch operation of the Inquisition in Spain, the so-called Tribunal of the Holy Office. Significantly, the pope delegated to the king and queen the power to appoint, remove, and replace the inquisitors, with the sole proviso that they must be priests over the age of forty. On Christmas Day in 1480, the newly appointed inquisitors arrived in Seville, and by February 6, 1481, the first *conversos* of Jewish ancestry had been arrested, tried, and convicted, the first auto-da-fé convened, and six men and women burned alive at the stake.

Such were the modest first efforts of the Spanish Inquisition, but its mere existence was enough to inspire panic among *conversos* throughout Spain. Some eight thousand fled the precincts of Seville for refuge in Cádiz, but they were promptly arrested and returned on the demand of the inquisitors. Later, when terrorized *conversos* crossed the border into France, the pope himself ordered that they be seized and returned to Spain. The Dominican convent in Seville, pressed into service as the center of operations, was soon overwhelmed with accused heretics, and the castle of Triana was put at the disposal of the friar-inquisitors. Within six months of the first auto, another 298 men and women had been burned alive, and some 1,500 had confessed, recanted, and received lesser penances, ranging from the wearing of crosses to life imprisonment. Following the example of the medieval Inquisition, the inquisitors resorted to the old practice of exhuming dead heretics and burning their bones or effigies.

All the old tools and techniques to be found in the inquisitor's handbooks were put to use by the Spanish Inquisition, but some new ones were required, too. Just as a pale complexion and an emaciated torso were once seen as telltale signs of a Cathar *perfectus,* certain external signs were regarded as evidence that a *converso* was a secret Jew. Washing one's hands before prayer, calling a child by a name from the Old Testament, and preparing a meal that did not include pork or shellfish were all regarded as suspicious acts according to the broadsheets that were published and distributed to alert the populace to the presence of secret Jews. Changing one's undergarments on Saturday, for example, was sufficient evidence to justify the arrest and interrogation under torture of a New Christian on charges of being a secret Jew.

The inquisitors hunted out their victims by every means available and wherever they could be found. Strictly speaking, as we have seen, Jews who had remained Jews were beyond the jurisdiction of the Spanish Inquisition, but the inquisitors ordered Spanish rabbis to use their influence, including the threat of excommunication, to compel their congregants to tell what they knew about *conversos* who had secretly remained in the faith or returned to it after their baptisms. According to the old Catch-22 that had caught so many other victims of the Inquisition, Jews who refused to act as informers were regarded as fautors and thus placed themselves under the authority of the Inquisition. They, too, were arrested, tortured, and burned for the crime of refusing to name names.

The ever-increasing number of victims prompted the appointment of additional inquisitors, the creation of tribunals in venues across Spain—a total of fifteen in all, ranging from the capital city of Madrid to the far-flung Balearic Islands—and eventually the establishment of an inquisitorial high command with responsibility for overseeing the work of the friar-inquisitors throughout Spain and around the world, *El Consejo de la Suprema y General Inquisición,* generally known as *La Suprema.* The musty old handbooks of Gui and Eymerich were reissued, but *La Suprema* also published its own manuals, known as *instrucciónes,* by which the inquisitors were briefed on the new and unique mission of the Spanish Inquisition.

Once in full operation, the friar-inquisitors followed the conquistadores all the way to the New World.

Torquemada was formally appointed as an inquisitor in 1482 and soon elevated to the high rank of grand inquisitor. The Dominican monk, a prideful ascetic who had taken the customary vows of poverty and obedience, was now supplied with a palace and a bodyguard of fifty mounted men and two hundred foot soldiers. Since the Spanish Inquisition did not hesitate to arrest, dispossess, and incinerate men and women who regarded themselves as powerful and influential—and since Torquemada was willing to quarrel with the emissaries of the pope himself—the grand inquisitor was fearful of assassination and took ample precautions to preserve his own life. As it turned out, he lived a long life and died peacefully in the safe confines of his bedchamber.

The Spanish Inquisition, as we have seen, was less concerned about Christian dissidents than about crypto-Jews, real or imagined. According to the inquisitors, the public conversion of a Jew to Christianity was likely to be a mere ruse, and even the distant descendants of a *converso* remained under suspicion. Any trace of Jewish origins, no matter how faint or remote, was enough to justify the accusation that the man or woman was a "Judaizer." For example, the bishop of Segovia, Juan Arias Dávila, a man of distant Jewish ancestry, dutifully hunted for the *conversos* who might be secretly practicing Judaism within his diocese, and he brought up sixteen Jews on charges based on the old blood libel. But the bishop himself was eventually arrested by the Inquisition on charges that he had arranged for the graves of his dead relatives to be exhumed, according to Roth, "in order to destroy proof of the fact that they had been interred in accordance with Jewish rites."[24]

High rank offered no immunity for the descendants of *conversos*. In fact, the most assimilated *converso* families may have been at even greater risk than crypto-Jews who actually practiced Judaism, if only because they possessed wealth that the inquisitors wanted to seize and posts that Old Christians wanted to hold. Among the victims of the Inquisition in the kingdom of Aragón, for example, were men from *converso* families who held the titles of master of the royal household, high treasurer, and assessor, all of whom were convicted of participating in a conspiracy to assassinate the inquisitor Pedro Arbués in 1485. The plot was successful—Arbués was stabbed to death as he knelt at the altar in the cathedral at Zaragoza, despite taking the precaution of wearing a coat of mail under his robes—but the act of resistance did nothing to stop the Inquisition. Indeed, more than two hundred victims were rounded up and executed in its aftermath, and the *conversos* found themselves at greater risk than before.

Nor was it easy for victims of the Spanish Inquisition to escape its long reach. Spanish Jews and *conversos* of Jewish origin who crossed the border into Portugal, for example, found themselves at risk from the tribunals that operated there. King Manuel had agreed to embrace the Spanish approach to the Jewish question in an effort to win the hand of the daughter of Ferdinand and Isabella, and a decree of expulsion was issued a week after their betrothal in 1496. In 1536, the Portuguese king successfully petitioned the pope for an inquisition of his own, and, again in imitation of Spain, the priest who served as royal confessor was named inquisitor general. Thereafter, the Inquisition in Spain and Portugal acted in parallel and, for the period when Spain conquered and ruled over Portugal, as a single unified operation.

Some Jewish families fled the Iberian Peninsula and eventually found refuge in Holland and England, Italy and Turkey, and later the Americas, including the ancestors of such luminaries as the philosopher Baruch Spinoza, the American jurist Benjamin Cardozo, and the British statesman Benjamin Disraeli.* But the Inquisition soon extended its jurisdiction to the Spanish and Portuguese colonies and dependencies around the world, including tribunals in Sicily, Goa, and Manila, and thriving branch offices in Mexico, Peru, and Colombia. The first auto on American soil was held in Mexico City in 1528, when two Marranos from Spain were burned alive. Not even the New World offered a safe refuge from the latest version of the inquisitorial war on heresy.

The year 1492 figures prominently in the history of Spain for more than one reason. In that year, of course, King Ferdinand and Queen Isabella dispatched Christopher Columbus on a voyage that was intended to reach

---

* Or so Disraeli boasted. Descent from Spanish Jewry (known as *Sephardim* after the Hebrew word for Spain, *Sepharad*) came to be regarded as a mark of distinction in Jewish circles, and Disraeli appears to have embellished or invented some of the details of his Sephardic roots.

Asia and ended up on the shores of a newly discovered continent. Then, too, the army of the Catholic Monarchs defeated the last Muslim ruler to reign on Spanish soil, thus completing the so-called Reconquista and bringing the Iberian Peninsula under exclusive Christian sovereignty for the first time since 711. And, finally, in 1492 Ferdinand and Isabella resolved to extend the mission of the Spanish Inquisition to its logical extreme by ridding Spain of *all* Jews. By royal decree, the Jewish population of Spain was offered a choice—convert to Christianity (and thus place itself at risk of the Inquisition) or depart from Spain.

An atrocity was tricked up to justify the expulsion and ease the concerns of any Spaniard who might take the idea of *convivencia* too seriously. A nameless baby was said to have been abducted in the town of Ávila in 1491 and then killed by a cabal of Jews and *conversos* to supply blood for one of those diabolical rituals that were the commonplace of anti-Semitic lore. Like other slanders directed at accused heretics across the ages, the foul deed had been wholly invented by a few hateful priests, but the lie was credible enough to prompt the arrest of some seventy new victims of the Inquisition. More important, the imaginary crime was described in lurid propaganda tracts circulated throughout Spain, thus provoking a new surge of fear and loathing directed toward Spanish Jewry.

On March 30, 1492, the formal decree of expulsion was issued by Ferdinand and Isabella. Only four months later, the Jews who declined to convert were forced to trudge across the border or embark by sea to their places of exile. Some sources place the total number of expelled Jews at 300,000 men, women, and children; others, at 800,000. According to the calculations of more recent and more exacting historians, however, the total Jewish population of Spain in 1492 was only slightly more than 80,000, and perhaps only half—40,000 or so—actually resettled outside Spain. Those who stayed behind complied with the royal decree by submitting to baptism, thus putting themselves in the same predicament that bedeviled the earlier generations of *conversos* and presenting the Inquisition with the opportunity to test the sincerity of their conversion.[25]

In fact, the expulsion of Spanish Jewry was yet another tool of persecution urged on the Catholic Monarchs by the grand inquisitor and the more radical elements among the Old Christians. Torquemada insisted that the inquisitors at work across Spain, no matter how zealous they might be, were unable to protect those *conversos* who aspired to be authentic Christians from the predations of professing Jews, "who always attempt in various ways to seduce faithful Christians from our Holy Catholic Faith." Torquemada advocated the expulsion of Spanish Jewry as a kind of radical surgery to excise a malignant growth from the body of Spain, thus reducing to manageable proportions the contagion that was the object of the Inquisition.[26]

A story is told that when a delegation representing the Jewish community petitioned King Ferdinand to withdraw the decree of expulsion—and offered a sizable gift by way of encouragement—Torquemada charged into the room and dramatically tossed thirty silver coins onto the table, "demanding to know for what price Christ was to be sold again to the Jews." The story is invented, but the fact remains that the king and queen were hesitant to expel "their" Jews and thus forfeit the considerable tax revenues that flowed directly into the royal coffers. Such was the will and guile of Torquemada, however, that the Catholic Monarchs submitted to his demands and issued the decree that he sought.[27] "The Holy Office of the Inquisition, seeing how some Christians are endangered by contact and communication with the Jews," wrote King Ferdinand by way of explanation, "has persuaded us to give our support and agreement to this, which we now do, because of our debts and obligations to the said Holy Office; and we do so despite the great harm to ourselves."[28]

The same fate later befell the Muslim communities of Spain. Just as most Spanish cities included a Judería, so too was there a Morería where the so-called Moors made their homes. Starting in 1501, and continuing with ever greater scope and severity, the Muslim population of Spain was presented with the same harsh choice that had been extended to the Jewish population: convert or depart. The Muslims who agreed to embrace Christianity were treated with no more credulity than the Jews had been, and the term Moriscos was coined to describe crypto-Muslims just as Marranos was used to describe crypto-Jews. "Lost souls stubborn in the sects of Moses and Mohammed" is how Jewish and Islamic communities were described by a Spanish historian of the sixteenth century, Fray José de Sigüenza, whose blend of piety and compassion prompted him to complain about the "evil custom prevalent in Spain of treating members of the sects worse after their conversion than before it."[29]

Thus did the *convivencia* that had prevailed during the Golden Age of Spain come to a final and tragic end. Muslims were subjected to baptism en masse, and mosques were converted into churches. Arabic books were seized and burned on royal command. All objects and practices that were associated with the Muslim community in Spain—their use of the Arabic language, their distinctive garb and adornments, and their rituals of circumcision and slaughter of animals—were solemnly condemned. By 1526, the war on Islam was complete and "the Muslim religion no longer existed in Spain officially," according to historian Henry Kamen.[30]

So it was that the Inquisition added Moriscos to its list of usual suspects on the assumption that Muslims, like Jews, were likely to feign a conversion to Christianity. Just as a New Christian with Jewish ancestry might come under suspicion for changing her underwear on Saturday, a New Christian of Moorish extraction was suspect if she decorated herself with henna. One woman was denounced to the Inquisition as a secret Muslim by her own lover because of "her habits in the matter of sexual hygiene," for example, and a few young men of Muslim ancestry were arrested in Toledo in 1538 because they were seen sharing a plate of couscous.[31]

By the beginning of the seventeenth century, Spain—once a rare example of cultural and religious diversity in the heart of Christendom—had expelled almost all its professing Jews and Muslims. But the Church was now confronting a powerful competitor for the hearts and minds of Christian believers—the Protestant Reformation. Martin Luther openly challenged the religious monopoly of the Roman Catholic church, and the inevitable result was a sudden profusion of new churches, clerics, and rituals, all of which were seen by the Vatican as deeply heretical. Here, too, the war on heresy was overlaid with political, economic, and cultural conflicts between Spain and England, who were old and bitter rivals for mastery of the high seas and the New World. The men and women who were charged, tried, and punished by the Spanish Inquisition for the crime of Protestantism were scapegoats in a culture war and a geopolitical standoff that started with the theological differences between Catholics and Protestants.[32]

The medieval Roman Catholic church regarded the translation of the Bible into vernacular languages as a threat to its own authority—indeed, the preference of the Cathars for Bibles in translation had been one of their supposed crimes—but the Protestant churches actively encouraged the practice. As early as 1521, Bibles printed abroad were subject to seizure at Spanish ports of entry, and the Spanish Inquisition later issued its own index of banned books that booksellers were required by law to keep in their shops.

Protestants joined the Jewish and Muslim *conversos* as principal targets of the Spanish Inquisition. In 1533, a priest who was charged with the seduction of a nun sought to appease the inquisitors by offering them the names of seventy men and women whom he denounced as "Lutheran heretics." By 1551, possession of a translation of the Bible in "the vulgar tongues"— that is, any language other than Greek or Latin—was a crime. The first Protestant burned for heresy by the Spanish Inquisition went to the stake in 1540, and twenty-six of the thirty accused heretics at an auto-da-fé at Toledo in 1559 were Protestants. On the way to the stake, one victim appealed to King Phillip II for mercy, but without success.[33] "I myself would bring the faggots to burn my own son," the king is said to have replied, "were he as perverse as you."[34]

When the meager supply of native-born Protestants ran low, the occasional English sailor or merchant was arrested—sometimes on Spanish soil and sometimes when an English ship was taken on the high seas—and tortured, tried, and punished by the Spanish Inquisition. The first Englishman to be burned alive as a heretic, a young man named John Tack, was judged and condemned by the Inquisition at Bilbao. An Englishman named John Massey, arriving at Seville in 1575, was sentenced to a term of seven years in an inquisitorial prison for the crime of possessing a Protestant prayer book titled *The Treasury of Gladness.* Thanks to the global reach of the Inquisition, a cousin of Sir Francis Drake was tried at an auto in Buenos Aires, and the son of Sir John Hawkins suffered the same fate in Lima.

Still, the Spanish Inquisition did not content itself with Marranos, Moriscos, and Protestants. Now and then, some more exotic heresy would excite the imagination of the inquisitors. A preacher in Guadalajara was condemned for teaching that "sexual union was union with God." A woman in Aragón claimed to be the bride of Christ but bedded down with her young male disciples. A priest in Seville was accused of conducting "indecent orgies" after mass and demanding that his female congregants lift their skirts for his pleasure as a form of penance. A band of Africans, pressed into slavery and baptized after their arrival in Spain, were charged as "votaries of hoodoo." All of these religious eccentrics were judged to be heretics and punished by the Spanish Inquisition.[35]

The inquisitors were uncomfortable with any variety of religious experience that they did not understand and endorse. The mystical practices of the so-called illuminists (*alumbrados*), by which the spiritual seeker supposedly achieved unity with God, drew the attention of the Spanish Inquisition, as did the teachings of Teresa of Ávila (1515–1582), a charismatic Carmelite nun who came under inquisitorial scrutiny several times during her lifetime because of her mystical practices and angelic visions. The fact that Teresa carried Jewish blood in her veins further excited the suspicions of the Inquisition. "Father, would that we could all be burnt for Christ," she remarked to a sympathetic priest when she was denounced as a heretic to the tribunal at Seville. Although Teresa was never formally condemned for heresy, the Inquisition refused to permit the publication of her famous memoir, *Life of Mother Teresa of Jesus,* until after her death in 1582.[36]

Still later, the inquisitors bestirred themselves to address the perceived danger of Freemasonry—"a horrid compound of sacrilege and many other abominable crimes," according to one inquisitorial document. One enterprising inquisitor succeeded in infiltrating a Masonic lodge to see for himself what manner of "occult depravity" went on there. He was sufficiently alarmed to bring formal charges against the members of nearly one hundred lodges in Spain. Yet again, the Inquisition acted to rid the Iberian Peninsula of what it regarded as the foul contagion of any idea not sanctioned by the Church and any living creature tainted by impure blood, and to do so at any cost in human suffering.[37]

The Inquisition served more than one function in Spain as it did elsewhere across the centuries and throughout western Europe. As an instrument of state terror, the Inquisition was a convenient tool for establishing the sovereignty of the newly created monarchy that ruled over what had been a collection of little kingdoms and principalities, including some places that had long been ruled by Muslim rather than Christian kings. A decree issued by the Inquisition during the upheavals of the War of Spanish Succession at the opening of the eighteenth century, for example, required that all good Catholics report to the Inquisition any priest who questioned the claim of Philip V to the Spanish crown. Nor was he the first or only Spanish monarch to put the inquisitors on the scent of a political enemy.

Not even the pope was capable of overmastering the Spanish monarchy when it came to the Inquisition. Complaints against the atrocities of the inquisitors were raised by men of purely Christian blood and practice, but when the popes attempted to temper the excesses of the Spanish Inquisition, they were generally ignored by the kings of Spain. Thus, for example, when Pope Leo X issued a bull in 1518 to curb a few of the procedural abuses of the Inquisition, Charles V prohibited its publication within the borders of Spain.* A Spanish proverb captured the chilling effect of the alliance between the crown and the Inquisition: *Con el rey y con la inquisición, chiton!*—"With King and Inquisition, silence!"[38]

Then, too, the Inquisition served as a means for the king to enrich himself at the expense of his subjects. An account by the Venetian ambassador to Madrid confirms the secondary gain that could be achieved by finding and burning rich *conversos* on charges of being secret Jews: "A fortnight ago last Sunday, an act was performed at Murcia, which is called at Toledo an act of the Inquisition, whereat twenty-nine individuals were burned as Jews," the ambassador wrote to the Doge. "Among them were some chief personages, so that the confiscation of their property will yield to the King upwards of 4,000,000 ducats." The Inquisition, too, routinely profited from whatever extortionate fines and seizures could be extracted from its victims; one wealthy financier was dispossessed of 300,000 ducats in gold and silver after he was charged by the inquisitors with the crime of being a secret Jew.[39]

Finally, the Spanish Inquisition, like its counterpart in Rome, provided the shock troops in a culture war against the values of the Enlightenment. The old ways of life that had prevailed during the High Middle Ages were being challenged by humanism in arts and letters, rationalism in science and technology, diversity and toleration in religious practice, and the movement toward representative democracy in government, all of which

---

* Charles (1500–1558) reigned as king of Spain and archduke of Austria under the name Charles I. He is better known as Charles V, the title he carried as Holy Roman emperor.

the Spanish monarchy and the Spanish Inquisition regarded as dangerous heresies. "If the Holy Office had not come to this realm, some of these people would have been like those in England," observed a Spanish priest, referring to the place where all the unsettling new ideas were being openly entertained and put into practice.[40]

So the inquisitors undertook to erect a wall around the Iberian Peninsula to keep out the contagion of people and ideas from what they called *tierras de herejes* (heretical nations), that is, any country that lay outside the Spanish empire. A visit by a Spanish subject to a foreign country was regarded as sufficient cause for suspicion of heresy and even an actionable crime in the eyes of the inquisitors. Agents of the Inquisition boarded foreign ships in Spanish ports and searched for forbidden books, which eventually included the works of such famous figures of the Enlightenment as Voltaire and Montesquieu, Rousseau and Locke.* Objectionable books were censored, sometimes by the simple expedient of tearing out pages, or consigned to the flames, and the recommended punishment for possession of a banned book was the stake.[41]

Even Cervantes felt the fearful chill of the Inquisition. Although only one line of *Don Quixote* was censored by the vigilant inquisitors in 1632, he is reported to have said that he "would have made the book more amusing had it not been for the Holy Office." As late as 1814, when the Spanish Inquisition had already been abolished in parts of Spain and was rapidly approaching its final collapse, Francisco Goya was condemned by the inquisitors for having painted the sensuous *Naked Maja*—a stunning portrait of a reclining nude woman—although he exacted a certain measure of revenge by documenting the sufferings of the Inquisition's victims in a series of memorable drawings.[42]

No offense against moral order was too trivial to escape the attention of the Spanish Inquisition. A quarrel between congregants during a Sunday mass, a curse uttered during a game of dice, a flirtatious remark offered to a

---

* When considering the three crimes that are "amongst us punished with fire"—witchcraft, heresy, and sodomy—Montesquieu observed how odd it was that "the first might easily be proved not to exist; the second to be susceptible of an infinite number of distinctions, interpretations and limitations [and] the third to be often obscure and uncertain." Quoted in Moore, *The Formation of a Persecuting Society*, 1.

young woman during a religious procession, the eating of meat on a Friday, and the failure to attend church services were all the subject of inquisitorial proceedings. Any opinion that struck the inquisitors as impious or impertinent might provoke a formal prosecution, as when one of the notaries on the inquisitorial staff was heard to say: "Tithes are ours, and the clergy are our servants, which is why we pay them tithes." For his daring words, the man was brought before the same tribunal that he had assisted in the prosecution of other accused heretics.[43]

As self-appointed moral guardians, the inquisitors were especially interested in what Christians did under the covers and behind closed doors. Bigamists, both men and women, were always at risk—the inquisitors reasoned that "bigamy implied a measure of heresy"—but the Inquisition extended its jurisdiction to almost every kind of sexual combination. A man and woman who shared a home after their formal betrothal but before their wedding could be prosecuted for "simple fornication." Since the Church was always hostile toward sexual practices that did not result in conception—one of the supposed crimes of the Cathars and various other heretical cults, real and imagined—the Spanish Inquisition in Aragón undertook to prosecute acts of bestiality and sodomy by both men and women, a policy that had the practical effect of equating homosexuality with heresy. Minors convicted of sodomy were whipped and condemned to forced labor, but the penalty for adults over the age of twenty-five who engaged in such sexual acts was burning at the stake.[44]

The Spanish Inquisition was not as vexed by fears of witchcraft as other inquisitors around Europe. After twenty-nine men and women were condemned as witches by the tribunal in Navarre in 1610—and six of them were burned alive—*La Suprema* dispatched one of its inquisitors, Alonzo Salazar y Frias, to conduct a formal investigation into the supposed dangers of sorcery in Spain. As we have already noted, Salazar y Frias concluded that the witch panic had been called into existence by the witch-hunters: "I have not found the slightest evidence," he reported, "from which to infer that a single act of witchcraft has really occurred." As a result of his findings, he welcomed nearly two thousand accused witches back into the Church, including children as young as nine years old.[45]

Aside from its admirable restraint in cases of witchcraft, however, the Spanish Inquisition steadily expanded its scope of operations, restlessly and anxiously searching for new heresies to condemn and new suspects to torture and burn. The victims of an auto-da-fé that took place in Seville on May 3, 1579, for example, included a Flemish bookbinder accused of embracing the new heresy of Lutheranism, an English gunner's mate who had been taken in a sea battle with a flotilla commanded by the great English commander Sir John Hawkins, a Morisco charged with continuing secretly to practice his Islamic faith, plus a few accused crypto-Jews, a miscellaneous assortment of defendants charged with blasphemy and sorcery, and a single bigamist, a total of thirty-eight in all. Significantly, only the bookbinder was burned alive at the stake, a measure of how threatening a Protestant man of letters was to the status quo of Spain. The rest were given milder "penances."

The old techniques of the medieval Inquisition were still in use in Spain. The inquisitors carried the title of Inquisitor Against Heresy and Apostolic Perversity, and they traveled throughout Spain in search of heretics. When they arrived in a town, they generally commenced the proceedings by publishing a so-called Edict of Grace, which invited all heretics to come forward and confess their crimes on the promise of mild penances. As was true during the medieval Inquisition, confession alone was insufficient; the naming of names was required.*

The long history and dire reputation of the Inquisition was itself a weapon. The inquisitors relied on the terror that it inspired to extract self-denunciation and the denunciation of others. Thus, for example, the Edict of Grace that was promulgated in Toledo in 1486 succeeded in summoning forth some 2,400 *conversos* of Jewish ancestry who were willing to confess to their own heresies and betray their friends, neighbors, and relations in order to escape the torture chamber and the stake, and another 2,689 Moriscos came forward to do the same in Valencia in 1568.[46] "We must remember that the main purpose of the trial and execution," wrote one

---

* The Edict of Grace offered the opportunity to avoid the worst punishments by voluntarily confessing. At some times and places, the inquisitors resorted to the so-called Edict of Faith, which omitted the promise of milder punishment in exchange for confession. Both forms of the inquisitorial edict, however, required the betrayal of others.

Spanish inquisitor in 1578 in a commentary on Eymerich's classic manual, "is not to save the soul of the accused but to achieve the public good and put fear into others."[47]

Every palace and prison of the Spanish Inquisition, of course, was equipped with a torture chamber. According to an English account published in 1600, the place of torture was both functional and theatrical; the inquisitors first posed their questions to the victim, and then if satisfactory answers were not forthcoming, they watched as the public executioner applied the instruments to the victim's flesh and bone. To enhance the terror, the torturer was dressed in a black linen robe, and his head was covered in a black hood with eyeholes, "this done to amaze the Patient, as if a devil came to punish his Misdeeds."[48]

The transcript of the interrogation of Elvira del Campo, charged as a secret Jew and tortured by the Inquisition at Toledo in 1568 after it was observed that she refrained from eating pork and changed her undergarments on Saturday, preserves a vivid example of how even a willing victim might find it hard to please the demanding inquisitors. "Tell me what you want for I don't know what to say," the naked woman pleaded, and then, as the inquisitor proceeded through the prescribed degrees of torture, she struggled to come up with a satisfactory confession: "Loosen me a little that I may remember what I have to tell; I don't know what I have done; I did not eat pork for it made me sick; I have done everything; loosen me and I will tell the truth. Lord, bear witness that they are killing me without my being able to confess!"[49]

The text of a typical Edict of Faith included a comprehensive and surprisingly accurate description of Jewish religious observances, and a good Christian was duty-bound to report to the Inquisition anyone who practiced them—those "who prepare on Fridays the food for Saturdays . . . who do not work on Friday evenings and Saturdays as on other days . . . who celebrate the festival of unleavened bread, eating unleavened bread and celery and bitter herbs . . . observe the fast of the Day of Atonement when they do not eat all day until the evening after star-rise . . . who slaughter poultry according to the Judaic law," and so on.[50]

Once a suspect was arrested, all the standard operating procedures of the medieval Inquisition were called into use. Apologists for the Spanish Inquisition point out that its victims were theoretically entitled to an advocate during the formal proceedings, a privilege that had been unavailable to victims of the medieval Inquisition. But the role of the attorney was so circumscribed that the assistance of counsel was ineffective or even "farcical." At first, victims was permitted to choose their own attorneys—if they could afford one and could find one willing to take the case—but the Inquisition later permitted only those attorneys who were approved in advance, "a fellow who would do only what the inquisitor wanted," according to a prisoner of the Inquisition in 1559.[51]

The proceedings of the Spanish Inquisition, in fact, cannot properly be called a trial at all. Rather, the inquisitors convened a series of "audiences" at which testimony was taken and evidence was presented, always behind closed doors and always with the names of witnesses withheld from the defendant. Anyone charged with the crime of heresy by the Inquisition was presumed to be guilty, and the burden of proving innocence fell wholly on the accused. During some periods of its long history, the Spanish Inquisition looked to a committee of inquisitors, priests, judges, and other experts in law and theology known as a *consulta de fé* to weigh the evidence, decide on guilt or innocence, and determine punishment. Later, however, the authority was removed to *La Suprema,* the council that oversaw the operations of the Spanish Inquisition and acted alone in deciding whether an accused heretic lived or died.[52]

Unlike the medieval Inquisition, which invariably condemned those whom it charged, the Spanish Inquisition was known to issue the occasional acquittal—an "absolution" in inquisitorial parlance. But since absolution implied that the accused heretic had been arrested and charged in error, the inquisitors preferred merely to suspend the proceedings rather than impugn the authority of the Inquisition by admitting that they had been wrong in the first place. Here was yet another catch in the workings of the inquisitorial machinery: an accused heretic whose trial was suspended remained at risk that the proceedings could be resumed at any moment, if and when the inquisitors were able to secure additional betrayals and denunciations from a victim of torture in another case. Thus did the victim fall into a kind of purgatory from which it was nearly impossible to escape.

The old definition of heresy—a thought-crime that consisted of believing something contrary to the dogma of the Church—was still used by the Spanish Inquisition. Thus, for example, a man named Luis de León was accused of heresy for teaching that the original Hebrew text of the Old Testament was more authoritative than the Latin translation used by the Church. But even more damning was the fact that he was distantly descended from a family of New Christians through his great-grandmother. De León was arrested along with another scholar named Garjal, also descended from a *converso* family of Jewish origin, which prompted the inquisitor to observe that both "must be intent on obscuring our Catholic faith and returning to their own law."

Indeed, the single greatest innovation of the Spanish Inquisition was to turn heresy from a thought-crime into a blood-crime, and the inquisitorial records now included detailed genealogical data that were used to measure the quantum of Jewish blood in the veins of a New Christian. The slightest trace was sufficient to bring a man or woman to the attention of the Inquisition, to raise the presumption of guilt as a crypto-Jew, and to send the victim to the stake.[53]

Not every *converso* in Spain fell victim to the Inquisition. Some of the newest of the New Christians of Jewish origin enjoyed the same upward mobility that an earlier generation of converted Jews had achieved. Thus, for example, three royal secretaries in service to the Catholic Monarchs were *conversos,* and so was one of the chaplains to Queen Isabella. Among the wealthy families who financed the voyages of Columbus were *conversos* whose religion may have changed but whose role in Spanish commerce did not.* Even the uncle of Tomás de Torquemada —Juan de Torquemada, a prince of the Church who wore the red miter of a cardinal—was reported to carry Jewish blood, although the grand inquisitor himself was held to suffer no such taint.

The ultimate irony of the Spanish Inquisition is that some of its assumptions about the Jewish identity of the *conversos* later came to be held by

---

* Some Spanish historians have argued that Christopher Columbus was a Marrano and have suggested that it was more than mere coincidence that he sailed from Spain in 1492, the year of the Jewish expulsion. The historical evidence supports no such claim, but some flesh-and-blood *conversos* did sail with Columbus, including one Luis de Torres who was formally converted to Christianity on the day before the voyage began.

certain strands of modern scholarship. Just as the archives of the Spanish Inquisition in Toledo preserve the testimony of a witness who insisted in 1483 that "all the *conversos* of this city were Jews," so, too, does historian Yitzhak Baer insist that "the *conversos* and Jews were one people, united by destiny," and Haim Beinart seconds the proposition: "[E]very converso did his best to fulfil Mosaic precepts, and one should regard as sincere the aim they *all* set themselves: to live as Jews."[54]

On the same assumption, Jewish tradition has enshrined the *conversos* who were condemned by the Inquisition for the crime of "Judaizing" as authentic martyrs for the Jewish faith. Some of the victims of the Spanish Inquisition were, in fact, unwilling converts to Christianity. A few of the men and women burned alive at an auto in Córdoba on September 29, 1684, for example, were heard to cry out "Moses, Moses" as they died at the stake. And the last prosecution of a *converso* of Jewish origin on charges of heresy did not take place until 1818, more than three centuries after the Spanish Inquisition had been explicitly charged by pope and king with the task of ridding Spain of its Jewish population.[55]

The reality of the Spanish Inquisition and the plight of Spanish Jewry are not quite what the conventional wisdom advertises them to be. The point has been made by Benzion Netanyahu, who confesses that he undertook the study of the Spanish Inquisition as a young historian in 1944 with the sure conviction that the Marranos were "moral heroes who courageously withstood the terrors of the Inquisition and adhered to their faith under grueling tortures, frequently unto death." In that fateful year, when the apparatus of the Holocaust was in full operation on European soil, Netanyahu saw the victims of the Spanish Inquisition in the context of Jewish martyrology: "Once again, I thought, the Jewish people, which produced the first religious martyrs in history and gave so many martyrs to the faith in the Middle Ages, demonstrated its capacity for suffering and self-sacrifice for its moral principles and religious convictions."[56]

But Netanyahu came to realize that the conventional wisdom about the Marranos was wrong. "To be sure, I found evidence that some of the Marranos were indeed secret adherents of Judaism," he writes in *The Origins of the Spanish Inquisition.* But his "idealistic conception and heroic image" of the Marranos were shattered by the documentary evidence that he gathered and studied: "[M]ost of the conversos were conscious assimilationists who wished to merge with the Christian society, educate their children as fully fledged Christians, and remove themselves from anything regarded as Jewish, especially in the field of religion." Thanks to the willing and even ardent embrace of Christianity by most Marranos, he insists, "the number of clandestine Jews among them was rapidly dwindling to the vanishing point."[57]

The crypto-Jews who actually existed—or at least the ones who came to the attention of the Inquisition—rarely practiced Judaism according to Jewish law and tradition. Rather, most of them cobbled together an "idiosyncratic" and "syncretistic" faith compounded of elements of both Judaism and Christianity in varying proportions and combinations. One *converso,* for example, confessed to the Inquisition that he recited the Paternoster on rising and then washed his hands and recited the morning prayers of Judaism, too. For some *conversos,* the only trace of Jewish practice was a lingering food taboo such as the avoidance of pork; for others, it was a prideful claim to biblical lineage, as when one *converso* reportedly altered the words of the Ave Maria to claim descent from Mary herself: "Holy Mary, Mother of God and my blood-relative, pray for us." Flesh-and-blood *conversos,* according to David M. Gitlitz in *Secrecy and Deceit,* could be found "along the spectrum that runs from wholly Christian to wholly Jewish."[58]

The *conversos* who practiced some form of Judaism were always few in number, however, and their numbers grew steadily smaller as the Inquisition continued to search out and send them to the stake. But the sparsity of real crypto-Jews never mattered to the inquisitors, who were quite content to persecute *conversos* whose only crime was the accident of a distant and long-forgotten Jewish relative. For the inquisitors, as for the Nazis in the twentieth century, blood mattered more than belief or practice. Thus did the Spanish Inquisition carry out "a holocaust of *conversos,*" many of whom went up in flames as authentic Christians falsely accused of being secret Jews.[59]

If most of the Marranos were, in fact, willing and earnest converts to Christianity, what explains the obsessive drive of the Spanish Inquisition to persecute and exterminate them?

One factor was the visceral anti-Semitism of Christian tradition, which was always a subtext of the inquisitorial project in Spain and prompted the inquisitors to regard Jewish blood as an ineradicable taint. Then, too, the opportunity to confiscate the wealth of accused heretics was a source of revenue for the Inquisition, both in Spain and elsewhere in Europe, and the *conversos* of Jewish origin provided a rich target. "The 'converso danger,'" explains Henry Kamen, "was invented to justify the spoliation of conversos." Above all, the Old Christians resented the rivalry of New Christians whose upward mobility in Spanish society had been so rapid and so remarkable, and they sought to remove these *arrivistes* from their positions of power and privilege by any means possible.[60]

All these motives combined to produce the obsession that distinguishes the Spanish version of the Inquisition from all others—the self-appointed mission of purging the Spanish population of Jewish and, later, Muslim contamination through the doctrine of *limpieza de sangre* (purity of blood). The medieval and Roman inquisitors had been concerned only with the purity of one's faith, and they were willing to spare accused heretics from the worst penalties if they repudiated the beliefs that the Church called heretical and embraced the ones that the Church prescribed for all good Catholics. The Spanish inquisitors, by contrast, were dubious that any New Christian was capable of authentic conversion or repentance if his or her blood was tainted by Jewish or Muslim ancestry, no matter how slight or how remote. Here begins a dangerous and deadly idea—the punishment of human beings for the crime of having been born with the wrong blood in their veins—that would reach its most horrific expression in the twentieth century.

One's blood was deemed to be pure, in fact, only if it was wholly untainted by Jewish or Muslim forebears, and only those whose blood was pure were entitled to the official designation of Old Christian. One important function of the Inquisition—and a source of revenue to fund its more brutal operations—was performing elaborate genealogical studies and issuing certificates that attested to one's purity of blood. Since New Christians came to be excluded from various posts and professions by a body of Spanish law called the Strictures of Purity of Blood, such a certificate was sometimes required to secure a professorship or a government job, to win a place in a military academy or the officer corps, to reassure the family of a prospective husband or wife, or to satisfy the curiosity of a suspicious inquisitor.

If one's purity of blood could not be documented, the label of New Christian would be imposed by law. Depending on the number and nearness of Jewish or Muslim relatives, one might be described as a Half New Christian, for example, or a Quarter New Christian. The quanta of tainted blood were measured and registered all the way down to a fraction of one-sixteenth, but even a single Jewish or Muslim relation on a distant branch of one's family tree was enough to mark one as "a part of the New Christian" and expose one to all the risks and disabilities imposed on *conversos* by the Strictures of Purity of Blood. Even if a man or woman escaped the Inquisition, he or she was still subject to the Spanish version of apartheid whenever and wherever the blood laws were in effect.[61]

The enemies of Spanish Jewry included deeply racist elements among the Old Christians who eventually recruited Ferdinand and Isabella to their radical program of ridding Spain of its Jewish population, not only all practicing Jews but anyone with even a trace of Jewish blood. "Old Christians came to treat the conversos as carriers of a lethal disease," explains Netanyahu. "What the racists proposed, then, was a large-scale bloodbath, mass extermination or, to use the language of our time, genocide." No such genocide took place, but the enactment of the blood laws, the expulsion of professing Jews, and the persecution of converted Jews by the Spanish Inquisition were all measures that were intended to achieve the same goal. Whenever a *converso* was sent to the stake by the inquisitors, it was another victory in the war of extermination against Judaism that began in Spain but did not end there.[62]

The burning of condemned heretics had been the occasion for a display of pomp and circumstance throughout the long history of the Inquisition, but the Spanish Inquisition aspired to new heights of grandeur and eventually raised the auto-da-fé to "a true art-form of the Baroque." A certain high point was reached on June 30, 1680, when King Charles II and his bride, Marie Louise, along with some fifty thousand other spectators, gathered in the Plaza Mayor in Madrid to enjoy an auto that started at 6:00 a.m. and ended more than twelve hours later. A total of 118 condemned heretics were paraded in front of the crowd to receive their penances, and 51 of them were "relaxed"—that is, burned at the stake.[63]

Some autos were small in scale and took place in private, but the celebrated spectacles of the Spanish Inquisition were elaborate events that required much preparation. A Sunday or a feast day would be chosen in order to build a suitably large crowd, and—for the same reason—the auto would be announced in advance from pulpits throughout the district. Carpenters and masons were summoned to build the platforms where the invited guests would sit and where the victims would be burned alive. A rehearsal might be held on the day before the big event. At dawn on the morning of the auto, the victims would be offered a last meal, perhaps a beaker of wine and a slice of fried bread with honey. With the tolling of church bells across the city and a solemn processional, the high ceremonial would finally begin.

Local priests and visiting prelates were invited to join the friar-inquisitors and other inquisitorial personnel in the parade, sometimes carrying lighted white tapers, and they were accompanied by soldiers, heralds, flag bearers, drummers, and trumpeters. On especially grand occasions, the procession would include a band and a choir to perform solemn hymns. The accused heretics followed behind, barefoot and bareheaded, and sometimes shaved down to bare skin. All of them assembled at the Palace of the Inquisition and formed up in ranks for the march to the place of judgment and then the place of burning, the dreaded *quemadero*.

Some of the accused wore ropes around their necks as signs of their imminent punishment, and the most defiant among them were gagged to prevent them from calling out to the crowd. The accused heretics were dressed in a loose-fitting yellow smock called a *sanbenito*—a corruption of *saco bendito* or "sacred sack"—and they wore the *coroza*, a tall dunce's cap fashioned out of yellow pasteboard. Crowds of spectators numbering in the tens of thousands might attend a well-orchestrated auto, and an elaborately printed program (known as a *lista*) was sometimes prepared to record the names and crimes of the condemned men and women.

According to the *lista* for an auto that took place in Lisbon on Sunday, June 17, 1731, for example, there were eighty-three victims, ranging from "persons who wear the *sanbenito*" to "persons handed over in the flesh"— that is, condemned heretics who had refused to confess, or had offered an insufficient confession, or had recanted and then later relapsed into heresy, and were now turned over to the civil authorities for burning. Thanks to the *lista,* we know that case 11 was a twenty-nine-year-old woman named María Méndes, native of Beja and resident of Moncarapacho, a New Christian who was described in the program in an urgent shorthand: "Convicted, refused to confess and obstinate." By contrast, a mule driver from Tondella named João Pereyra, age thirty-two, described as "half New Christian," was charged with "Judaizing and other sins" and sentenced to "perpetual wearing of the *sanbenito* and imprisonment without remission" as well as a five-year exile in the Portuguese colony of Angola.[64]

The *sanbenito* and the *coroza* were Spain's unique contributions to the iconography of the Inquisition. On the *sanbenitos* were painted scenes and figures that indicated the crime and fate of the wearer. For example, if a man or woman had been convicted of "formal" heresy, the *sanbenito* was decorated with a black cross with one transverse arm; two arms were reserved for more egregious forms of heresy. The *sanbenito* worn by those condemned to die was black, and the others were yellow. Also painted on the *sanbenito* and the *coroza* were garish scenes of devils and flames; if the flames climbed upward, the wearer was condemned to die; if the flames pointed downward, the wearer had confessed and faced a lesser penance. Sometimes the garment or headgear was made to fit a specific crime, as when a bigamist who had taken fifteen wives was required to wear a *coroza* on which were painted the figures of fifteen women. "The procession presented an artistically loathsome dissonance of red and yellow hues," wrote one English propagandist in the nineteenth century, "as it defiled to the infernal music of growled psalms and screams and moanings, beneath the torrid blaze of Spanish sunlight."[65]

The ranks of the processional often swelled with various functionaries and honorees. At the famous Madrid auto of 1680, for example, the Company of Coal Merchants, all of them bearing pikes and muskets, were invited to join the procession in recognition of their crucial contribution to the festivities—"the Wood with which the Criminals are burnt." On that occasion, the Duke of Medina-Celi was given the honor of carrying the official banner of the Inquisition, which depicted a cross, a branch, and a sword to symbolize the heretic's choice between the Church and the pyre, and the words *Justitia et misericordia* (Justice and Mercy). Other participants carried pasteboard effigies of escaped or missing heretics who were to be burned in absentia, or trunks containing the remains of defunct heretics who had been posthumously condemned to the stake.[66]

The inquisitorial parade eventually arrived in the public square where two platforms had been erected, one to accommodate the accused heretics, the attending priests, and the guards, the other for the comfort of honored guests from both the Church and the royal court, assorted nobles of various ranks, public officials, and the occasional ambassador, although the highest chair was reserved for the grand inquisitor, who dressed for the occasion in a purple robe. Between these two stages was a pulpit from which a Mass was conducted and a sermon preached to the crowd by one of the inquisitors, always an occasion for excoriating the accused heretics and sternly cautioning everyone else against the crime of heresy. Then, as the accused heretics were brought to the pulpit, sometimes one by one and sometimes in groups, the inquisitor recited the charges, announced the verdict, and pronounced the sentence against each, including the effigies and corpses as well as the flesh-and-blood victims.

The lesser punishments might include the obligation to wear the *sanbenito* to church services every Sunday—a Spanish variant on the medieval practice of requiring heretics to wear yellow crosses—but more severe penances were more commonly imposed, including a public lashing of up to two hundred strokes, forced labor as a galley-slave aboard one of the royal men-of-war, or "perpetual and irremissible" imprisonment. Sometimes the inquisitors devised a punishment that was, at once, both painful and whimsical, as when one victim of the Inquisition in Mexico was anointed with honey, covered with feathers, and left to stand in the sun for four hours.[67]

The climax of the auto-da-fé, of course, was the execution of condemned heretics. At the auto attended by King Charles II and Marie Louise, the ceremonies began early in the day and it was not until midnight that the burnings began. Still, it was a much-sought-after spectacle. According to the time-honored legal fiction of the Inquisition, the burnings were conducted by the public executioner rather than the inquisitors, and the actual conflagration took place at a site outside the city walls known as the *quemadero* (place of burning). The victims were conducted from the public square to the *quemadero* on the backs of donkeys; the friar-inquisitors were close at hand, urging them to recant while it was still possible, and the crowd followed behind. A high scaffold had been erected at the place of execution to improve the sightlines, and the owners of houses overlooking the pyre are said to have sold window seats at a handsome price.

The victims mounted the platform, followed by the priests who continued to encourage them to confess. At some autos, the victims were made to climb a ladder and seat themselves on a small wooden board affixed at the top of the stake—another effort aimed at improving the view and thus enhancing the pleasure of the crowd. The priests would follow the victims up the ladder, but if the victims still refused to recant, the priests withdrew and the executioners took their place, binding each of the victims to the stake with ropes or chains. Then the priests mounted the ladder again for one last effort at conversion, and if the final plea was rebuffed, "they leave them to the Devil," wrote one contemporary observer, "who is standing below ready to receive their souls and carry them with him into the flames of hell-fire, as soon as they are out of their bodies." To taunt the victims—and to encourage a confession before it was too late—some executioners would playfully burn off the beards of the male victims with a torch before touching it to the pyre.[68]

If, on the other hand, a condemned heretic offered a satisfactory confession at the last moment, he or she was granted what the inquisitors apparently regarded as a final act of mercy: the victim would be strangled with a garrote before being burned. Sometimes a bag of gunpowder might be hung around the neck of the victim, both as a gesture of mercy—once ignited by the mounting flames, the resulting explosion would bring his ordeal to a quick end and possibly even take off his head—and as a pyrotechnic effect to please the crowd. Then, at last, the executioner put the torch to the brushwood and charcoal that had been neatly arranged around the stakes, igniting the fuel at each of the four corners to ensure that the flames burned evenly on all sides. As a final theatrical touch, the corpses and effigies, also dressed in the *sanbenito* and the *coroza,* were burned along with the living victims.

"To make these holocausts of human beings more ghastly," wrote one nineteenth-century historian, "artificial dolls and decomposed bodies, with grinning lips and mouldy foreheads, were hauled to the huge bonfire, side by side with living men, women and children."[69]

The sight of men, women, and children being slowly burned to death was apparently a crowd-pleaser, and "the shrieks of dying heretics sounded as sweet music in the ears of blameless adherents of the Church," according to Cecil Roth's bitterly sarcastic description of the scene. At the auto in 1680, one of the victims, a girl still in adolescence, is said to have addressed a heartrending plea to Marie Louise as she passed the royal gallery: "Noble Queen! Cannot your royal presence save me from this?" the girl cried out. "I sucked in my religion with my mother's milk; why must I now die for it!" But the young queen remained silent and aloof. Indeed, the king himself was invited to ignite the torch that was used to kindle the flames, and the girl was burned alive along with the rest of the victims.[70]

Not every spectator was quite so cool about the carnage. A private letter written by one of the queen's attendants, the Marquise de Villars, betrays a degree of compassion that apparently escaped the others: "The cruelties which were witnessed at the death of these poor wretches it is impossible for me to describe." Yet the writer also confirms the principle of terror that the Inquisition applied not only to its victims but to the populace at large. "It was necessary to put in an appearance from beginning to end, unless one had a medical certificate, for otherwise one would have been considered a heretic," she reports. "Indeed, people thought very ill of me that I did not seem to enjoy everything that was happening."[71]

As the flames did their grisly work, the victims were incinerated along with their clothing and headgear. If they had been bound to the stakes with ropes rather than chains, the blackened bodies would fall into the flames at the foot of the stake as the ropes burned away. Sometimes a trapdoor was built into the structure so that the charred bodies would drop into a bed of embers. The goal was to burn the bodies to ashes, which were then collected and scattered on waste ground or dumped into a nearby river, all in order to avoid a burial place where the victim might be remembered and honored. The mission of the Spanish Inquisition was not merely to murder but also to obliterate the condemned heretic.

But the victims of the auto were not entirely forgotten. According to the *instrucciones* of the Spanish Inquisition issued in 1561, *sanbenitos* on which the names and crimes of condemned heretics had been written were to be hung like trophies in the churches of the towns where they had once lived.

When the old garments had turned brittle and the lettering had faded away, they were to be replaced with fresh ones "in order that there may be perpetual memory of the infamy of the heretics and their descendants." Thus did the Inquisition unwittingly create and maintain enduring memorials of its own infamy.[72]

The death toll of the Spanish Inquisition has been estimated as high as 30,000, with another 17,000 burned in effigy and nearly 300,000 "penanced" in various other ways. Another 40,000 victims were persecuted by the tribunals of the Inquisition in Portugal. Even if the numbers are "suspicious," as modern historians agree, and even if the mythification of the Inquisition had begun even while the friar-inquisitors were still at work, the fact remains that Spanish Inquisition offers plenty of authentic horrors.[73]

Children as young as ten were charged by the tribunal at Toledo in 1659, and a ninety-six-year-old woman named María Bárbara Carillo was sent to the stake at Madrid in 1721. Indeed, it has been suggested that a disproportionate number of women were victimized by the Spanish Inquisition, but the inquisitors were perfectly willing to torture and burn accused heretics of both genders and every age. Although the victims included Muslims and Protestants, mystics and eccentrics, bigamists and homosexuals, the casualties of the Spanish Inquisition were mostly men and women of Jewish ancestry, including a few who were secretly practicing their original faith and many more who remained earnest Christians until their deaths. Of all the victims of the inquisitorial tribunal at Barcelona between 1488 and 1505, for example, more than 99 percent were Jewish *conversos*.

The death toll declined slowly but steadily after the Spanish Inquisition reached its zenith in the mid–seventeenth century. At the very moment in history when the Inquisition was held up by progressives in western Europe and North America as a symbol of everything that was wrong with the *ancien régime* and religious true belief, it was already on its way to irrelevance. A ballad titled "The Loyal Martyrs, or Bloody Inquisitor," for example, was published in England in 1700 to condemn "the mercenary and inhuman barbarities transacted in the Inquisition of Spain." At roughly the same moment in history, when a grandson of Louis XIV crossed the border from France to Spain to ascend the Spanish throne as King Philip V in 1701, the

new monarch signaled the obsolescence of the Inquisition by pointedly refusing to attend an auto that had been organized in his honor, the very first
Spanish monarch to have done so.[74]

"There is no need to attribute this to the growth of tolerance," explains
Henry Kamen. "The simple reason was that heretics had been purged out of
existence, so depriving the tribunal of combustible material for its fires."[75]

Still, a few dedicated inquisitors in Spain and Portugal continued to
send their victims to the stake even as the freshening winds of the Enlightenment were stirring elsewhere in Europe, and at least 150 autos were
recorded during the first half of the eighteenth century. The Portuguese
Inquisition burned its last condemned heretic in 1761. The Spanish Inquisition ran low on Marranos and thereafter contented itself with the occasional religious eccentric or political dissenter, blasphemer, or bigamist.
Starting in 1780, however, the events of the French Revolution stirred the
Spanish Inquisition into a new spasm of activity as it struggled to preserve
the monarchy and the Church from the dangerous new ideas that had top-
pled the French king. The friar-inquisitors were right to fear the French:
the army of Napoleon entered Madrid in 1808, and Napoleon himself issued the decree by which the Inquisition was formally abolished. The Palace of the Inquisition was demolished, and its voluminous records thrown
into disorder.

The story is told that French troops entering the Palace of the Inquisition were greeted by the grand inquisitor himself, who welcomed them to
the opulent premises but cagily refused to show them the way to the notorious torture chambers where so much of the inquisitorial business was
conducted. An enterprising French soldier poured water on the marble
floors and saw where the fluid ran through the cracks of a secret hatchway
that led to the dungeons. There the liberators found the bones and corpses
of dead victims, a hundred or so naked convicts, and the notorious instruments of torture, which they applied to the skulking inquisitors who were
now their prisoners.

The story, however, is invented, an exercise of the imagination not unlike
Edgar Allan Poe's equally lurid story "The Pit and the Pendulum," which
depicts a victim of the Inquisition who is spared the gruesome (and wholly
imaginary) torture described in the title by the timely arrival of the French
army. The truth is rather less spectacular. Napoleon's decree was effective

only where French troops were present to enforce it, and the Inquisition continued to operate elsewhere in Spain. After the defeat of Napoleon, Spain suffered a long period of intermittent political upheaval and civil war during which the Spanish parliament, known as the Cortes, would occasionally bestir itself to adopt a resolution by which the Inquisition was abolished, and then the king would annul it. King Ferdinand VII, for example, first abolished the Inquisition, later annulled his own decree, and still later reinstated it. Meanwhile, a few more victims were charged with heresy—a priest turned political insurgent named José María Morelos, for example, was tried and executed in 1815 in Mexico City on charges of being a "Deist, Atheist, Voltairean and Hobbesan"—but not even the most zealous inquisitor dared to convene a public auto.[76]

Clearly, the Inquisition was dying a lingering death. The inquisitors were reduced to clerical housekeeping chores, as when one priest in Seville was penanced for the crime of having improperly raised the wafer during Mass. One by one, the inquisitorial tribunals went out of business—first Goa in 1812, then Mexico, Peru, and Cartagena in 1820, and Portugal in 1821. Only in Spain itself did the antique machinery of persecution, just like the contraption depicted in Kafka's *In the Penal Colony*, continue to grind up the occasional victim. But the apparatus, again as in Kafka's story, was in disrepair. Vacancies on some tribunals went unfilled, and others no longer operated at all; many of the meticulous and voluminous records dating back to the fifteenth century were scattered; and when the inquisitorial palaces were thrown open to public inspection, they were subjected to "an orgy of destruction."[77]

On July 26, 1826, fully six centuries after the first heretic was burned by the newly created Inquisition, the inquisitors took their last human life. A schoolteacher named Cayetano Ripoll was charged as a heretic because he had professed the principles of Deism, and he was "relaxed" like countless thousands before him. The last of the inquisitors could not bring themselves to burn him alive, and the death sentence was administered by strangling him with a garrote. To affirm their solidarity with the old and enduring traditions of the Inquisition, however, the dead body was stuffed into a wooden barrel decorated with painted red flames and buried in unconsecrated ground—a purely symbolic auto-da-fé but one whose point was not lost on the rest of the world.

Cayetano Ripoll had committed no greater crime than any of the other men, women, and children who were victimized by the Inquisition simply because, according to the prescribed language of the handbooks, they had supposedly failed "to hold and believe all that the Holy Mother Church of Rome holds, believes and teaches." But his death marks the last homicide committed by the inquisitors in the name of God. The Spanish Inquisition itself continued to exist, if only on paper, for a few more years after the garishly painted barrel containing Ripoll's mortal remains was buried. On the death of Ferdinand VII, a child-queen named Isabella II took the throne, and her mother, Cristina, ruled in her name as regent and queen mother. To Cristina belongs the credit for bringing to an end what Pope Innocent III had begun six hundred years before.[78] "It is declared," she decreed on July 15, 1834, "that the Tribunal of the Inquisition is definitely suppressed."[79]

So ended the Inquisition as a fact of history. But the inquisitorial idea, first conceived by the lawyer-popes and then put into operation by the friar-inquisitors, was too powerful and too useful to be wholly abandoned. Indeed, the same deadly idea reached its most ambitious and horrific expression only in the twentieth century and, as we shall see, it is not yet dead and gone.

7.

THE ETERNAL INQUISITOR

[W]e must not try to excuse things for which
there is no real excuse. . . . To ignore the question
of human responsibility would make all history
meaningless.

G. G. COULTON, *The Inquisition*

The Inquisition has always been a moving target. Indeed, its history was already being rewritten long before the friar-inquisitors burned their last heretic, and the revisionism shows no sign of ending soon. The Inquisition continues to generate hot fires of controversy among modern commentators who, remarkably, struggle to explain away its worst outrages. But there are dangers in the effort to reverse the verdict of history, if only because the imitators of the Inquisition have shown themselves willing and able to commit ever more outrageous crimes against humanity by embracing the ideology and techniques of the first inquisitors.

Within twenty years after Joan of Arc was burned at the stake in 1431, King Charles VII found it politically expedient to convene a posthumous retrial in order to prove that he did not owe his crown to a witch and a heretic. Not surprisingly, the Maid of Orléans was acquitted, and the new verdict "broke the authority of the Inquisition in France." Only in 1869, however, did the Church tacitly acknowledge the errors of the inquisitors who had burned her alive by commencing the long process of canonization, and not until 1920 was she was finally elevated to sainthood. By then, Saint Joan had been transformed from a troubled adolescent who suffered from spooky aural hallucinations into a stirring icon of French patriotism. Even so, Saint Joan was regarded as a heroine of French resistance to foreign aggression rather than a symbolic victim of the Inquisition.[1]

The ghost of Galileo, by contrast, is still awaiting an acquittal or, at least, an apology from the Church for what has been called "the greatest scandal in Christendom." His books remained on the Index until 1822, and it was not until 1979 that Pope John Paul II appointed a papal commission of historians, scientists, and theologians to reconsider the verdict that had been handed down more than three centuries earlier. When the commissioners finally concluded their work after thirteen years of dilatory effort, they conceded only that the Inquisition had committed a "subjective error of judgment." The pope himself expressed sympathy with their findings, but the original conviction of Galileo by the Inquisition on charges of heresy has never been formally reversed.[2]

The office long known as the Sacred Congregation of the Holy Roman and Universal Inquisition still exists today, although it was renamed the Congregation of the Holy Office in 1908 and then the Sacred Congregation for the Doctrine of the Faith in 1965. Until recently, as we have already noted, the cardinal in charge of the office was Joseph Ratzinger (b. 1927), who was elevated to the papal throne as Pope Benedict XVI in 2005. Although no one is at risk of torture or imprisonment by the "reformed inquisition," the office is still charged with the enforcement of church dogma and "canonical discipline." As recently as 1981, the Sacred Congregation reaffirmed an old decree of excommunication against Catholics who dare to join the Freemasons, the same fraternity that the Spanish Inquisition had found so threatening. So the distinction between permissible and impermissible beliefs—if not the rack and the wheel—survives in the bureaucracy of the Roman Catholic church in the third millennium of the common era.[3] "[W]ith its image improved and its name twice changed, the Inquisition still exists and functions today," concludes Edward Burman, "the heir to a tradition of over seven hundred years."[4]

Remarkably, the verdict on the Inquisition itself is still open. To be sure, a whole literature of outrage was produced by French, English, and American propagandists even while the Inquisition was in active operation, and some of the imaginary atrocities that they conjured up still blur the line between fact and fiction. Henry Charles Lea—"the great denouncer of the Inquisition," according to Giorgio de Santillana—voted to convict the inquisitors on all counts: "It was a system which might well seem the invention of demons," writes Lea in one characteristic rhetorical flourish, "and was fitly characterized by Sir John Fortescue as the Road to Hell."[5]

But the academic historians who have studied and debated the Inquisition over the last two hundred years have failed to reach a moral or historical consensus. The events and personalities of the Inquisition have been reconsidered by each new generation of critics and scholars, an enterprise in the rewriting of history that is still going on today. According to some of its apologists, the Inquisition was a well-meaning and mostly lawful if also sometimes flawed institution, and even the revisionists who concede that the Inquisition was a machine of persecution insist that it never operated quite as well as its inventors had hoped.

The Inquisition, however, is not merely a point of academic interest. Although the historical Inquisition may not have been quite what it was advertised to be by "the great denouncer," the fact remains that the grand inquisitors aspired to create a Brave New World of authoritarian mind-control, and their example has inspired the same Orwellian dreams in successive generations—not only in Nazi Germany and Stalinist Russia but even here in America. The inquisitorial toolkit has remained open and in active use, and the modern inquisitors have been even more ruthless than the original ones. Indeed, as we shall see, the machinery of persecution was applied in the twentieth century to produce atrocities on a scale that would have beggared even the fertile imagination of the first men to carry the title of Inquisitors into Heretical Depravity.

The crimes of the Inquisition, as we have now seen in sometimes gruesome detail, begin with the persecution of men, women, and children for nothing more than entertaining a private thought that the Church condemned as heretical. In some cases, the victims were arrested, imprisoned, tortured, and burned for an offense that existed only in the minds of the inquisitors, as in the case of the Witch Craze, or for the accident of having a distant Jewish ancestor, as in the case of the Spanish Inquisition. The fundamental fact that real human beings suffered and died at the hands of the inquisitors for nothing more than a thought-crime—or for no crime at all—is sometimes overlooked in the scholarly debate over the Inquisition. Now and then, we need to recall the ordeal of the Jewish *converso* named Elvira del Campo, stripped naked and put to torture by the Spanish Inquisition in 1568 because eating pork made her sick to the stomach, if only to remind ourselves of the human face of the Inquisition: "Lord," she cried, "bear witness that they are killing me without my being able to confess!"[6] "

To keep these abominations out of sight," observes G. G. Coulton, "is the same offence as to describe the French Revolution without the guillotine."[7]

The case against the Inquisition goes beyond its flesh-and-blood victims. For example, the routine use of torture as a tool of criminal justice by civil police and courts throughout Europe, starting in the Middle Ages and continuing for five hundred years, has been attributed to the example set by the Inquisition. Even the apparent superiority of northern Europe over southern Europe in commerce, scholarship, science, and technology is sometimes explained as a result of the chilling effect of the Inquisition in the places where it lasted the longest and exercised the greatest authority. It is no accident, in other words, that Galileo's writings were banned in Italy even as they were being published in Holland, or that Spain remained the sick man of western Europe for a century after the Inquisition was formally abolished: "The Dead Hand of the Holy Office," explains Cecil Roth, "was pressing slowly on the vital arteries of Spanish intellectual life."[8]

Yet the Inquisition has its defenders, as we have already seen, and even those who reluctantly admit that the Inquisition was capable of excess also suggest that it was never as fearful as historians such as Lea, Coulton, and Roth have depicted it. Those who seek to justify or explain away the Inquisition argue that it was governed by the rule of law, at least in theory, and they insist that its atrocities and excesses were the exception rather than the rule. They point out that "the Inquisition" is a term that meant different things at different times and places across history, ranging from a freelance papal inquisitor like Robert le Bougre in thirteenth-century France to the elaborate bureaucracy of the grand inquisitor and *La Suprema* in Spain after the fifteenth century.

Above all, the revisionists contend that the Inquisition never really fulfilled its mission, if only because the friar-inquisitors lacked the means to carry out the task of ridding Christendom of every heresy and every heretic. When Henry Charles Lea condemns the Inquisition for creating "a system unspeakably atrocious," the revisionists retort, he is focusing on the grandiose ambitions of the inquisitors and overlooking their meager achievements. The sorry if also sordid reality, they insist, is something quite different from the carnage that we find in so many accounts of the Inquisition, both in history books and in storybooks.[9]

"For the Inquisition to have been as powerful as suggested, the fifty or so inquisitors in Spain would need to have had an extensive bureaucracy, a reliable system of informers, regular income and the cooperation of the secular and ecclesiastical authorities," writes Henry Kamen, a leading modern historian of the Spanish Inquisition. "At no time did it have any of these."[10]

So we are invited to regard the Inquisition as a sporadic, quixotic, often hapless, and ultimately futile enterprise. The revisionists point out, by way of example, that the inquisitors were always running short of funds if not of heretics and heresies: "Your Majesty should above all provide that the expenses of the Holy Office do not come from the property of the condemned," wrote one daring *converso* to Charles V in 1538, "because it is a repugnant thing if inquisitors cannot eat unless they burn." Ironically, the defenders are able to cite "the great denouncer" for the proposition that the Inquisition was so ineffectual that it could do nothing to stop the single greatest challenge to the authority of the Roman Catholic church, the Protestant Reformation.[11] "Had it existed in Germany in good working order, Luther's career would have been short," Lea quips. "An Inquisitor like Bernard Gui would have speedily silenced him."[12]

Sometimes the apologia offered by modern commentators seems overly generous, if not downright bizarre, in light of the facts available to us. "It was not a drumhead court, a chamber of horrors, or a judicial labyrinth from which escape was impossible," write Renaissance historians John and Anne Tedeschi about the Roman Inquisition in the introduction to their translation of Carlo Ginzburg's *The Cheese and the Worms: The Cosmos of a Sixteenth-Century Miller.* "Capricious and arbitrary decisions, misuse of authority, and wanton abuse of human rights were not tolerated. Rome watched over the provincial tribunals, enforced the observance of what was, for the times, an essentially moderate code of law, and maintained, to the extent that a consensus existed, uniformity of practice."[13]

Yet, as we learn from Carlo Ginzburg's account of one flesh-and-blood victim of the Inquisition, the miller called Menocchio was twice arrested, tried, and convicted on charges of heresy because, among the weightier items of evidence cited against him, he possessed a vernacular translation of the Bible, a book that might or might not have been a copy of the Koran, and a fatally loose tongue. "He was always arguing with somebody about the faith just for the sake of arguing," one witness testified against him. Like all victims of the Inquisition, Menocchio was required to name names, and when his answers were deemed unsatisfactory, he was tortured with the strappado. "Oh Jesus, oh Jesus," the old man cried as the inquisitorial notary took down his every anguished word. "Oh poor me, oh poor me." On his second conviction, Menocchio was sent to the stake as a relapsed heretic, but only after the vigilant bureaucrats of the Holy Office had pointedly reminded the local inquisitors of their sacred duty to burn the old man alive.[14] "[Y]ou must not fail to proceed with that diligence required by the gravity of the case, so that he may not go unpunished for his horrible and execrable excesses," went the merciless message from Rome, "but that he may serve as an example to others in those parts by receiving a just and severe punishment. Therefore do not fail to carry it out with all the promptness and rigor of mind demanded by the importance of the case."[15]

The burning of a talkative religious eccentric, as the Tedeschis readily concede, cannot be seen as an act of "moral justice" but they still see it as an example of "legal justice," at least as the notion was understood and applied in the sixteenth century. They urge us to look at the Inquisition in its historical context, an era in which Europe turned into "a persecuting society," according to R. I. Moore, with victims that included not only religious dissidents but anyone whose ancestry, appearance, sexual practices, or gender orientation was perceived to be different and therefore dangerous. To apply our modern notions of liberty and due process of law to the Inquisition, some historians suggest, is a pointless anachronism, and they insist that it is possible to explain the peculiarities of the past without condoning them. The proper role of the historian, as Moore explains it, is "with Spinoza, not to ridicule men's actions, or bewail them, or despise them, but to understand."[16]

Yet there is a terrible risk in dismissing of the Inquisition as an antique curiosity that can be safely contained between the covers of a history book. Precisely because the Inquisition provides a blueprint for building and operating the machinery of persecution—and a rationale for using the same apparatus to exterminate one's enemies—the Inquisition was and still is a danger to human life and human liberty.

So the Inquisition must be seen as both a fact of history and an idea that transcends history. Edward Peters, for example, argues that the inquisitions as they actually existed and operated—he pointedly insists on the lower case *i* and the plural noun—"were transformed by polemic and fiction into a myth" and then into "an indictment, by the modern world, of an earlier Europe for its crushing of the human spirit." The fact and the idea of the Inquisition are distinguishable, and that is what a revisionist historian like Peters insists that we must do.

But the Inquisition is more than a lens through which to look at the events of the far-distant past. Rather, as Peters reminds us, the Inquisition has come to be "woven tightly into the fabric of modern consciousness," and it has continued to inspire new generations of persecutors long after the last of the friar-inquisitors were dead and buried. In that sense, the inquisitorial idea has been at work in the world ever since it was first conceived in the thirteenth century, never more so than in the twentieth century and even in our own times.[17] Indeed, as we shall see, the inquisitorial apparatus was constantly improved and put to new uses against new victims even as the Inquisition faded into history.

The Inquisition first articulated and embraced the daring idea of eradicating all heresies and exterminating all heretics, an elastic term that came to include Jews, Muslims, homosexuals, radical priests, female mystics, and even the occasional midwife or miller whose eccentricities were unsettling to one inquisitor or another. "Several popes and kings in the high and late Middle Ages had the cast of mind to effect these holocausts," explains Norman F. Cantor in *Inventing the Middle Ages,* and only the primitive state of medieval technology and statecraft prevented them from doing so.

So the argument that the Inquisition was rather less ghastly than it aspired to be may be historically accurate, but it is morally sterile. The medieval inquisitors lacked only the means and not the will to rid the world of everyone they regarded as "heretical filth," and so Cantor concludes that "the indictment against the Middle Ages runs."[18]

Within a century after the last victim of the Spanish Inquisition was put to the flames, a new generation of inquisitors came to power in Europe. They enjoyed access to the technology of the twentieth century—railroads, chemical pesticides, automatic weapons, radio transmitters, and much else besides—and they swore themselves to serve rulers who enjoyed far more authority than any pope or king of the Middle Ages. But they embraced the same hateful idea that was the raison d'être of the Inquisition, and so they were able to update and automate the medieval equipment and set it into operation on an industrial scale. "The modern totalitarian state in Nazi Germany and the Leninist-Stalinist Soviet Union and its satellites was a realization of a medieval nightmare," writes Cantor. "The result was Auschwitz and the Gulag, World War II, and the death of at least twenty million civilians at the hands of the Nazi and Bolshevik governments."[19]

To be sure, the willingness to torture and kill one's fellow human beings because of some trivial difference in appearance or habit or belief hardly began with the Inquisition. The first heretic to be burned alive in Spain, for example, was Priscillian of Ávila, who was sent to the stake on charges of witchcraft in 383, more than a thousand years before the Spanish Inquisition came into existence. The persecutorial impulse—"the urge to purify the world through the annihilation of some category of human beings imagined as agents of corruption and incarnations of evil"—seems to be hardwired into Western civilization. Sad to say, human beings as a species have never failed to find reasons to regard one another with fear and loathing and thus to offer violence to one another.[20]

But the Inquisition transformed these ugly and tragic impulses into something vastly more powerful and thus more perilous by draping them in the trappings of law and theology and creating a bureaucracy to organize and administer the bloodshed. Once available, the inquisitorial toolbox could be put to use by any authoritarian regime with the will and the means to unpack and use it. "Here, then, was an engine so constructed that it might be turned effectually to any purpose," explains Coulton. "Good purpose or bad purpose depended only upon the policy or the caprice of the man or the group who had this tribunal at command."[21] The "engine" to which Coulton is referring is the medieval Inquisition, but his words apply with equal force to the lowercase inquisitions of the twentieth century and, as we shall see, the opening decades of the third millennium, too.

When a young SS officer named Adolf Eichmann (1906–1962) first showed up for work at the Main Office for the Security of the Reich in Berlin, he was promptly sworn to secrecy and then ushered into a locked room in the headquarters of the Gestapo in the ornate Prinz-Albrecht-Palais. "Then I saw what we would be doing," he later recalled, "and it gave me the creeps." What gave Eichmann the creeps, as it turns out, had nothing to do with the crimes against humanity for which he was later tried and hanged by the state of Israel. But it had everything to do with the machinery of persecution that had been borrowed from the Inquisition and put to use in Nazi Germany.

"We had to put the card files in alphabetical order," Eichmann told the Israeli police captain who interrogated him in advance of his trial. "It was all about Freemasons. We sorted and sorted. Always taking care to keep the right letters together, the C's with the C's and so on. I'd never even heard of the Freemasons, I had no idea what they were."[22]

Eichmann's reminiscences—yet another scene that must be described as Kafkaesque—reveal something important about the Inquisition and the long shadow that it casts across history. Like the friar-inquisitors who came before them, the dutiful bureaucrats who operated the Nazi version of the machinery of persecution were avid collectors of information, which they also gathered from spies, informers, and prisoners interrogated under torture. Both the Inquisition and the Nazi regime were fearful of any idea or practice that fell outside the narrow circle of dogma; thus, for example, both turned their attention to Freemasons, homosexuals, and Jews, among other victims. Both were obsessed with their self-appointed mission of imposing a rigid authoritarian order on an unruly world, always putting "the C's with the C's." Tragically, the similarities do not stop there.

When Eichmann was later transferred to what he called "the Jews department," he was handed a copy of Theodor Herzl's *The Jewish State* and told "to make an abstract of it to serve as an orientation booklet for the General SS"—a kind of latter-day inquisitor's manual. Even after Eichmann had been promoted to the upper ranks of the bureaucracy whose job it was to find and kill Jews, his underlings were still collecting and sorting index cards (*Judenkartei* or "Jew cards") that were "intended to identify every Jew living in the Reich," a task the Nazi regime deemed necessary "for a successful internal struggle against Jewry."[23]

Just as the Roman Inquisition was headquartered in the Vatican and the Spanish Inquisition was governed by *La Suprema* in the Palace of the Inquisition in Madrid, their counterpart in Nazi Germany was administered from a complex of stately buildings in Berlin, the same site where Eichmann was first assigned to sort index cards. Working under the command of a failed chicken farmer named Heinrich Himmler (1900–1945) who rose to the lofty rank of Reichsführer, the dutiful Nazi bureaucrats supervised the day-to-day operations of the secret state police (Geheime Staatspolizei, better known as the Gestapo), the criminal police, the security service of the SS, and the various other departments in charge of the mundane tasks required to carry out a well-organized genocide. Together they aspired to create and operate "an entirely integrated system of surveillance, reporting and arrests," according to historian and Holocaust survivor Saul Friedländer, with the ultimate goal of supplying "combustible material" for the crematoria.[24]

To accomplish these tasks, the Nazis used many of the same instruments of torture that would have been found in any inquisitorial dungeon. The Gestapo, for example, contrived its own version of the strappado by suspending the victim from a rope threaded through his or her handcuffs, and then dangling and jerking the victim at the pleasure of the questioning officer. The ordeal by water was applied by forcibly submerging the victim in a tub of cold water or by leaving the victim in a barrel of water placed outside in cold weather until he or she was nearly frozen, and the ordeal by fire was administered by use of a soldering iron.

The Nazis were enchanted with medieval legend and lore, as we shall see, but they were not content with medieval technology, and so they encouraged innovation and invention in the application of torture. A favorite technique of the Gestapo was to apply electrical shocks conveyed through wires attached to the penis and the anus of the victim. Like the Renaissance artisan who fashioned the Pear as a tool for the torture of heretics, some nameless German inventor in service to the Nazi regime devised a cunning little metal box with a thread-and-screw device that allowed the Gestapo torturer to slowly crush the testicles of his victim during questioning.

All the while, a female clerk-typist fulfilled the role of the medieval notary, taking down every word uttered by the victim of torture. A Gestapo doctor was occasionally summoned to the torture chamber, but for strictly functional rather than compassionate reasons: "[T]hey are not to render any medical aid, but only to determine whether the prisoner may still be beaten," reported the authors of *The Brown Book of the Hitler Terror* in 1933. "They are like the doctors of the Inquisition: the torture is stopped when there is a danger of the victim dying." Once the victim was revived, the questioning could begin again.[25]

The point of such devices and techniques was never merely to extract a confession of wrongdoing—the Nazis were perfectly willing to murder their victims without cause—but rather to compel the victim to name names. Thus, for example, one resistance fighter was kept alive and repeatedly tortured by the Gestapo over a period of more than two years only because his tormentors imagined that he would finally betray the names and whereabouts of other members of the underground. Only when the Nazis were finally convinced that there was nothing that he could or would reveal did the Gestapo finally put him out of his misery. But then, even a victim of torture who eventually consented to betray his comrades generally suffered the same fate.

Of course, it was not always necessary for the Gestapo to resort to torture to compel a man or woman to betray a friend or neighbor. Whether out of fear or malice or self-interest, a network of willing informers was available to the Gestapo as it had been to the Inquisition. Just as a woman working as a midwife might find herself denounced to the Inquisition as a witch by a jealous business rival, ordinary Germans were often willing to volunteer some damning item of information, whether real or invented, to the Gestapo. "Angry neighbors, bitter in-laws, and disgruntled work colleagues," states historian Eric A. Johnson, "frequently used the state's secret police apparatus to settle their personal and often petty scores."[26]

Again like the Inquisition, the Nazi regime refused to call any of its crimes by their rightful names. An ordinary beating was known in Gestapo

documents as "Rigorous Examination," and the more inventive and excruciating forms of torture were called "Especially Rigorous Interrogations."
Just as "relaxing" a condemned heretic meant burning him alive in inquisitorial jargon, the Nazis devised a whole vocabulary of euphemisms to refer
obliquely to the arrest, incarceration, and murder of their Jewish victims:
"deportation," "evacuation," "resettlement," and "redistribution" all meant
the same thing. The use of such circumlocutions is the best evidence that
those who participated in crimes against humanity during the Holocaust
knew exactly what they were doing and actively sought to cover it up.[27]
"This is a page of glory in our history," Himmler declared to a secret meet-
ing of SS generals in 1943, "which has never been written and is never to be
written."[28]

Indeed, the violence that Nazi Germany did to language was always intimately linked to the violence it did to its victims. A distinction was made
in official German documents between Jews who were assigned to "labor
service"—that is, slave labor on starvation rations, a kind of murder in slow
motion—and those designated for "special treatment." Yet the distinction
between these two fates was never spoken aloud by the bureaucrats who
decided between them. Only during his interrogation by an Israeli police
captain long after the war did Eichmann finally decode the phrase: "Special
treatment," he conceded, "was killing."And the whole ghastly enterprise
that resulted in the mass murder of six million Jewish men, women, and
children was concealed behind an oblique bureaucratic euphemism that
would have appealed to any grand inquisitor for whom the Latin phrases of
canon law provided a similar moral fig leaf: "The Final Solution of the Jewish Problem." [29]

The Strictures of Purity of Blood that were enacted in Spain in the fifteenth
century, as we have seen, represented an escalation in the war on heresy,
one that was based on blood rather than belief. Nazi Germany embraced
the same ominous notion in the so-called Nuremberg Laws, which were
announced by Adolf Hitler (1889–1945) at a Nazi party rally in that city in
1935. Thus did Judaism itself come to be regarded in modern Germany as
a blood crime for which the only proper punishment was death. In that
sense, the Nuremberg Laws can be seen as the first draft of the Holocaust

in much the same way that the canons of the Fourth Lateran Council were the "first sketch" of the Inquisition.[30]

The centerpiece of the Nuremburg Laws was the Reich Citizenship Law, which formally withdrew the legal rights of citizenship from the Jewish population and reduced them to the status of "subjects" of the Third Reich. A second element was the Law for the Protection of German Blood and Honor, which criminalized sexual contact of any kind between Jews and non-Jews. As the law was later applied in German courts, not only intercourse but also "mutual masturbation" and even kissing were regarded as criminal acts. And, as if to add insult to injury, the Reich Flag Law adopted the swastika-marked banner of the Nazi party as the national colors of Germany and solemnly forbade any Jew from raising the German flag. With the announcement of these decrees, and the steady accumulation of other anti-Jewish laws aimed at the "purification" of Germany, the Nazis provided themselves with the legal rationale for their war on the Jews.[31]

Behind the legalese of the Nuremberg Laws can be seen the recrudescence of the same visceral anti-Semitism that had blighted medieval Europe and prompted some of the worst excesses of the Spanish Inquisition. According to the ideologues of the Nazi regime in Germany, starting with Adolf Hitler himself, Jews were an alien and malignant element that had infiltrated Christian civilization and must now be ruthlessly excised. They were condemned as poisoners and parasites, both subhuman and superhuman, an existential threat not only to Germany but to the whole world. Just as the Inquisition sought to rid Christendom of "heretical filth" by every available means, Nazi Germany now declared total war on the Jews.

Jews were demonized as ravening beasts whose appetites prompted them to stalk their human prey. Thus did the Nuremberg Laws prohibit Jews from employing German women under the age of forty-five on the assumption that a younger woman would be at risk of sexual assault by her Jewish employer. "The Jew systematically defiles the maidens and women of Aryan peoples," shrilled one of the "orientation bulletins" issued by the SS to its rank and file, thus priming them for their crucial role in the Holocaust. "He is equally driven by cold calculation and uninhibited animal lust."[32]

At the same time, Hitler saw the Jews as both guileful and powerful. He characterized them as agents of a vast international conspiracy bent on world domination, sometimes working their will as a cabal of bankers and sometimes under the banner of Bolshevism—"the 'gold' and the 'red' internationals"—but always with the goal of overmastering and destroying Western civilization. "[W]e must recognize that there is no good or bad Jew," insisted Hitler. "He is a Jew: he is driven only by one single thought: how do I raise my nation to become the dominating nation?"[33]

So the Nazis looked on the Jewish population of Germany—an accomplished and highly assimilated community—as both dangerous criminals and a source of contamination and disease. They were neither shy nor subtle in announcing their intention to punish the Jewish people for their imaginary crimes. "Without fear, we want to point the finger at the Jew as the inspirer, the author, and the beneficiary of this terrible catastrophe," ranted Nazi propaganda chief Joseph Goebbels (1897–1945) during a public address in 1937. "Look, this is the enemy of the world, the destroyer of cultures, the parasite among the nations, the son of chaos, the incarnation of evil, the ferment of decomposition, the visible demon of the decay of humanity." In his private journal, Goebbels was even more explicit: "This Jewish pestilence must be eradicated," he wrote. "Totally. None of it should remain."[34]

The image of Jews as pests and parasites is yet another borrowing from the vocabulary of medieval anti-Semitism, but it took on an entirely new and wholly literal meaning in Nazi Germany. Zyklon B, the brand name for the pellets of prussic acid used to kill Jewish men, women, and children in the gas chambers at Auschwitz and other death camps, was originally designed for use as an insecticide for delousing garments and disinfecting freight cars. Ironically, Zyklon B was invented by a Nobel Prize–winning Jewish industrial chemist who managed to escape from Germany in 1933 and did not live to see the use of his invention to murder his fellow Jews, including some of his own blood relations.

None of Adolf Hitler's hateful ideas about Judaism were wholly new or unique. Christians had been forbidden to employ Jewish wet-nurses in the Middle Ages, as we have seen, and sexual contact between Jews and non-Jews was prosecuted under the medieval laws against bestiality. The Nazi iconography of the Jew—and even the specific words and phrases of the sputtering diatribe delivered by Goebbels in 1937—was borrowed from the cracked and yellowing tracts of medieval anti-Semites. The Nuremberg Laws of 1935 can be traced all the way back to the Jewry Law of 1268: "The Jews are deprived of the protection of their natural rights and condemned to eternal misery for their sins." But, as we shall see, the Nazi regime was capable of accomplishing what even the most visionary medieval anti-Semites could have only dreamed of doing.[35]

After the enactment of the Nuremberg Laws in 1935, the Nazi bureaucracy promptly turned itself to the task of identifying and marking Jews. Like the Spanish Inquisition, which issued certificates of blood purity to Old Christians and ascertained the degree of Jewish blood in the veins of *conversos,* the Gestapo studied baptismal records and other public archives to determine the racial purity of the German population. Here, too, the Nazis updated the old inquisitorial methods by setting up such pseudoscientific institutions as the Reich Office for Kinship Research and the Institute for Racial Science and Ethnology, and pressing anthropologists and geneticists into service in making the deadly distinctions between "full" Jews (*Volljuden*) and fractional Jews (*Mischlinge*). Any man, woman, or child with a single Jewish grandparent (known as "a *Mischlinge* of the second degree") was at risk of arrest and execution, but "for most party members and officials," writes Eric A. Johnson, "anyone with a drop of Jewish blood was a Jew."[36]

Many of the *Mischlinge,* like the *conversos* of Spain, were professing Christians, either because of their own conversions or because they were descendants of converts. Cardinal Eugenio Pacelli (1876–1958), then serving as secretary of state in the Vatican and later to reign as Pope Pius XII, echoed the admonitions issued by the Church when the Spanish Inquisition started burning *conversos* who insisted that they were earnest converts to Christianity: "The Holy See takes this occasion to add a word on behalf of those German Catholics who themselves have gone over from Judaism to the Christian religion or who are descended in the first generation, or more remotely, from Jews who adopted the Catholic faith," Pacelli wrote in a note to the German *chargé d'affaires* in Rome in 1933. Tragically, "a word" was all that the Vatican was able to muster, then or later, although some of the clergy were willing to risk their lives to shelter a few Jews in convents and monasteries during the worst years of the Holocaust. The Church itself made peace with Nazi Germany and turned a blind eye to the murder of both Jews and converted Christians of Jewish ancestry.[37]

Thanks to the assimilation and intermarriage of German and other European Jews that began in the nineteenth century, discerning a Jew from a non-Jew was even more difficult in Nazi Germany than it had been in medieval Europe, and so the "Jew badge" of medieval usage was revived in Nazi Germany in the form of a yellow Star of David with the word *Jude* (Jew) imprinted in black stylized lettering that was meant to suggest the Hebrew alphabet. Later, the same Jew badge was used throughout occupied Europe: *Jood* appeared on the badges used in Holland, for example, and *Juif* in France. By 1941, every Jewish man, woman, and child over the age of six in Nazi Germany was required by law to wear the Star of David, and it was a crime in itself to conceal the star with a handbag or a folded newspaper. Again, we are reminded of the Inquisition, which punished any convicted heretic who failed to prominently display the "heretic's cross" and relied on its own network of informers to track down every offender.

Jewish men, women, and children were subjected to increasingly brutal measures that were expressly designed to identify them as Jews and isolate them from ordinary Germans. Along with the wearing of the yellow star, all Jews were required to append the name Abraham or Sarah to their given names unless they were already known by names that the Nazi regime deemed to be recognizably Jewish, a list that included such rarely used biblical names as Absalom and Ahab. They were required to post signs that marked their businesses as Jewish-owned, and their passports and identity cards were stamped with the telltale letter *J*. As a practical matter, the new visibility exposed Jews to insults and assaults on the public streets, but the Nazi authorities actually discouraged such acts of impromptu violence because it only interfered with their ambitious plans to rid Germany of its Jewish population.[38] "Violent mob anti-Semitism must be avoided," one Nazi officer commented in a secret memo. "One does not fight rats with guns, but with poison and gas."[39]

Just as Jewish *conversos* in Spain were banned by law from various institutions and occupations, Jews in Germany were now excluded from enrollment in public schools and universities, employment as civil servants, the practice of law or medicine, and ownership of farms. They were forbidden to work in the media or the entertainment industry, and later they were refused entry to cinemas, cabarets, circuses, concert halls, museums, libraries, swimming pools, bathhouses, and ice-skating rinks. They were still permitted to ride trains, but they could not enter dining cars or sleeping cars. Various streets and even whole districts were eventually declared off-limits to living Jews, and defunct Jews were denied burial in German cemeteries. The small and ever-diminishing remnant of Jews who survived in Germany after the commencement of Allied bombing during World War II was denied access to bomb shelters.

The Nazis repeatedly and intentionally followed the example of medieval anti-Semitism in general and the Inquisition in particular. Shortly after the Nazis came to power in 1933, for example, ceremonial book-burnings were organized in Berlin and elsewhere around Germany; some twenty thousand volumes, many of them by Jewish authors ranging from Sholem Asch to Stefan Zweig, were tossed on the bonfires by torch-bearing Nazi youth in Berlin, and thousands more were burned in other cities. The notoriously pornographic Nazi newspaper *Der Stürmer* published a special issue in 1934 devoted to the age-old blood libel: "The Jewish Murder Plot Against Non-Jewish Humanity Is Uncovered." A Nazi propaganda film released in 1941, *The Eternal Jew,* was a remake of the legend of the Wandering Jew. Ominously, the medieval ghetto was put back into use in twentieth-century Europe, although the walled-off Jewish districts in Lodz, Vilna, Warsaw, and elsewhere in German-occupied lands were only holding areas for Jewish men, women, and children awaiting transit to the death camps.[40]

Nazi Germany also learned a valuable lesson from the Inquisition when it came to turning persecution into a paying enterprise. Germany systematically looted its Jewish victims by compelling them to sell their land, businesses, artwork, jewelry, and stock at nominal prices, confiscating their homes when they were arrested and "deported," and imposing collective fines to be paid by the Jewish population, as when the Jews were made to pay one billion marks for the replacement of window-glass smashed during the state-sponsored pogrom in 1938 known as *Kristallnacht* or Night of the Broken Glass. The Nazi regime charged its Jewish victims for conveying them in cattle cars to the death camps at the "standard rate for third-class travel," that is, four *pfennigs* per kilometer with children traveling free of charge. Even the corpses of dead Jews were a source of revenue for Nazi Germany: gold dental work was pulled from the mouths of dead Jews, melted down into ingots, and sent to the Reichsbank in Berlin.[41]

All the while, Nazi Germany also followed the example of the Inquisition by draping itself in the thin fabric of "legal justice" and thus rationalizing its worst crimes as the dutiful observance of law. Since the Nuremberg Laws had formally stripped the German Jews of the rights of citizenship, the stateless Jews—according to the reasoning of German jurists—could be arrested, imprisoned, tortured, and murdered without offense to German law or legal procedure. "The Jews were placed outside of the German community because of the laws," explained one Gestapo commander by way of defense at his war-crimes trial. "This was indeed wrong, as I now know, but at the time it was the law of the land."[42]

At least one of the weapons used against Spanish Jewry during the Inquisition was considered but later rejected by Nazi Germany. The Nazis toyed with the idea of the mass expulsion of the Jewish population, a project assigned to the so-called Central Office for Jewish Emigration under Adolf Eichmann. Some Jewish families were allowed to leave Germany during the early years of the Nazi regime but only after they had been looted of their property and wealth.

The Nazis soon realized, however, that expulsion was an unsatisfactory answer to "the Jewish question." After all, no country in the world was willing to accept Jewish refugees from Germany in significant numbers, and the Nazis opposed the creation of a Jewish homeland in Palestine because of their fear that it would serve as a sactuary and a base of operations for Jewish resistance. After Germany invaded Poland in 1939—the tripwire that finally triggered the outbreak of the Second World War—the rapid conquest of new territory in both eastern and western Europe meant that Jews who had managed to escape in the years before the war suddenly found themselves once again on German-occupied soil.[43]

So Nazi Germany decided that the "Final Solution of the Jewish Problem" required a still more radical approach: the murder of every Jewish man, woman, and child within its long reach. The resources that the Nazi regime had assembled to identify and mark the Jewish population—the index cards, the Jew badges, the passports stamped with the red letter *J*—now enabled the Nazi security apparatus to round up its victims with speed and efficiency. Like the Spanish inquisitors, the Nazis did not inquire whether people now forced to call themselves Abraham or Sarah were, in fact, practicing Jews; all that mattered in the end was whether he or she possessed at least one Jewish grandparent.[44] *"In extremis,* when the Inquisitors extend their torches or the Nazis tip the canisters of Zyklon B gas," explains historian David Gitlitz, "this external definition is the one that counts."[45]

Jews were not the only victims of the new inquisitors in Nazi Germany. Gypsies (as the Sinti and Roma people were called) and homosexuals, too, were regarded by the Nazis as suitable only for extermination. Communists and socialists, partisans and Christian resisters were also arrested, tortured, and killed by Nazi Germany and its collaborators. And the death toll included countless millions who died in the various countries that Germany oppressed during World War II, whether because they were punished for acts of resistance or selected for reprisal executions, or simply because of the privation, maltreatment, and bombardment that were the inevitable consequences of German occupation. Even a full-blooded German who suffered from a disease or a disability was subject to sterilization under the Law for the Prevention of Genetically Diseased Offspring, and the technology that would be used to kill Jews was first tested on German mental patients.

But the fate of the Jews was something different and something unique, not only because of the sheer numbers who were murdered—and not only because of the nightmarish cruelties and indignities that accompanied their murders—but also because the war against the Jews was seen by Nazi Germany, just as the Inquisition had regarded the war on heresy, as "a confrontation of apocalyptic proportions." In that sense, the Nazis managed to convince themselves that they were acting in the interest of both moral *and* legal justice when they committed what the rest of the world called crimes against humanity. Hitler himself plainly announced that he intended to exterminate the Jewish people, and he explained why he believed the war against the Jews was a holy war.[46] In a public address delivered in the Reichstag on January 30, 1939, he declared:

> I have often in my life been a prophet, and usually people laughed at me. Let me be a prophet again today: If international financial Jewry, in Europe

and beyond, should succeed in plunging the nations into another world war, the result will not be the Bolshevization of the world, and thus the victory of Jewry, but the destruction of the Jewish race in Europe.[47]

The inquisitorial apparatus of the Nazi regime was essential for carrying out the crusade that Hitler preached to the German people. But the theology of the Inquisition was also essential in motivating German police officers, soldiers, bureaucrats, and various other workers (and their collaborators in various occupied countries) to carry out mass murder on an industrial scale. Surely it takes more than an order from on high to give an ordinary human being the will and the stomach for killing other human beings—men and women, children and babies—hour after hour, day after day, year after year.

By following the example of the Inquisition, which had demonstrated how to dehumanize the victim as nothing more than "heretical filth" and, at the same time, how to demonize the victim as a "traitor to God," the Nazi regime was able to convince its population—or, at least, the hundreds of thousands of men and women who participated in the Holocaust—that torture and murder could be seen as a proud and righteous act.

So Nazi Germany serves as the worst-case scenario of what can happen when the resources of a modern totalitarian state are put in service to a hateful idea. From the moment the Nazi party came to power in Germany, the slanders against the Jewish people were advertised by some of the most gifted propagandists of the twentieth century. The Jews were "the most evil world enemy of all times," as Hitler himself put it, and "will forever remain beneath humankind, as the rats are beneath the animals," according to one German newspaper, "parasites, poison carriers, and subversive scroungers." Meanwhile, all the moving parts of the machinery of persecution were being carefully assembled and lubricated, and once kicked into operation, they did not cease until Germany was utterly defeated by force of arms.[48]

For some Germans assigned to operate the gas chambers at Auschwitz, then, the task was no more unsettling than delousing a shipment of old clothing; after all, wasn't Zyklon B intended for use on pests and parasites? For other Germans (and their collaborators in various occupied countries), it was an opportunity to take revenge on "the most evil world enemy of all times," which may explain why young men in uniform took such apparent pleasure in afflicting their victims with wholly gratuitous acts of violence. Thus, for example, German soldiers were seen to use torches to burn off the beards of observant Jewish men who were being sent to die in the gas chambers, just as the executioners of the Spanish Inquisition had done to their own victims before burning them alive.[49]

When Cecil Roth's *The Spanish Inquisition* was first published in 1937, the author added an urgent note to reflect events that were taking place even as the book was being set into type. "The Spanish Inquisition was until yesterday an antiquarian diversion," wrote Roth in a note dated September 1937. "The events of the past few years, and above all of the past few months, have converted it into a dreadful warning." Roth felt obliged to point out that his work "is not intended as a satire on present-day conditions," and he observed that the Inquisition seemed to have risen from its grave to stalk the earth yet again.[50]

"Its spirit has recently been revived outside Spain," wrote Roth, "and in certain parts of the world has achieved in the course of the present generation a triumph ostensibly more instantaneous and more remarkable than Torquemada could ever have hoped."[51]

Roth's words were inspired by a remarkable spectacle that was being presented to the Russian people and the rest of the world in a Moscow courtroom—the trial of a handful of Old Bolsheviks who had been present at the creation of the Soviet Union and now stood accused of conspiring to destroy it. So shocking was the sight of the Russian Revolution turning on its own makers that even the highest leadership of Nazi Germany found it noteworthy. "Again a show trial in Moscow," Goebbels wrote in his journal on January 25, 1937, and he did not fail to notice that the principal defendants were Jewish in origin. "Maybe Stalin does want to smoke the Jews out."[52]

The Nazis did not feel obliged to observe any fussy legal niceties before murdering their victims, nor did they deem it advantageous to stage what came to be known as a show trial, that is, a meticulously stage-managed trial that served as a tool of propaganda rather than an act of "legal justice." Even when Hitler resolved to exterminate a rival faction of the Nazi party in 1934, thus consolidating the machinery of terror in the hands of the SS, he ordered his former comrades to be seized and murdered without any formalities, much less a trial, an event known as the Night of the Long Knives. The same principle applied when it came to the murder of his various other victims, ranging from German mental patients to the Jewish population of Europe.*

Joseph Stalin (1879–1953), by contrast, seemed to take special pleasure in the spectacle of the show trial, a distinctive feature of the Soviet version of the machinery of persecution. Apart from such moments of high drama, the Soviet secret police (known at various times as the Cheka, the GPU, the OGPU, the NKVD, the MVD, and the KGB) used many of the same tools and techniques as the Gestapo. The program of repression directed against the Soviet population lasted from the outset of the Bolshevik Revolution in 1917 until long after Stalin's death in 1953, and its victims must be counted in the tens of millions. But the apparatus was occasionally kicked into high gear when whim or circumstance inspired Stalin to focus on one or another of the bogeymen who haunted his imagination. The Soviet equivalent of the Witch Craze took place between 1936 and 1938—a sustained spasm of violence that has come to be called the Great Terror— and Stalin, a former seminary student, assumed the power and function once reserved to the grand inquisitors.

The rationale for the Great Terror was the supposed discovery of a diabolical conspiracy whose object was nothing less than the destruction of the Soviet Union, a notion that echoes the rationale of the Inquisition in its long war on heresy. The conspirators were accused of putting themselves in service to the worst enemies of the Bolshevik Revolution, including Nazi Germany and imperial Japan. The reality is that "the whole alleged plot was a vast cycle of frame-ups by Stalin and his entourage," all of it intended to eliminate his rivals and strengthen his authority as the absolute dictator of

---

* The only notable exception was the trial of Marinus van der Lubbe (1909–1934), the young man who was convicted at a show trial and then beheaded on charges of setting fire to the Reichstag, a crime that provided the Nazis with a pretext for doing away with the last vestiges of democracy in Germany in 1933. Whether van der Lubbe acted alone—and whether his co-conspirators, if any, were Nazis or Communists—is still debated. His codefendants, all Communists from Bulgaria, were acquitted, a fact that prompted Hitler to create the Nazi tribunal known as the People's Court to ensure the conviction of those few victims whom the regime decided to offer a trial.

the Soviet Union. Significantly, the arch-villains in Stalin's show trials were men whose roles in the Bolshevik Revolution had been equal to or arguably even greater than his own, including Leon Trotsky (1876–1940)*, Grigory Zinoviev (1883–1936), Lev Kamenev (1883–1936), and Nikolai Bukharin (1888–1938).[53]

The Moscow show trials, like the autos-da-fé of the Inquisition, can be seen as high ceremonials in which arch-heretics were tried and punished as a caution to the rest of the population. Just as Cathars were put on display in the cathedrals and public squares of medieval Europe to abjure their false beliefs before going to the stake, a few prominent Communists were given an opportunity to confess to wholly imaginary crimes in the chandelier-hung Hall of Columns before being returned to the underground cells of the NKVD where death sentences were carried out with a single shot to the back of the head. Such were the improbable scenes that obliged Cecil Roth to warn his readers that *The Spanish Inquisition* was a work of history rather than parody.

World public opinion—not excluding the Nazi leadership and especially the cadres of the Communist party in Russia and elsewhere throughout the world—was staggered when the celebrated heroes of the Bolshevik Revolution stood up in open court and confessed to every imaginable crime against their comrades and Stalin himself. "I, together with Zinoviev and Trotsky, was the organizer and leader of a terrorist plot which planned and prepared a number of terroristic attempts on the lives of the leaders of the government and the Party of our country," declared Kamenev. "For ten years, if not more, I waged a struggle against the Party, against the government of the land of Soviets, and against Stalin personally." The confessions were so surreal that the defendants themselves seemed to understand the Kafkaesque quality of the scene they were made to play.[54]

"Who will believe a single word of ours?" asked one of the defendants in

---

* Leon Trotsky was in exile from the Soviet Union during the Great Terror, but the "cloven hoof of Trotsky" was detected by the prosecutors in the various conspiracies that figured in the Moscow show trials. Trotsky and his son, Lev Sedov, were declared by the Soviet judges in 1936 to be "convicted by the evidence" and "subject, in the event of their being discovered on the territory of the U.S.S.R., to immediate arrest and trial." Trotsky was assassinated in Mexico in 1940. Quoted in People's Commissariat, 130, 180.

the course of his confession, perhaps in a brave effort at irony. "Who will believe us, we who are facing the Court as a counter-revolutionary gang of bandits, as allies of fascism, of the Gestapo?"[55]

Even as the trials were in progress—and long after they were over—comparisons were made between the Great Terror and the Inquisition. Indeed, the analogy has come full circle, and some historians now describe the medieval Inquisition as a "proto-Stalinist" phenomenon. Just as the Cathars and Waldensians were condemned as "heretical filth," the Old Bolsheviks on trial in Moscow were condemned as "filthy scum." The torturers in service to the NKVD, like their counterparts in the Gestapo, resorted to such old-school techniques as the strappado, which was known as "the swallow" in the parlance of the Soviet secret police. And the Moscow show trials help us understand how wholly innocent men and women—Catholic priests no less than Bolshevik commissars—could be made to confess to any grotesque misdeed that an interrogator might dream up, whether by promise of leniency, application of torture, or threat of death.[56]

The defendants in the Moscow show trials were charged with acts of wrongdoing that would have been recognizable as violations of law if they had actually taken place—not only assassination, sabotage, and treason but "every possible sordid and shameful crime," as the notorious Soviet prosecutor, Andrei Vishinsky (1833–1954), put it. Not unlike the accounts of sodomy and sex orgies and infant cannibalism that enlivened the proceedings of the Inquisition, most of the allegations against the defendants in the Moscow show trials were wholly imaginary. Yet the defendants were willing to stand up in open court and confess to even the most unlikely and implausible accusations against them, a fact that has always baffled those who struggle to make sense of the spectacle.[57]

The threat of torture and death is the most obvious explanation, of course, but a different and more illuminating one can be found in the single most striking similarity between the Inquisition and the Great Terror—the religiosity of the cult of personality that was erected around Stalin. The Soviet Union was avowedly atheist, of course, but Stalinism in practice took on all the trappings of religious true belief; thus, for example, the long list of malefactions charged against the defendants in the Moscow show trials included the crime of "sacrilege." Soviet citizens were required to conform to the party line in the same way that good Catholics were required to embrace the dogma of the Church, a principle that even such adversaries as Stalin and Trotsky apparently agreed upon.[58] "None of us desires or is able to dispute the will of the Party," declared Trotsky in the years before his estrangement from Stalin and the resulting exile and assassination. "Clearly, the Party is always right."[59]

The Inquisition demanded that accused heretics recant and repudiate their supposed heresies before they could be readmitted to the Church, and the Communist party required the same of the defendants in the show trials. "Their constant avowals of political sin, their admissions that Stalin was, after all, right," explains Robert Conquest in *The Great Terror*, "were based on the idea that it was correct to 'crawl in the dust,' suffer any humiliation, to remain in or return to the Party." Some defendants were such true believers that they were willing to confess to crimes that they did not commit in the deluded hope that their own death and disgrace would serve some higher purpose. The point is made by Arthur Koestler in *Darkness at Noon,* a novel whose principal character is a composite of several of the Old Bolsheviks who figured in the Moscow show trials.[60] "Some were silenced by physical fear . . .; some hoped to save their heads; others at least to save their wives or sons . . . ," Koestler writes of the fictionalized victims of Soviet terror. "The best of them kept silent in order to do a last service to the Party, by letting themselves be sacrificed as scapegoats."[61]

Indeed, a certain complicity between the inquisitors and their victims—and sometimes a glimmer of subtle but defiant wit—can be discerned in the transcripts of the show trials as the players speak the lines that had been prepared for them, sometimes with Stalin's active participation as a kind of executive producer. The interrogation of Kamenev, an Old Bolshevik and an early rival of Stalin, by Vishinsky, Stalin's handpicked prosecutor, in the 1936 trial, for example, may have been scripted, but the leading actor in the scene succeeds in injecting a note of irony into his performance:

VISHINSKY: What appraisal should be given the articles and statements you wrote in 1933, in which you expressed loyalty to the party? Deception?

KAMENEV: No, worse than deception.

VISHINSKY: Perfidy?

KAMENEV: Worse!

VISHINSKY: Worse than deception; worse than perfidy—find the
                word. Treason?

KAMENEV: You have found the word![62]

After five days of sputtering rhetoric by the state prosecutor and staged confessions by the defendants in the first of the great show trials in 1936, Vishinsky asked for the death penalty—"I demand that dogs gone mad should be shot, every one of them!"—and the judges dutifully delivered the foreordained verdicts. They adopted yet another inquisitorial flourish when they not only sentenced the defendants to "the supreme penalty" but also decreed that "all property personally belonging to them [is] to be confiscated." After the public executioners had finished their work, the slugs were dug out of the victims' skulls, carefully labeled to identify which bullet had killed which Bolshevik, and preserved as relics somewhere in the archives of the NKVD—a final gesture of piety by the Soviet inquisition.[63]

The Moscow show trials featured only the most famous victims, the ones whose public confession and humiliation Stalin regarded as a useful propaganda tool. Indeed, a curious intimacy existed between the persecutors and the persecuted, many of whom had struggled together in earlier, happier days when they victimized their adversaries rather than one another. Thus, Stalin himself not only decreed in advance that a particular defendant was to be found guilty but also edited the formal verdict before it was announced in court: "It needs stylistic polishing," he explained to a subordinate about one such document. And some of the defendants were bold (and desperate) enough to scribble personal appeals for mercy to their former comrade-in-arms who now sat in the Kremlin.[64]

Bukharin, for example, had sought to put himself back in favor by penning a paean titled "A Poem About Stalin in Seven Cantos" and sending it to Stalin. After his conviction in the last of the show trials in 1938, Bukharin begged Stalin to permit him to take his own life with an overdose of morphine rather than take a bullet in the back of the head. Although the plea went unanswered—and Bukharin was shot like a dog, just as Vishinsky demanded—Stalin kept Bukharin's last note in a desk drawer for the rest of his life: "Koba," the Old Bolshevik had written, using Stalin's revolutionary alias, "why do you need my life?"[65]

By far the greatest number of victims of the Great Terror, however, consisted of obscure party cadres, officers of the Red Army, apparatchiks of the Soviet bureaucracy, and members of the intelligentsia whose loyalty to the Stalinist regime was doubted, if only by Stalin himself. Countless thousands of men and women were arrested and punished in absolute secrecy, whether by summary execution or by long sentences at slave labor in the vast complex of camps and prisons called the Gulag, a Russian acronym for the bureaucracy blandly known as the Main Camp Administration. The Great Terror afforded the ruler of Soviet Russia an opportunity to purge his regime of all its enemies—actual or potential, real or imagined—just as the Inquisition had provided both a theological rationale and a prosecutorial toolkit that allowed the king of France to eliminate the Knights Templar and the king of Spain to eliminate the Jews and the Jewish *conversos.*[66]

The Great Terror, in fact, can be seen as the Soviet counterpart of the medieval Inquisition in many of its particulars. The Soviet inquisitors, for example, devised their own set of useful codes and tropes to avoid speaking plainly about their atrocities. Arrest was called "isolation," confinement in a labor camp was "the second category" of punishment, and death was called "the first category." The victims of the Great Terror were commonly demonized as "enemies of the people," "counter-revolutionaries," and "wreckers," all of which were used as loosely as "heretic" or "witch" had been during the Middle Ages. The purging of such malefactors was described as a process of "ongoing purification" by which the Soviet Union resolved to rid itself of "vermin" and "pollution."[67]

Just as a Cathar was called a "traitor to God," a victim of the Great Terror might be condemned as a "traitor to the fatherland." Although they were often accused of committing (or conspiring in) acts of terrorism, their real crime was a thought-crime; the twentieth-century heretics of the Soviet Union were "deviationists" who had strayed, whether willfully or inadvertently, from the ever-shifting party line. Like the *conversos* of Spain, whose conversion to Christianity was seen as inauthentic by the Inquisition, the victims of the Great Terror were condemned as insincere Communists who "crawl[ed] stealthily into socialism," according to Stalin, "even though [they] 'secretly did not mean it.'"[68]

No one was safe from the Soviet inquisitors during the Great Terror, an era in which "the Revolution devoured its children"—sometimes figuratively and sometimes quite literally. Children were encouraged to inform on their parents, parents on their children, wives on their husbands, and they were praised when they did so. One aggrieved student denounced his teacher for assigning too much homework and was singled out for admission to an elite school in Moscow. Once a man or woman had been seized by the secret police, his or her relations were at heightened risk of arrest as a "Member of the Family of a Traitor to the Fatherland," a newly coined status crime that recalls the penalties imposed by the Inquisition on the children and grandchildren of convicted heretics.[69]

Not even the triggermen and torturers of the Great Terror were beyond the reach of the Soviet inquisition. Thus, the chief of the Soviet secret police, Genrikh Yagoda (1898–1938), was himself arrested and sentenced to die, a moment of rough justice for the man who had directed the work of the agents, jailors, and executioners during the first two years of the Great Terror. "I fall to my knees before the People and the Party," pleaded Yagoda, who must have known all too well that his words were pointless, "and ask them to pardon me, to save my life." Yagoda's plea was unavailing—his life, like those of countless thousands of his victims, ended with a bullet in the back of the head—and he was helpless to protect his wife, parents, siblings, and even more distant relatives, all of whom were arrested by Yagoda's successor.[70]

A vast network of spies and snitches—and the fact that some other victim would be tortured into naming names—put every Soviet citizen at risk. A history professor named Konstantin Shteppa, for example, first came to the attention of the secret police when he was overheard to describe Joan of Arc as "nervous and highly strung," a notion that was held to be at odds with the then-prevailing party line, which regarded the Maid of Orléans as "a heroine of a national resistance movement." Shteppa was arrested in 1938 and subjected to fifty days of "severe interrogation." Although he managed to survive, he later recalled the atmosphere of fear and distrust that was the whole point of the Great Terror: "I was naturally sorry for my friends, but I was not only sorry for them," said Shteppa, "I was afraid of them."[71]

The men and women who operated the machinery of persecution in the Soviet Union—just like the rank and file of the Inquisition or, for that matter, the Holocaust—were assured (and reassured themselves) that they were serving the interests of "legal justice." But only a few victims of the Great Terror were afforded even the parody of due process that constituted a show trial. Most were condemned to prison, slave labor, or death by order of the roving three-man tribunals, known as troikas, that operated across Russia in much the same manner as the flying squads of the medieval Inquisition, passing sentence on their victims in absentia and "without benefit of judge, jury, lawyers, or trial." On September 30, 1937, by way of example, a troika set up operations in a labor camp in the Karelian Republic and issued 231 sentences in a single day.[72]

"Assuming a ten-hour workday, with no breaks," observes Anne Applebaum in *Gulag*, "less than three minutes would have been spent considering the fate of each prisoner."[73]

By the end of 1938, after some 750,000 men and women had been put to death, Stalin ordered an abrupt halt to the Great Terror. He was apparently satisfied that the ranks of the party, the armed forces, the bureaucracy, and the intelligentsia had been sufficiently purged of wreckers and deviationists to preserve his absolute authority over the Soviet Union. Or perhaps a better explanation is that Stalin finally awakened to the fact that his counterpart in Berlin was actively preparing for war, and the time had come for him to do the same.

Even if the show trials and summary executions now abated, however, the Soviet secret police and the Gulag continued to operate without pause through Stalin's death in 1953, and Soviet citizens in the countless millions continued to be arrested and sentenced to hard (and sometimes killing) labor. Although the absolute number of victims is still debated, as many as 18 million men and women may have passed through the Gulag between 1929 and 1953, and Applebaum proposes a total of 28.7 million when all Soviet victims of forced labor are included. The death toll, which surely numbers in the millions, is simply uncountable.

According to such calculations, the Soviet inquisitors were Stakhanovites who outperformed not only their medieval counterparts but also their rivals across the fighting front in Nazi Germany. But the core idea of the Stalinist war on "wreckers" and "deviationists"—as with Nazi Germany's war against the Jews—had occurred to the popes and grand inquisitors of the Middle Ages seven centuries earlier. In that sense, the Stalinist and Nazi models of the machinery of persecution are unique only in their industrial-scale production capacity and not in their purpose.

Still, we are morally obliged to ask if any distinctions can be drawn between the two great secular inquisitions of the twentieth century, if only to extract some meaning out of these nightmares of history. The question has been even more hotly argued than the Inquisition itself, and the debate forces us to confront the vexing issue of whether we are, as Spanish poet and philosopher George Santayana famously suggested, condemned to repeat the past. To ignore the question renders history itself meaningless.

On the surface, Nazi Germany and Stalinist Russia can be seen as a pair of opposites, each the mirror image of the other. Both Hitler and Stalin were dangerous and even deluded visionaries, capable of acting out of true belief even when realpolitik might have suggested a compromise of principles. On a less exalted level of comparison, the Gestapo and the NKVD resorted to the same tools and techniques in service to their masters, including even the use of the medieval "queen of torments," the reliable old strappado. Indeed, many of the parallels between these two totalitarian states owe something to the fact that the machinery of persecution can be readily repurposed and put to use by any totalitarian regime in the service of any ideology.[74]

Other similarities between Nazi Germany and Stalinist Russia are even more striking because they seem to transcend the purely practical problems that all persecutors are forced to address. Both the Gestapo and the NKVD understood that ordinary men and women can be made to confess to extraordinary acts of wrongdoing if only they are properly tortured, which explains why both resorted to the strappado. But some other explanation must be sought for the fact that both Hitler and Stalin, like Torquemada, singled out Jews for special treatment. Here, too, is a clue to perhaps the single most dangerous component of the inquisitorial project—the willingness to punish anyone whose faith, ethnicity, nationality, sexual orientation, or physical appearance is somehow different from that of those who enjoy the power to decide what is permitted and what is forbidden.

To be sure, Soviet anti-Semitism was deeply rooted in history. Imperial Russia had its own long and ugly tradition of Jew hatred, including official segregation in the so-called Pale of Settlement, state-sponsored mob violence in the form of pogroms, and exclusion of Jews from land ownership, the professions, the universities, and the government. The revolutionary movement in Russia had attracted Jewish participation precisely because it offered an opportunity to overthrow a system that had oppressed the Jewish people for centuries. But the stain of anti-Semitism can be detected in the Stalinist regime no less than in the tsarist one it replaced, and it was no accident that Jewish defendants figured prominently in the Great Terror, a fact that did not escape the attention of Joseph Goebbels.

The story is told that the execution of Kamenev and Zinoviev was sometimes reenacted for the amusement of Stalin in the privacy of his dacha, with his own bodyguard in the role of Zinoviev, "begging for Stalin to be fetched and then crying out 'Hear O Israel.'" Even after the Great Terror subsided, Yiddish culture in general and Jewish writers in particular were repeatedly targeted by the Soviet secret police. After the defeat of Nazi Germany, a new wave of persecution was directed against the Jewish population of the Soviet Union, and Jewish figures in the Communist regimes of various satellite countries in Eastern Europe were put on display in a whole new round of show trials.[75]

A new purge was being prepared for the Jewish population of the Soviet Union in the last years of Stalin's life. The signs of the impending catastrophe could be read between the lines in *Pravda,* where the phrase "rootless cosmopolitans" was adopted as a code for "Jews"—yet another repurposing of the figure of the Wandering Jew—and Jewish men and women were pointedly identified in print by their original family names in addition to their adopted revolutionary ones. The medieval slander of the Jew as a poisoner was revived in a campaign against the Jewish doctors serving on the medical staff of the Kremlin, who were accused of conspiring to murder the Soviet leadership en masse. Only the death of Stalin in 1953 prevented these seeds of anti-Semitism from flowering into yet another Great Terror.

It is also true, however, that both Hitler and Stalin singled out various other victims for mass arrest, deportation, and execution. Hitler persecuted homosexuals, Gypsies, Jehovah's Witnesses, and otherwise good Germans who suffered from birth defects and mental illness; Stalin persecuted the landowning peasantry called the kulaks, the Polish officer corps, and various national minorities—the Balts, Chechens, and Tartars. What the victims actually believed and what they actually did were ultimately less important than the fact that they provoked fear and loathing in these two powerful men. Here, then, is yet another example of how the inquisitorial apparatus can be repurposed and redirected at will: "[T]he task of the totalitarian police is not to discover crimes," as Hannah Arendt puts its, "but to be on hand when the government decides to arrest a certain category of the population."[76]

What Hitler and Stalin had in common was the same aspiration that animated the first inquisitors—the simple but deadly notion that it was both possible and desirable to rid the world of anyone whom the regime deemed to be unworthy of life. Significantly, Hitler, Stalin, and Pope Innocent III all used the word *filth* to apply to a different set of victims, but each saw himself as the ordained agent of purification, each arrogated to himself the absolute power to decide who lived and died, and each was convinced of both the rightness and the inevitability of his role in history. If all three were arguably suffering from symptoms of megalomania, it is also true that all of them found a way to validate their madness in the inquisitorial idea.

On a few other points, though, useful distinctions can and should be made between Nazism and Stalinism. Like the medieval and Roman Inquisitions, the Stalinist regime insisted only on correct belief— at least in theory if not always in practice—and was willing to entertain the prospect that "deviationists" might recant their thought-crimes and return to the party line; but the Nazis, like the Spanish inquisitors, saw Jewish blood as a crime for which no expiation was possible. Again like the first inquisitors but unlike their Nazi counterparts, the Soviet secret police more often imprisoned and enslaved their victims rather than simply murdering them. And the Soviets felt obliged to preserve a faint semblance of "legal justice," even if it was strained and sometimes wholly symbolic—a burden of conscience that never seemed to trouble the German police and soldiers who served in the death squads or the men and women who staffed the death camps.

"No one tried and sentenced the Jews in Nazi-occupied Europe, but the vast majority of inmates in Soviet camps had been interrogated (however cursorily), tried (however farcically) and found guilty (even if it took less than a minute)," observes Anne Applebaum. "Undoubtedly, the conviction that they were acting within the law was part of what motivated those working within the security services."[77]

Yet there is a certain moral risk to making such fine distinctions in the culpability of torturers and executioners. We might conclude that one practitioner of terror is more egregious than all the others and thus more worthy of our condemnation. But if the long history of the Inquisition teaches us anything at all, it is that the machinery of persecution, once switched on, cannot be easily slowed or directed, much less stopped. Nor does the machinery require the high technology of a modern industrial state; little inquisitions have been conducted by impoverished regimes throughout the Third World, and we have seen for ourselves in recent years that it is quite possible to carry out a campaign of genocide in a jungle or a desert with nothing more than clubs and machetes.

Above all, we cannot and should not try to distance ourselves from any of these inquisitions by reassuring ourselves that no abuse of "moral justice" could occur in the American democracy. The naming of names as a test of earnest confession is hardly unique to the Inquisition, and neither is the insistence on referring to "harsh interrogation techniques" when we are talking about torture. We need only pause and reflect on the plain fact that at least one of the tools that was used for six centuries by the hooded friar-inquisitors has also been used more recently by young men and women in American uniforms. We call it "waterboarding," they called it "ordeal by water," but torture under any name is still torture, even if the inquisitorial habit of mind has always preferred a euphemism over plain speech.

8.

AMERICAN INQUISITION

There is prodigious danger in the seeking of
loose spirits. I fear it, I fear it. Let us rather blame
ourselves. . . .

ARTHUR MILLER,
The Crucible

Only once did the Inquisition operate on the soil of England, and
then only because the pope prevailed upon a reluctant English
king to grant permission to a flying squad of inquisitors to complete the destruction of the Knights Templar. Like other Templars across
Europe, some 229 English members of the order were arrested and interrogated under torture on the same charges of heresy, blasphemy, and sexual
perversion that resulted in the burning of so many of their fellow warrior-
monks. With the exception of the Templars, the only other English victims
of the Inquisition were a few inoffensive merchants and sailors who showed
up in a Spanish port with an English translation of the Bible in their baggage and thus faced prosecution for the heresy of being Protestants.

The fact remains, however, that England had its own sorry tradition of
terror in the name of God. The Jewish community of York, sheltering from
a mob in the keep of a castle, was massacred en masse in 1190. A man who
had converted to Judaism was burned at the stake as a heretic in Oxford in

1222, and every Jew in England was expelled by royal decree in 1290, more than two hundred years before the same idea occurred to Ferdinand and Isabella. The preaching of the Lollards, who resembled the Waldensians in their defiance of the Roman Catholic church and their insistence on the right to translate the Bible into vernacular languages, prompted Parliament to adopt the death penalty as "a settled punishment for heresy" in 1400. The persecution of religious dissenters ran so deep in England in the six-teenth century that one London goldsmith made a bequest in his will "to buy faggots for the burning of heretics."[1]

Women accused of witchcraft fared no better in England than they did on the continent during the Witch Craze. Even without the assistance of the Inquisition, the civil courts were not reluctant to pass judgment on poor, eccentric, or troubled women who were imagined to have trafficked with the Devil and worked various kinds of diabolical mischief on their neighbors. So it was that the land of the Magna Carta also produced such horrors as the burning of a pregnant young woman on charges of sorcery in 1555—she suffered a miscarriage at the stake, and the baby, still alive, was "tossed back into the flames as an offspring of Satan."[2]

Defenders of the Inquisition like to point out that England, so proud to have avoided the worst excesses of the inquisitors, was hardly kind or gen-tle when it came to the use of torture and capital punishment. "The Span-ish Inquisition was certainly no worse than contemporary secular courts in other countries," writes one historian, "including England." Defendants who refused to plead guilty or not guilty when charged with a crime un-der English common law, for example, were subjected to a form of torture called *peine forte et dure* ("strong and hard pain") in which stones were piled on the victim's chest until he or she answered or died. Convicted criminals were still being drawn and quartered—and hangings still served as a grue-some form of popular entertainment—well into the nineteenth century. Not until 1868, in fact, did the practice of public hanging come to an end in England.[3]

Along with the common law and certain notions of civil liberty, all of these uglier traditions were carried to the New World in the baggage of the Pilgrim Fathers. Indeed, the Puritans were true believers and theocrats who sought religious liberty for themselves but refused to grant the same liberty to anyone else. One of the dirty little secrets of American history is the fact that the Quakers were ruthlessly persecuted in the Massachusetts Bay Colony in the seventeenth century. Quaker men and women were flogged for their defiance of Puritan law—like the Cathars, they refused to recognize clerical authority and declined to take oaths on religious principle—and they were ultimately ordered to leave the colony on pain of death. A few of the Quakers who defied the order of expulsion were tried and hanged by the civil courts of Massachusetts as thought-criminals in a brave new world.

It was the first American inquisition, but not the last.

"Who torments you?" is the simple question that set off a witch panic in Salem Village in the winter of 1692, the single most notorious example of how the machinery of persecution can be made to operate at any place and time, even here in America.

A clutch of bored teenage girls in the settlement of Salem began to spend their idle hours in the company of a household slave named Tituba, who amused them with some of the "tricks and spells" she recalled from her childhood in Barbados. Back home in their own strict households, the girls began to act out in strange and unsettling ways, barking like dogs and braying like donkeys, screaming and stamping their feet to drown out the words of the family at prayer. Surely these outbreaks of adolescent hysteria were evidence of nothing more than a guilty conscience; after all, if Quakerism was a capital crime in the Massachusetts Bay Colony, the consequences of dabbling in black magic must have shaken the hearts of the Puritan girls who played in Tituba's kitchen.[4]

"Who torments you?" asked the credulous ministers and magistrates who assembled in Salem to investigate the curious phenomenon. Surely, they thought, the grotesque behavior was best explained as demon possession at the behest of a cult of Devil worshippers, and they wanted the girls to name names. At first, the girls were silent, but when their interrogators began to suggest a few likely culprits—including not only Tituba, an obvious suspect, but also various other citizens of Salem, all eccentric or unpopular—they saw a way to spare themselves by blaming others. They readily affirmed that Tituba was one of their tormentors, and they went on to denounce the wife of a common laborer who was thought to be "shrewish, idle, and above all slovenly," and then a widow who was suspected of taking her handyman as a lover before marrying him. The list of accused witches and wizards grew ever longer, ranging from a five-year-old girl to an eighty-year-old man.[5]

"They should be at the whipping post," said a skeptical farmer named John Procter about the chorus of accusers. "If they are let alone we should all be devils and witches."[6]

Procter's anxiety, as it turned out, was well founded. After the first few accused witches were formally put on trial in civil court on charges of sorcery, both Procter and his wife were denounced by the girls, who claimed that the diabolical couple was invisibly afflicting them even as they sat in the courtroom. "Why he can pinch as well as she!" one of the girls cried out. Such was the quality of "spectral evidence"—more accurately described by author Marion L. Starkey as "the crazed fantasies of wenches in their teens"—on which the judges were content to find the Procters and other defendants guilty of the crime of sorcery. A few of the accused witches managed to escape the gibbet by offering their own abject confessions, and when prompted by the prosecutors, the confessors were pressed to denounce yet others, the same chain of betrayal that had so often operated the gears of the inquisitorial apparatus in other times and places.[7]

"There are wheels within wheels in this village," one of the characters in Arthur Miller's *The Crucible* is made to say, "and fires within fires."[8]

As with the Inquisition, not even spouses were safe from each other during the Salem witch trials. A woman named Martha Cory fell under suspicion when she reacted to the first news of the adolescent coven in Tituba's kitchen by laughing out loud. Her eighty-year-old husband, Giles, was called as a witness at her trial, where he allowed that he found it hard to pray when she was around—an ambiguous remark, as was all his testimony, but damning words in the judges' ears. Later, Giles himself was accused of witchcraft, and—perhaps because he had been so easily manipulated into betraying his wife—he fell silent in the face of the magistrates. So Giles was subjected to the traditional English torture of *peine forte et dure* in an effort to extract a plea from the stubborn old man; by refusing to answer as stones were piled on his chest, he effectively prevented the court from exercising its jurisdiction over him. According to tradition, if not the historical record, Giles Cory uttered only two words as he was crushed to death: "More weight."[9]

Other victims did not succeed in cheating the public executioner, and they were put to death by hanging on Gallows Hills, a spectacle designed to warn any other witches who had gone undetected against the consequences of trafficking with the Devil. The girls who had accused them in the first place were brought along to taunt the "firebrands of hell" one last time. When the cart carrying the condemned prisoners to one such hanging was momentarily stuck on the steep road, the girls shrilled that they could see the spectral figure of the Devil at work yet again. But the Devil was powerless to prevent the hangings, the last auto-da-fé to be conducted on American soil.[10]

Soon after the hangings, some of the Puritan witch-hunters found themselves afflicted yet again. What tormented them now, however, was a troubled conscience rather than an invisible agent of the Devil. Another 150 victims of the witch panic, some as young as eight years old, were still awaiting trial on accusations that were based on nothing more than slander, gossip, and the rantings of frightened and vengeful children. Now, at last, a few sensible voices could be heard over the clamor of the accusers: "It is better that ten suspected witches should escape than one innocent person should be condemned," observed the renowned Puritan preacher Increase Mather (1639–1723), neatly reversing the bloodthirsty declaration of the Abbot of Cîteaux during the Albigensian Crusade ("Kill them all; God will know his own").[11]

A new rule was now applied by which "spectral evidence" was excluded and the confessions previously extracted from various terrified defendants were put aside. Suddenly, the cases against the accused witches "melted like moonshine at daybreak," as Marion L. Starkey writes in *The Devil in Massachusetts*. A general pardon was issued, and the remaining defendants were released, two of them carrying babies who had been born while they were behind bars. Even Tituba was delivered from jail, although she was promptly sold into slavery to a new master to raise money for the prison fees that every defendant was obliged to pay before being discharged. One of the pardoned women who was unable to scrape up the money died in prison, a debtor rather than a convicted witch.[12]

As the years passed, some efforts at reparation were undertaken. Five years after the hangings, a day of fasting was declared in Massachusetts as a gesture of regret and repentance. On that occasion, Samuel Sewall, one of the nine judges of the Court of Oyer and Terminer who had sent the accused men and women to the gallows, offered an apology for "bring[ing] upon ourselves the guilt of innocent blood." Ann Putnam, one of the adolescent accusers, waited until 1706 to acknowledge that the "spectral evidence" she had given "was a great delusion of Satan" and to "earnestly beg forgiveness of all those whom I have given just cause of sorrow and offence." In 1711, the sum of 598 pounds and 12 shillings was appropriated by the state of Massachusetts for distribution to the surviving victims and their descendants. The following year, in a final and purely symbolic act of contrition, the excommunication of Giles Cory was formally revoked by the First Church of Salem.[13]

If the Salem witch trials of 1692 can be compared to the Inquisition, they amount only to an inquisition in miniature. The whole ordeal lasted fifteen months, only fourteen women and six men were put to death, and—even counting the men, women, and children who were imprisoned rather than executed—the total number of victims was equal to a single day's work by the friar-inquisitors at an auto-da-fé during the Spanish Inquisition. None of the grand inquisitors was ever moved to the act of moral justice that Judge Sewall performed when he stood up in church and apologized for the spilling of "innocent blood."

But the points of similarity should not be overlooked. Like the Inquisition, the Salem witch trials were set in motion by whispered rumors and fabricated evidence; they were fueled by confessions extracted under the threat of torture and execution; their victims were demonized, quite literally, as agents of Satan; and the whole enterprise was carried out not by a lynch mob but by constables, magistrates, jailors, and executioners on the public payroll, all of whom acted in the name of the state as the ultimate guardian of law and order. Indeed, the most alarming fact about what happened in Salem in 1692 is the sure conviction of the civil authorities that extraordinary means were justified because of the dire threat posed to the sleepy village of Salem—"the Rendezvous of Devils," as one panic-stricken preacher put it, "where they Muster their infernal sources."[14]

The Inquisition, as we have seen, was brought into existence on the same dire assumptions and for the same weighty purpose—it was "an organ of repression," according to Giorgio de Santillana, "conceived for situations of emergency." What constitutes an emergency, however, is always in the eye of the beholder. For Pope Innocent III, it was the pale and emaciated Cathar *perfectus;* for Torquemada, it was the bishop whose great-grandfather may or may not have been Jewish; for Cardinal Bellarmine, the Hammer of Heretics, it was a scientist who insisted that the earth revolved around the sun. For the town fathers of Salem Village, the emergency took the carnal form of any man, woman, or child whom Ann Putnam and her hysterical girlfriends might denounce as a witch.[15]

More recently, of course, America has confronted other emergencies, some of them quite real and others that exist, as the witches of Salem existed, only in our imaginations. And here we confront the deadly and inevitable peril of the inquisitorial impulse: sometimes we do not know the difference between an authentic threat and an imaginary one until it is too late.

America was at war with a flesh-and-blood enemy in 1942 when Franklin Delano Roosevelt issued Executive Order 9066, a presidential decree that empowered military commanders to arrest, imprison, and confiscate the property of every man, woman, and child of Japanese ancestry along the Pacific seaboard from Washington to California. As early as 1939, the FBI had begun preparing a list of "enemy aliens," and the first arrests were made on the same day that Pearl Harbor was attacked by the Japanese armed forces. Even infants with "one drop of Japanese blood" were to be sent to the internment camps: "A Jap's a Jap," declared the general who directed the operation. No hearings were held to determine whether, in fact, the victims of Executive Order 9066 actually posed a threat to national security, although the Supreme Court ruled in 1944 that the internment was justified by "pressing public necessity." Not a single Japanese-American was arrested for an act of sabotage or espionage, however, and the 120,000 internees were wholly innocent of wrongdoing.[16]

Imperial Japan's military threat against America was real, of course, but the fear of Japanese-Americans turned out to be wholly imaginary.

Precisely the same phenomenon was still at work in America only a few years later when Senator Joseph R. McCarthy (1908–1957) and the congressmen who served on the House Un-American Activities Committee (better known as HUAC) undertook a crusade to defend the country against what they claimed was a vast conspiracy to establish "Communist totalitarian dictatorship throughout the world" through "treachery, deceit, infiltration" as well as "espionage, terrorism and any other means deemed necessary," according to the Internal Security Act of 1950.[17]

By 1950, China was ruled by a Communist regime, the United States was at war against North Korea, the Soviet Union had acquired nuclear weapons with the assistance of a few spies in the Manhattan Project, and the threat of Communism was plausible enough to plant a terrifying idea in the collective imagination of American government, media, and business— "the fear of a Red tank on Pennsylvania Avenue," as Lillian Hellman put it. But the red-baiting politicians and propagandists of the McCarthy era were not only afraid of Soviet aggression. Like the inquisitors of medieval Europe and the witch-hunters of colonial Salem, they sought to portray Communists and their fellow travelers in America as invisible and inhuman, "almost a separate species of mankind," or, even worse, something both pestilential and apocalyptic, "the germ of death for our society," a "political cancer" that had infected "every phase of American life."[18]

So a new model of the machinery of persecution was tinkered together and kicked into operation in America. No one was tortured or burned alive by HUAC and its senatorial counterpart, of course, but some of the old inquisitorial tools were unpacked and put to use. Testimony was taken in secret from anonymous informants, known euphemistically as "friendly witnesses," as the congressional tribunals ranged across America, and then used in public hearings that functioned as the latter-day American equivalent of the auto-da-fé, some of them televised. Abject confessions were much sought after: "I want to humbly apologize for the grave error which I have committed," pleaded writer Nicholas Bela, sounding like one of the defendants in the Moscow show trials, "and beg of you to forgive me." Potential targets were hounded tirelessly by congressional investigators and federal law enforcement officers—like the FBI agent who showed up at Charlie Chaplin's front door, a stenographer at his side, ready to interrogate the famous man on his own doorstep.[19]

Above all, the men and women who were called to testify by HUAC and other congressional committees were judged not by their willingness to confess their own membership in the Communist party, past or present, but by their readiness to denounce their fellow members. Indeed, a Communist who had recanted and abjured his or her party membership was also obliged to identify those who had merely attended a party gathering or made a contribution to a so-called Communist-front organization, the modern version of the medieval crime of fautorship. Precisely like the tribunals of the Inquisition, HUAC subscribed to the principle that the failure of a witness to betray friends, relations, and co-workers rendered the witness's own confession defective and unacceptable. To make matters worse, if a witness under subpoena was willing to answer some but not all questions—to confess his or her own political sins but not the sins of others—the witness forfeited the legal protection of the Fifth Amendment, and so the refusal to name names was treated as a crime in itself.

"The ultimate test of the credibility of a witness," declared Congressman Donald L. Jackson, a member of HUAC, "is the extent to which he is willing to cooperate with the Committee in giving full details as to not only the place of activities, but also the names of those who participated with him in the Communist Party."[20]

The result of the Communist witch-hunt was not only an "orgy of informing," as journalist Victor Navasky puts it, but "a Cecil B. DeMille–sized one." Indeed, HUAC was especially successful when its attention turned to the entertainment industry. Actor Sterling Hayden gave up the name of a former lover to the tribunal. A screenwriter named Martin Berkeley (*My Friend Flicka*) may have set a record when he offered a total of 161 names. Director Elia Kazan paid for an advertisement in the *New York Times* to explain his reasons for naming names and to encourage others to follow his example. Among the "unfriendly" witnesses who refused to name names was playwright Lillian Hellman, who declared that betraying others to save herself would be "inhuman and indecent and dishonorable" and famously told the committee that she "cannot and will not cut my conscience to fit this year's fashions." Hellman summed up the moral climate of the whole sordid era in the title of her memoir: *Scoundrel Time*.[21]

Like the victims of the historical Inquisition and its other modern equivalents, the men and women who were targeted during the McCarthy era were not guilty of any wrongful acts; rather, they were accused only of thought-crimes. McCarthy and his fellow witch-hunters, like the grand inquisitors of the Middle Ages, defined a circle of approved beliefs and associations and condemned anyone who, by their lights, had crossed the line into heresy. "It was not enough to be American in citizenship or residence—one must be American in one's thoughts. And lack of right thinking could make an American citizen un-American," explains Garry Wills. "These latter can be harassed, spied on, forced to register, deprived of government jobs, and other kinds of work."[22]

The American red-baiters, like every other inquisitor, were quick to appeal to every ugly prejudice in order to turn public opinion against their victims. Ten of the first nineteen witnesses called by HUAC in its investigation of Hollywood were Jewish, and a stench of anti-Semitism hung over the proceedings. When a planeload of celebrities flew to Washington to show their support for the Hollywood witnesses, for example, Congressman John Rankin rose on the floor of the House of Representatives to reveal their given names, precisely the same ploy being used at that very moment by *Pravda* when it printed the Jewish-sounding names of the victims of Stalinist purges. Danny Kaye's real name was David Daniel Kaminsky, the congressman announced, and Melvyn Douglas was actually Melvyn Hesselberg. "There are others too numerous to mention," ranted Rankin. "They are attacking the committee for doing its duty to protect this country, and save the American people from the horrible fate the Communists have meted out to the unfortunate Christian people of Europe."[23]

Some victims of the Communist witch craze ended up behind bars; the so-called Hollywood Ten, for example, were writers and directors (including Dalton Trumbo and Ring Lardner Jr.) who were cited for contempt of Congress and sent to prison after they appeared before HUAC but refused to answer questions about their political beliefs. Victims who readily confessed their own membership in the Communist party or "Communist-front" organizations were punished when they refused to incriminate others; novelist Dashiell Hammett, for example, spent six months in a cell because he refused to divulge the names of contributors to a defense fund for victims of McCarthyism.

By far the greatest number of victims managed to stay out of prison but were fired from their jobs because their names appeared on one of several blacklists whose existence was officially denied. Some were already in ill health when the subpoenas were served, and the stress has been blamed for accelerating their deaths. A few were so demoralized that they took their own lives; one victim committed suicide on the night before he was scheduled to testify before HUAC, declaring himself to have been "assassinated by publicity."[24]

Because the House Un-American Activities Committee sought so many of its victims in the entertainment industry, the Communist witch-hunt of the McCarthy era is refracted in the work of more than a few celebrated writers. Bertolt Brecht's *Galileo,* first staged at a small playhouse in Los Angeles in 1947, characterizes Galileo as a moral and physical coward, a fact that has prompted some critics to observe that "the Galileo of his drama is Zinoviev or Bukharin . . . dressed up in historical costume." When Galileo is asked why he went on his knees before the Inquisition, Brecht makes him say: "I recanted because I was afraid of physical pain." And his depiction of Galileo prefigures Brecht's own strange and tortured performance when he was subpoenaed by HUAC only weeks after the premiere of *Galileo.*[25]

Brecht, in fact, was among the first witnesses summoned to testify at the 1947 hearings on Communist influence in the entertainment industry, and he followed the last of the Hollywood Ten to the witness stand. Rather like Galileo before the friar-inquisitors of the Roman Inquisition, Brecht did not openly defy his interrogators. Instead, he took advantage of a thick accent and an imperfect command of English to confound them, and his testimony began to resemble an Abbott and Costello routine.

Q: Have you attended any Communist party meetings?
A: No, I don't think so. . . .
Q: Well, aren't you certain?
A: No—I am certain, yes.
Q: You are certain you have never been to Communist party meetings?
A: Yes, I think so. . . .
Q: You are certain?
A: I think I am certain.[26]

But when Brecht was finally cornered on the question of whether he had ever applied for membership in the Communist party, he suddenly demonstrated his mastery of the English language: "No, no, no, no, no," Brecht declared. "Never." He also denied that his writings were "based on the philosophy of Marx and Lenin," a disingenuous answer that amounted to the disavowal of his life's work. At the end of the session, the committee chairman thanked him for his cooperation and cited him as "a good example" to the unfriendly witnesses. Then, quite literally, Brecht caught the next plane out of town and spent the rest of his life behind the Iron Curtain.[27]

An openly defiant commentary on the Communist witch-hunt can be read between the lines of *The Crucible* by Arthur Miller, a play that was first produced just as the McCarthy era was reaching its zenith in 1953. "I speak my own sins," says the character John Procter, who pointedly refuses to betray his friends and neighbors to save his own life, "I cannot judge another." When Miller himself was subpoenaed by HUAC, he offered to testify about his own flirtation with the Communist party—"I have had to go to hell to meet the devil," said Miller—but he refused to name names, a stance that earned him a contempt citation. Later, he warned about the dangerous consequences of seeing demons where none exist.[28] "No man lives who has not got a panic button," observed Miller, "and when it is pressed by the clean white hand of moral duty, a certain murderous train is set in motion."[29]

None of the victims of the Communist witch-hunt were, in fact, the kind of "wreckers" they were made out to be by McCarthy and his gang of red-baiters. About the worst crime that HUAC could imagine was the insinuation of Communist propaganda into the movies that the Hollywood studio system cranked out in the 1930s and 1940s, but even these offenses existed only in the eye of the beholder. Apart from the much-abused *Mission to Moscow*—a war movie made at the encouragement of the White House at a time when the Soviet Union was an ally of the United States and doing most of the fighting against Nazi Germany—the red-baiters were unable to discover a single instance in which the party line had found its way into a Hollywood movie. "It was hard to insert proletarian class consciousness," cracks historian Ellen Schrecker, "into such vehicles as *Sweetheart of the Campus, Charlie Chan's Greatest Case,* or *Our Blushing Brides.*"[30]

The actors, directors, and writers whose names ended up on the Hollywood blacklist were the most publicized victims of the McCarthy era. But diplomats, bureaucrats, librarians, university professors, classroom teachers, labor union officials, and serving officers of the armed forces—almost all of them obscure and unnoticed by the media—were also the objects of persecution as the tribunals of the Communist witch-hunt ranged across the country in search of subversives. The Hollywood blacklists were notorious, but even the New York City school system maintained a little list of its own. "From Hollywood to Harvard," writes Schrecker, "the anticommunist crusade blighted thousands of lives, careers, and marriages."[31]

One such victim was a man named Milo Radulovich, a twenty-seven-year-old Air Force reserve officer who lived in a little town in Michigan and held down two part-time jobs while studying physics at the University of Michigan. He was taking care of his two young children while his wife was at work when a pair of Air Force officers showed up at his door. Radulovich was officially notified that he had been denounced as a "security risk" and now faced a dishonorable discharge on the grounds that his father subscribed to a socialist newspaper and his sister had once participated in a demonstration to protest the refusal of a Detroit hotel to rent a room to the African-American singer, actor, and activist Paul Robeson. "I had done nothing," Radulovich later explained. "Guilt by blood, of all things."[32]

When Radulovich consulted an attorney, he was advised to "disavow" his father and sister in order to save himself. Fatefully, the Radulovich case caught the attention of CBS journalist Edward R. Murrow, who featured the young soldier's dilemma in a report on the news program *See It Now.* A month later, the Air Force officially exonerated Radulovich, and Murrow went on to prepare the famous broadcast that finally called Joe McCarthy to account for his groundless accusations against innocent Americans. The Senate formally censured McCarthy for his excesses in 1954, and the inquisitorial machinery in America finally began to sputter and stall.

Still, the American inquisition, like its Spanish counterpart, was not easy to dismantle. Arthur Miller, for example, was not subpoenaed by HUAC until 1956, and his citation for contempt of Congress was upheld by a federal judge in 1957. The Hollywood blacklist was not decisively broken until 1960, when Dalton Trumbo was openly credited as the screenwriter of *Spartacus*. HUAC remained in formal existence until 1975, although—rather like the Roman Inquisition—it was renamed as the House Committee on Internal Security in 1969 in a belated and ultimately futile effort to repair its appalling reputation.

Even now that HUAC and McCarthy himself are both long gone, however, the inquisitorial impulse is still deeply imprinted on the American democracy, and the machinery of persecution remains available. And whenever new events and personalities strike us as a Rendezvous of Devils, we are tempted to hit the panic button.

A revival of *The Crucible* was staged on Broadway in the spring of 2002. After the final lines of dialogue were spoken—"You are pulling Heaven down," cries John Procter, "and raising up a whore!"—the audience was presented with a spectacular stage effect. The elaborate wooden set was made to collapse upon itself, and the last piece of debris to fall was artfully designed to resemble a fragment of the distinctive façade of the World Trade Center, a familiar image borrowed from the daily newspapers and news broadcasts. The play itself, of course, uses the Salem witch trials as a stand-in for the McCarthy era, and now the producers were reminding us of yet another and more recent moment in American history.[33]

The visual reference to the horrific events of September 11, 2001, in a performance of *The Crucible* was a daring gesture, especially when human remains were still being dug out of the ruins at Ground Zero. But it was also a Brechtian moment that forces us to ponder the linkage between the war on witchcraft in colonial America, the Red Scare of the McCarthy era, and the newly declared war on terror in contemporary America, all of which are examples of "what can happen when fears and anxieties [are] combined to create hysteria in public and political life," as journalist Haynes Johnson observes in *The Age of Anxiety*. The same "devil's brew of fear, suspicion and paranoia," along with a dollop of "cynical political opportunity," created the historical Inquisition and now threatens to set the machinery of persecution back into operation.[34]

To be sure, the attack on America on September 11 was just as real as the one that took place on December 7, 1941. And it prompted the same sense that the ground had shifted under our feet, the same righteous indignation, the same call for vengeance against the aggressor. Thus did George W. Bush preach a "crusade" to "rid the world of evildoers." But it is also true that America hit the panic button in the aftermath of both attacks, and the result has been the victimization of men and women who pose no real threat to America. Like the 120,000 Japanese-Americans who were arrested and interned during World War II, thousands of men and women whose only apparent crime is their Arabic or Islamic ancestry have been targeted for arrest, incarceration, and interrogation. Americans of every race, color, and creed also pay a price whenever a new inquisition is cranked up.[35]

More than a few unsettling parallels can be drawn between the medieval Inquisition and the modern war on terror. The FBI reportedly considered a plan to secretly monitor the sales of Middle Eastern foods in grocery stores in order to detect the presence of Muslim terrorists in America; the FBI later denied the report, but the whole notion echoes the readiness of the Spanish Inquisition to arrest young men of Muslim ancestry who were seen eating couscous. Federal law enforcement officers were, in fact, "ordered to search out and interview Muslim and Arab men between the ages of eighteen and thirty-three," an *inquisitio generalis* that was intended to flush out a vast and secret conspiracy of alien terrorists. So far, however, only a handful of malefactors have been detected, even fewer have been convicted of a crime, and the conspiracy that seemed so real and so urgent on September 12, 2001, may have existed only in our collective imagination.[36]

Like the canons of the Fourth Lateran Council, the Patriot Act and related federal legislation enacted in the wake of 9/11 have provided a legal framework for the war on terror. Secret trials were mandated for foreign nationals whom the federal authorities sought to deport—the real targets, of course, were men and women from Muslim countries—and the evidence on which the government relied could be withheld from their attorneys. Of the 13,740 foreigners who were prosecuted under these new laws, according to the American Civil Liberties Union, "not a single one of these individuals was ever publicly charged with terrorism." Of the estimated 5,000 foreign nationals who were rounded up by federal agents during the investigation of the attack on the Pentagon and the World Trade Center—most of them from Arab or South Asian countries, and nearly all of them Muslim—"not one was convicted of a terrorist crime."[37]

The parallels are even more striking when it comes to American military and intelligence operations in Afghanistan, Iraq, and elsewhere around the world. Like the war on heresy in the Middle Ages, the war on terror has been the occasion for coining new and evasive phrases: "extraordinary rendition," for example, refers to kidnapping a suspect off the streets and sending him to a secret prison in a "third country" where he can be subjected to "harsh interrogation techniques," a euphemism for torture. Indeed, the technique now called waterboarding is precisely the same one that the friar-inquisitors of the Middle Ages called the ordeal by water, and the same one used by the Gestapo and the NKVD. The spirited debate among attorneys, politicians, and pundits over whether waterboarding is or is not torture is yet another Kafkaesque moment in the long history of the inquisitorial enterprise.*

The inquisitorial prisons, where victims could be held for years or even decades and tortured at will, find their counterparts in the Abu Ghraib prison in Baghdad and the detention facilities at the U.S. military base at Guantánamo Bay in Cuba. The notorious photograph of a naked and shackled Iraqi prisoner taken in a cellblock at Abu Ghraib features a specific item of apparel that was a favorite of the friar-inquisitors—the Iraqi man has been crowned with a conical "dunce's cap" that resembles the *coroza* worn by victims of the Spanish Inquisition at an auto-da-fé. In both cases, the point of the headgear was to degrade and humiliate the victim.

When it comes to the war on terror, "legal justice" means something quite different than what we expect in an American courtroom. A presidential decree signed two months after the 9/11 attacks subjected the "enemy combatants" in U.S. custody to the jurisdiction of secret military tribunals that were empowered to judge and punish the prisoners without a public trial, the assistance of an attorney, the right of appeal, or any of the other presumptions and protections guaranteed under American constitutional law. Like the victims of the Inquisition, the defendants are not even en-

---

* Wordplay in the war on terror extends to the Patriot Act, whose formal title reduces to the acronym USA-PATRIOT: "Uniting and Strengthening America by Providing Appropriate Tools Required to Intercept and Obstruct Terrorism." Congressman Bob Barr observed that "he hoped the bill's supporters spent as much time on the bill itself as they did coining the acronym." Quoted in Bovard, 89.

titled to be told what crimes they are accused of committing or what evidence the government has relied upon in arresting and holding them. And yet, even though the prosecutors had relieved themselves of these burdens of procedural due process, they did not bestir themselves actually to try and convict their prisoners.

"We've cleared whole forests of paper developing procedures for these tribunals, and no one has been tried yet," a former government attorney told the *New York Times* in 2004. "They just ended up in this Kafkaesque sort of purgatory."[38]

Hyper-vigilance in the war on terror is not limited to foreigners from Muslim countries and Americans of Muslim faith. The Patriot Act permits the government to "read your medical records, screen your credit card bills, search your home or business without telling you, patrol your Internet use, wiretap your phone, spy on you and your house of worship, examine your travel records, inspect your bookstore purchases, snoop on your library records, [and] monitor your political activities," according to a civil rights group in opposition to the act, and all without regard to race, color, creed, religion, or national origin. Law enforcement maintains "watch lists" and "no-fly lists" that have been used, for example, to detain a couple of middle-aged activists with the thoroughly American names of Jan Adams and Rebecca Gordon when they tried to fly to Boston to visit relatives. A project known by the Orwellian phrase "Total Information Awareness"— a database of electronic surveillance that is the high-tech equivalent of the notarial transcripts of the Inquisition and the index card files of the twentieth century—has been described by one of its critics as "the most sweeping threat to civil liberties since the Japanese-American internment."[39]

Like the Inquisition, the war on terror is conducted throughout the world by a vast army of civilian and military personnel, all of them intent on collecting and preserving data of all kinds in the hope that it might someday yield the name of an actual terrorist. The Department of Homeland Security, newly created in the wake of 9/11, is an aggregation of federal agencies with a total staff of some 200,000 men and women. To extend their considerable reach, the Justice Department announced its intention to create a Terrorism Information and Prevention System (TIPS) by which "millions of American truckers, letter carriers, train conductors, ship captains, utility employees and others" would be afforded "a formal way to report suspicious terrorist activity," and the proposal was withdrawn only after it was denounced for what it was—a "snitch system."[40]

All the weaponry and tactics that have been deployed in the war on terror are justified by precisely the same theological stance once invoked in the war on heresy. Nowadays, of course, Osama bin Laden is the Devil whose cloven hoof is detected behind every act of terrorism around the world, but all concerns about the impact of the war on terror on our civil liberties are checkmated by the same theological absolutism that the grand inquisitors once invoked: "Either you're with us, or you're with the enemy," declared George W. Bush in the run-up to the invasion of Iraq. "Either you're with those who love freedom, or you're with those who hate innocent life." When the argument was made by the Inquisition, the enemy consisted of men and women who preferred to read the Bible in translation, or who were persuaded that the sun revolved around the earth, or who saw some merit in herbal remedies, or who happened to have a distant Jewish relative. Nowadays, we might ask ourselves whether the victims of the war on terror might not include more than a few innocents, too.[41]

The history of terror in the name of God is not confined to the medieval Inquisition or its modern successors. But it is a healthy caution to remind ourselves that the Inquisition was "called into existence to meet a national emergency." The first inquisitors saw themselves as crusaders in a holy war against "a monstrous, anti-human conspiracy," and they saw their adversaries as "a devoted underground elite" in service to the Devil. They claimed to act in the name of "legal justice," and they were willing to "kill them all" and let God sort out the carnage. Such is the "murderous engine" that is set in motion whenever we hit the panic button. If a moment of reflection on that sorry history stays our hand, we will have achieved some measure of moral justice.[42]

ACKNOWLEDGMENTS

As with all of my books, I was sustained on my journey to the Middle Ages and back to the here and now by my cherished wife, Ann Benjamin Kirsch, and our beloved children, Jennifer Rachel Kirsch and Adam Benjamin Kirsch. Along the way, Adam and his wife, Remy, presented Ann and me with our first grandchild, Charles Ezra Kirsch, a history-making moment in our family.

For their roles in inspiring and shaping this book, I express my deepest appreciation to my agent, Laurie Fox; my editor, Gideon Weil, and his colleagues at HarperOne, Michael Maudlin, Mark Tauber, Claudia Boutote, Jan Weed, Terri Leonard, Jim Warner, Laina Adler, Carolyn Allison-Holland, Anne C. Collins, Annette Jarvie, and Kris Ashley.

My colleague and cherished friend, Judy Woo, supports and encourages my work literally every day, always showing the greatest patience and dexterity in dealing with the little mountains of reference material that hinder her way across our offices.

I salute my fellow author and attorney, Leslie S. Klinger, a constant source of camaraderie and inspiration in both of the fields of endeavor that we share.

I affirm my enduring gratitude to Jack Miles and Karen Armstrong, whom I am proud to claim as my mentors, and the other scholars who have extended their generosity and support over the years, including Don

Akenson, David Noel Freedman, (who passed away while this book was in press), David Rosenberg, Leonard Shlain, and John M. Barry.

To my friends, family, and colleagues, I once again express my heartfelt appreciation:

My beloved daughter-in-law, Remy Elizabeth Holzer, and her family, Harold, Edith, and Meg Holzer.

Lillian Conrad Heller, Marya and Ron Shiflett, Paul and Caroline Kirsch, Heather Kirsch, and Joshua, Jenny, and Hazel Kirsch.

Eui Sook (Angie) Yoon, Charlie Alexiev, and Stefan Johnson, my friends and colleagues.

Susan Pollyea, Ralph Ehrenpreis, and Harland Braun, my much-admired colleagues in the practice of law.

Dora Levy Mossanen and Nader Mossanen, Candace Barrett Birk and Raye Birk, Maryann Rosenfeld and Shelly Kadish, Pat and Len Solomon, John Rechy and Michael Ewing, Diane Leslie and Fred Huffman, Doug and Penny Dutton, and Jacob Gabay.

K. C. Cole, Janet Fitch, Carolyn See, Bernadette Shih, Rhoda Huffey, and Dolores Sloan.

Linda Chester and her colleagues at the Linda Chester Agency.

David Ulin, Nick Owchar, Orli Low, Kristina Lindgren, Sara Lippincott, Susan Salter Reynolds, and Janice Dawson at the *Los Angeles Times Book Review*.

Doug Brown, Ann Binney, David Nelson, Barbara Morrow, Maret Orliss, and Kristine Erbstoesser at the *Los Angeles Times*.

Terry Nathan at the Publishers Marketing Association.

Sarah Spitz and Ruth Seymour at KCRW-FM.

Larry Mantle, Patt Morrison, Aimee Machado, Jackie Oclaray, Linda Othenin-Girard, and Polly Sveda at KPCC-FM.

Rob Eshman at *The Jewish Journal*.

Connie Martinson, host of *Connie Martinson Talks Books*.

NOTES

AUTHOR'S NOTE: Citations are collected in a single endnote that appears at the end of a paragraph or portion of a paragraph in which material is quoted. I have taken the liberty of omitting brackets and ellipses to mark the minor changes I have made in some (but not all) quoted material, including changes in spelling, capitalization, italicization, punctuation, and omissions that do not materially change the meaning of the quoted text. In every instance where I have done so, however, the quotation is identified as "adapted" in the endnote where the source is cited. Quotations from the Bible are attributed to the specific translation from which they are taken according to the following acronyms: KJV (King James Version), NKJ (New King James Version), and RSV (Revised Standard Version).

I. THE *PIETÀ* AND THE PEAR

1. Robert Held, *Inquisition: A Bilingual Guide to the Exhibition of Torture Instruments from the Middle Ages to the Industrial Era* (Florence: Qua d'Arno, 1985), 18 ("delectable to the Holy Trinity . . ."). The author is referring here to the burning of heretics at the stake.

2. Edward Peters, *Inquisition* (Berkeley: University of California Press, 1989), Plate 5 (following p. 90).

3. 1 Cor. 11:19, NKJ.

4. Fydor Dostoyevsky, *The Brothers Karamazov,* trans. Constance Garnett (New York: Modern Library, n.d.), 270 (adapted).

5. Henry Charles Lea, *The Imquisition of the Middle Ages,* (New York: Citadel Press, 1961) 60, 97 (adapted).

6. Quoted in Lea, 126 (adapted).

7. Lea, 61, 192 (adapted).

8. George Orwell, *1984* (New York: Signet, 1981) 7.

9. Quoted in Lea, 107 (adapted).

10. G.G. Coulton, *The Medieval Village, Manor and Monastery* (New York: Harper & Row, 1960), 347 (adapted). Emphasis added.

11. Lea, 96 (adapted).

12. Norman Cohn, *Europe's Inner Demons: An Enquiry Inspired by the Great Witch-Hunt* (New York: Basic Books, 1975), 17, 20 (adapted).

13. Cohn, 17.

14. Cohn, 49 ("a monstrous, anti-human conspiracy"); Malcolm Lambert, *Medieval Heresy: Popular Movements from the Gregorian Reform to the Reformation*, 2d ed. (Cambridge, MA: Blackwell, 1992), 151 ("a devoted underground elite"); Edward Burman, *The Inquisition: The Hammer of Heresy* (New York: Dorset Press, 1992; orig. pub. 1984), quoting Henry Kamen, *The Spanish Inquisition: A Historical Revision* (New Haven: Yale Univ. Press, 1997), 150–51 ("called into existence . . ."); Edward Peters, *Torture* (New York: Basil Blackwell, 1985), 54 ("traitors to God"), paraphrasing the papal decretal *Vergentis in senium*, 1199, and 65 (" thieves and murderers . . ."), paraphrasing *Ad extirpanda*, 1252.

15. Dietrich von Nieheim, Bishop of Verden, *De schismate libri III* (1411), quoted in Arthur Koestler, *Darkness at Noon*, trans. Daphne Hardy (New York: Macmillan, 1958), 95.

16. Quoted in Burman, 36 ("heretical depravity"); quoted in Karen Armstrong, *Holy War: The Crusades and Their Impact on Today's World* (New York: Anchor Books, 2001), 393 ("gives birth continually" and harmful filth"); Deborah Root, "Speaking Christian: Orthodoxy and Difference in Sixteenth Century Spain," *Representations* 23 (Summer 1988): 118–34, at 130 ("evil weeds").

17. Father Aznar Cordona, *Expulsión justificada de los moriscos españoles*, quoted in Root, 118.

18. Graham Greene, *The Power and the Glory* (New York: Penguin Books, 2003), 131.

19. Quoted in Burman, 66 ("one insanely led to reject . . ."); quoted in Lambert, 177–88 ("good doctors").

20. Strictures of the Purity of Blood, 1449, quoted in Armstrong, 460 ("purity of blood"); "The Canons of the Fourth Lateran Council, 1215," in *Internet Medieval Sourcebook*, ed. Paul Halsall, http://www.fordham.edu/halsall/basis/lateran4.html ("purity of faith"); R. I. Moore, *The Formation of a Persecuting Society: Power and Deviance in Western Europe, 950–1250* (Oxford, UK, and Cambridge, MA: Blackwell, 1987), 10 ("machinery of persecution").

21. Quoted in Lea, 230.

22. Henry Ansgar Kelly, "Inquisition and the Prosecution of Heresy: Misconceptions and Abuses," *Church History* 58 (1989): 439.

23. John and Anne Tedeschi, in Carlo Ginzburg, *The Cheese and the Worms: The Cosmos of a Sixteenth-Century Miller*, trans. John and Anne Tedeschi (New York: Penguin Books, 1982), ix ("legal justice" and "moral justice") (adapted).

24. Franz Kafka, *The Complete Stories*, ed. Nahum N. Glatzer (New York: Schocken Books, 1976), 140, 144, 145, 147, 150 (adapted).

25. Cynthia Ozick, "The Impossibility of Being Kafka," in *Quarrel & Quandary* (New York: Alfred A. Knopf, 2000), 53 (quoting *The Trial* by Franz Kafka) and ("an Alice-in-Wonderland arbitrariness").

26. G.G. Coulton, *Inquisition and Liberty* (Boston: Beacon Press, 1959), 316–17 (adapted).

27. Lea, 126.

28. Quoted in Armstrong, 396–97.

2. THE CATHAR KISS

1. Quoted in Lambert, 10 (adapted).

2. Lambert, 11.

3. Lambert, 11.

4. Quoted in Lambert, 11–12.

5. Quoted in Lambert, 11–12.

6. Lambert, 11–12.

7. See *God Against the Gods: A History of the War Between Monotheism and Polytheism,* (Viking, 2004) by Jonathan Kirsch.

8. Armstrong, 385–86 (adapted).

9. Quoted in Sean Martin, *The Cathars: The Most Successful Heresy of the Middle Ages* (New York: Thunder's Mouth Press, 2005), 76–77 (adapted).

10. Coulton, 259, quoting Archbishop Peckham ("The ignorance of the priests . . .") (adapted) and Bishop Guillaume le Maire of Angers ("contemptible persons . . ." and "the lay folk hold the priests . . .") (adapted).

11. Coulton, quoting author, *Dives and Paupers,* 273 (adapted).

12. Quoted in Coulton, 266 (adapted).

13. Quoted in Coulton, 263.

14. Burman, 16.

15. Lambert, 29.

16. Luke 9:58; 10:4, 8, RSV.

17. Mary T. Malone, *From 1000 to the Reformation,* vol. 2 of *Women and Christianity* (Maryknoll, NY: Orbis Books, 2002), 48.

18. Lambert, 38.

19. Quoted in Walter L. Wakefield, *Heresy, Crusade and Inquisition in Southern France, 1100–1250* (Berkeley and Los Angeles: Univ. of California Press, 1974), 45.

20. Quoted in Wakefield, 45.

21. Lambert, 56.

22. Cohn, 17.

23. Quoted in Cohn, 19 (adapted).

24. Wakefield, 102 ("riff-raff").

25. Cohn, xii ("exotic and non-Christian").

26. Lambert, 119. Emphasis added.

27. Lambert, 121.

28. Wakefield, 38.

29. Lambert, 139.

30. Wakefield, 38.

31. Lambert, 107.

32. Everwin of Steinfeld, quoted in Lambert, 56, and alluding to Matt. 10:16.

33. Quoted in Lambert, 109.

34. Lambert, 139.

35. Quoted in Martin, 7.

36. Wakefield, 42 ("Ardent believers married . . .").

37. Lambert, 114.

38. Lambert, 114.

39. The derivation of Cathar from *cattus* is proposed by Alain de Lille in *Against the Heretics of His Times,* written between 1179 and 1202. Kissing the anus of a cat also is described by Guillaume d'Auvergne, bishop of Paris, in a work written between 1231 and 1236. Cohn, 22.

40. Hos. 4:14, RSV.

41. Lambert, 9, n. 1.

42. Wakefield, 41.

43. Quoted in John R. Sommerfeldt, *Bernard of Clairvaux: On the Spirituality of Relationship* (Mahwah, NJ: The Newman Press, 2004), 82.

44. Lambert, 15 ("the fictions of carnal men . . ."); quoted in Stephen C. Ferruolo, *The Origins of the University: The Schools of Paris and Their Critics, 1100–1215* (Stanford, CA: Stanford University Press, 1985), 55 ("The woods and stones will teach you. . .").

45. Quoted in Burman, 27.

46. Quoted in Lambert, 59 ("were not bishops and priests but ravening wolves . . .") (adapted); quoted in Martin, 128 ("was only good for batting away flies . . ."); Martin, 128 ("have God in their bowels . . .").

47. Quoted in Armstrong, 393.

48. Armstrong, 393.

49. Wakefield, 30.

50. Quoted in Emmanuel Le Roy Ladurie, *Montaillou: Cathars and Catholics in a French Village, 1294–1324,* trans. Barbara Bray (New York: Penguin Books, 1980), 223, 320–21.

51. Ladurie, 223.

52. Lambert, 98.

53. Caesarius of Heisterbach (ca. 1180–1240), *Dialogue on Miracles,* quoted in Wakefield, 197. The reference is to 2 Tim. 2:19, RSV ("The Lord knows those who are his.").

54. Martin, 90.

55. Martin, 96.

56. Wakefield, 120.

57. Wakefield, 121.

58. Quoted in Wakefield, 120.

59. Lea, 65.

3. THE HAMMER OF HERETICS

1. Arthur Griffiths, *In Spanish Prisons: The Inquisition at Home and Abroad; Prisons Past and Present* (New York: Dorset Press, 1991; orig. pub. 1894), 15.

2. Lea, 24.

3. Lea, 51 (adapted).

4. Lea, 7.

5. Lea, 2.

6. Quoted in Burman, 25.

7. Cohn, 25 ("self-appointed inquisitors . . . ," etc.); Burman, 35 ("on papal license").
8. Quoted in Cohn, 26.
9. Lambert, 148–49, 165 (adapted).
10. Burman, 29–30, quoting Achille Luchaire, *Innocent III.*
11. "Canons of the Fourth Lateran Council, 1215," Canon 4 ("conform themselves like obedient sons . . ."), Canon 68 ("thus it happens at times . . ."), Canon 71 ("to liberate the Holy Land . . ."), Internet Medieval Sourcebook, www.fordham.edu/halsall/basis/lateran4.html.
12. "Canons of the Fourth Lateran Council, 1215," Canon 1.
13. "Canons of the Fourth Lateran Council, 1215," Canon 3.
14. "Canons of the Fourth Lateran Council, 1215," Canon 3 (adapted).
15. "Canons of the Fourth Lateran Council, 1215," Canon 3.
16. Burman, 21, 30.
17. "[I]t cannot be disputed that the creation of a permanent tribunal, staffed by Dominican friars who worked from a fixed base in conjunction with the episcopate and were endowed with generous authority, occurred first in Languedoc in 1233–1234. . . ." Wakefield, 140.
18. Burman, 28, 34 ("an integral part . . . ," "an act of love . . . ," etc.).
19. Quoted in Kelly, 439, n. 2.
20. Quoted in Burman, 18–19.
21. Quoted in Lea, 27.
22. Burman, 53.
23. Quoted in Lea, 63–64.
24. Quoted in Lea, 63–64.
25. Burman, 81.
26. Lea, 69, 125. The words attributed to Sir John Fortescue are paraphrased by Lea and slightly adapted here.
27. Burman, 37, 38.
28. Giorgio de Santillana, *The Crime of Galileo* (New York: Time Inc., 1955; orig. pub. Univ. of Chicago Press), 27, n. 2.
29. Lambert, 177 ("zealous, hard-working bureaucrats").
30. Pope Gregory IX, *Ille humani generis,* 1231, quoted in Burman, 35–36. Although addressed to Conrad of Marburg, "it provides the first sketch of the procedure that later became standard for inquisitors."
31. Burman, 55 (adapted).
32. Lea, 69 ("the authorities . . ."); Bernard Gui, *The Inquisitor's Guide: A Medieval Manual on Heretics,* trans. and ed. Janet Shirley (Welwyn Garden City, UK: Ravenhall Books, 2006), 10 ("Most Reverent").
33. Lea, 82, 83.
34. Lea, 104, 105, 114.
35. Lea, 61.
36. Lea, 113.
37. Lea, 75.
38. Lambert, 98.
39. Wakefield, 133 (adapted).
40. Kelly, 441.

41. Gui, 30.

42. Lea, 106–7.

43. Lambert, 137.

44. Lea, 128.

45. Quoted in Lea, 112 ("How often have you confessed . . ."); quoted in Wakefield, 151–52, n. 10 ("Does a woman conceive through the act of God . . .").

46. Gui, quoted in Lea, 108–9 (adapted).

47. Lea, 99.

48. Lea, 127 (adapted), 153.

49. Lea, 72–73.

50. Quoted in Lea, 72.

51. Lea, 74.

52. Lambert, 101.

53. Burman, 54.

54. Kelly, 448.

55. Lea, 141.

56. Lea, 72, citing Zanghino Ugolini ("utterly ignorant of the law"), and Eymerich ("should always associate himself. . .").

57. Lea, 144.

58. Quoted in Ozick, 53.

59. Lea, 192.

60. Quoted in Lea, 192–93.

61. Kelly, 444, 450–51.

62. Lea, 83, 84, 85.

63. Lea, 149 (adapted).

64. Wakefield, 188 ("canonical irregularities . . .").

65. Lea, 148 ("devices and deceits," referring specifically to the rights of appeal), 72, 73 ("The inquisitors were a law unto themselves . . .") (adapted); Kelly, 450 ("[t]hings had come to a sorry pass . . .").

66. Burman, 46, 66.

67. Burman, 50, paraphrasing Mariano da Alatri.

68. Wakefield, 141–42.

69. William of Pelhisson, quoted in Wakefield, 224.

70. William of Pelhisson, quoted in Wakefield, 218–19.

71. William of Pelhisson, quoted in Wakefield, 218–19.

72. William of Pelhisson, quoted in Wakefield, 216–17 (adapted).

73. Burman, 40.

74. Lea, 42, 43 (adapted).

75. Wakefield, 142.

76. Wakefield, 184, citing Yves Dossat. Wakefield reports that twenty-one victims in the diocese of Toulouse were formally sentenced to death and suggests that five additional victims who were recorded as "relapsed" heretics probably suffered capital punishment, too.

77. Burman, 93 ("infested with heretics").

78. Burman, 54.

79. Lea, 78 ("pointed knives, etc.) and 79 ("armed familiars . . ."), citing Pope John XXII.
80. Lea, 80, citing Nicholas Eymerich.
81. Quoted in Burman, 66, and paraphrased in Lea, 154, 157.

4. CRIME AND PUNISHMENT

1. Quoted in Brian Innes, *The History of Torture* (Leicester, England: Blitz Editions, 1999), 43. Innes cites the account of a sixteenth-century Florentine attorney called Paulus Grillandus who specifically describes the use of the strappado.
2. Burman, 41.
3. Quoted in Peters, 1985, 65 (adapted).
4. Held, 18 ("delectable to the Holy Trinity . . .") (the author is referring here to the burning of heretics at the stake); quoted in Innes, 41 ("By the grace of God . . .").
5. Malise Ruthven, *Torture: The Grand Conspiracy* (London: Weidenfeld & Nicolson, 1978), 51 (adapted).
6. Ruthven, 51.
7. Burman, 59.
8. Quoted in Burman, 148 (adapted).
9. Paraphrased in Lea, 104 (adapted).
10. Dostoyevsky, 270 (adapted).
11. Quoted in Burman, 60, 70 (adapted).
12. Lea, 114–55.
13. Lea, 114.
14. Lea, 114.
15. Quoted in Innes, 41.
16. Quoted in Peters, 1985, 42.
17. Quoted in Peters, 1985, 1 (adapted). The Latin word *quaestio* appears in the original text and is translated by Peters as "torture."
18. Lea, 2.
19. Ruthven, 47 (adapted).
20. *Directorium Inquisitorium,* quoted in Ruthven, 54.
21. Ruthven, 55 ("with a general reputation for heresy," etc.); Peters, 1985, 67 ("facial expressions . . .").
22. Burman, 148.
23. Nigel Cawthorne, *Witch Hunt: History of a Persecution* (New York: Barnes & Noble, 2004), 174–75.
24. Ruthven, 58.
25. Burman, 63. Strictly speaking, these were the standard measurements for the water ordeal as used in Italy.
26. Burman, 63 ("for fresh questioning . . ."); Cecil Roth, *The Spanish Inquisition* (New York: Norton, 1964; orig. pub. 1937), 107 ("A man might . . .").
27. Quoted in Anthony Grafton, "Say Anything: What the Renaissance Teaches Us About Torture," *The New Republic,* Nov. 5, 2007, 23 ("jump" and "dance"); Burman, 64 ("Only a confession . . . ," etc.); Peters, 1985, 68 ("queen of torments").

28. Ruthven, 59 ("the space of one or two Misereres"); Innes, 43 ("weights were attached . . .").

29. Lea, 114.

30. Held, 78.

31. Held, 17 (adapted).

32. Peters, 1989, 218.

33. Burman, 63.

34. Quoted in Burman, 63, 146.

35. Quoted in Burman, 63.

36. Burman, 63.

37. Burman, 62.

38. Lea, quoted in Burman, 65.

39. *Processus inquisitionis,* quoted in Wakefield, 255 ("The bearer sinned . . .") (adapted).

40. Quoted in Burman, 47.

41. Burman, 58.

42. *Processus inquisitionis,* quoted in Wakefield, 183, 255.

43. Wakefield, 183 ("ostentatious dress . . ."); Lea, 113 ("His body . . .")

44. Lea, 229.

45. Lea, 211.

46. Lea, 168.

47. Lea, 219.

48. Lea, 229.

49. Lea, 217.

50. Quoted in Burman, 54 ("perpetual imprisonment . . ."); Lea, 184 ("frightful abodes . . .").

51. Quoted in Burman, 41.

52. Lea, 180.

53. Lea, 184.

54. Lea, 185.

55. Wakefield, 239.

56. *Processus inquisitionis,* quoted in Wakefield, 256 (adapted).

57. Coulton, 189 (adapted).

58. Burman. 37.

59. Ladurie, 142, n. 3.

60. Held, 82.

61. Lea, 249.

62. Quoted in Lambert, 15 ("laughed as they were bound . . ."); quoted in Burman, 155 ("thrust their hands . . .").

63. Lambert, 15 ("a strange state . . .").

64. See *A History of the End of the World: How the Most Controversial Book in the Bible Changed the Course of Western Civilization,* by Jonathan Kirsch (HarperOne, 2006).

65. Quoted in Burman, 37.

5. THE INQUISITOR'S MANUAL

1. Quoted in Lambert, 362.
2. Peters, 1985, 65.
3. Quoted in Lambert, 211.
4. Lambert, 193 ("poverty fanatics"); Wakefield, 190 ("mystics. . .")(adapted).
5. Lambert, 185–86, 187.
6. Burman, 104 (adapted).
7. Burman 105 ("to enquire into the beliefs . . .").
8. Gui, 95, 122 (adapted).
9. Burman, 103 ("no Rule and no authority . . ."); Lambert, 184 ("So little obvious was the heresy . . .").
10. Kelly, 448.
11. Quoted in Burman, 95 ("in the name of the Inquisition"); quoted in Cohn, 85 ("a detestable crime . . .").
12. Cohn, 77.
13. Cohn, 83.
14. Cohn, 80.
15. Quoted in Burman, 95.
16. Lambert, 180 ("extraordinary farrago of nonsense"); Cohn, 86 ("absolutely without foundation").
17. Cohn, 85, 88.
18. Cohn, 87, 88, 91 ("indecent" and "beautiful young girls" and "encrusted with jewels"); Cawthorne, 45 ("a goat endowed . . .").
19. Cohn, 87.
20. Cohn, 92 ("reduced the pope . . .").
21. Cohn, 87.
22. Quoted in Cohn, 85 (adapted).
23. Cohn, 96.
24. Exod. 22:18, KJV; quoted in Cawthorne, 35 ("wizardry and sorcery . . .") (adapted), 35–36 ("believe and openly profess").
25. Cohn, 177 ("he had seized and read many books . . ."); Burman, 121 ("love-magic").
26. Pope John XXII, *Summis desiderantes affectibus,* 1484, quoted in Cawthorne, 39–40 ("correction, imprisonment and punishment . . ." and "They blasphemously renounce . . .") (adapted); Cohn, 252 ("a secret, conspiratorial body . . .").
27. Burman, 121.
28. Jeffrey Burton Russell, quoted in Burman, 129–30 (adapted).
29. Lambert, 187 ("verbal exhibitionists")(adapted).
30. Salazar y Frias, quoted in Burman, 182 ("There were neither witches . . .").
31. Montague Summers, ed. and trans., *The "Malleus Maleficarum" of Heinrich Kramer and James Sprenger* (New York: Dover, 1971; orig. pub. 1928), 194, 195 (adapted).
32. Summers, 44–45, 47 (adapted); Sydney Anglo, quoted in Burman, 131 ("scholastic pornography"); Grafton, 24 ("an amalgam of . . .").
33. Summers, 56.
34. Burman, 116.

35. Cohn, 102.

36. Cohn, 102.

37. Quoted in Burman, 180.

38. Cohn, 117.

39. Cohn, 56, 59, 104; Gui, 149 ("sorcerers, fortune-tellers . . .").

40. Barbara Ehrenreich and Deidre English, *Witches, Midwives and Nurses: A History of Women Healers* (New York: Feminist Press at the City Univ. of New York, 1973), 12 ("trading herbal lore . . ."); Anne Llewellyn Barstow, *Witchcraze: A New History of the European Witch Hunts* (New York: Pandora, 1994), 109 ("were not in fact riding broomsticks . . .") (adapted).

41. Alonzo Salazar y Frias, 1612, quoted in Burman, 182 ("I have not found . . ."); Johann Wier, 1564, quoted in Burman, 182 ("witches were persons . . .").

42. Quoted in Cohn, 240.

43. Barstow, 1994, 25 ("80 percent of the accused . . ."); Cohn, 249 ("solitary, eccentric, or bad-tempered . . . ," etc.); quoted in Cohn, 250 ("she had done nothing . . .").

44. Summers, 223 (adapted).

45. Barstow, 1994, 10, 11, 12, 15, 21.

46. Burman, 179 ("reliably"); Cohn, 253 ("fantastic exaggerations"); Barstow, 1994, 23 ("is off by . . .").

47. Cohn, 254 ("and all, without exception . . .") (adapted); Ehrenreich and English, 8 ("two villages were left . . ."). Cohn debunks the outright forgeries on which much early historical writing on the Inquisition and the Witch Craze was based, especially Étienne-Léon de Lamothe-Langon's *Histoire de l'Inquisition en France,* first published in Paris in 1829.

48. Quoted in Coulton, 262.

49. Quoted in Coulton, 262–63, and Barstow, Anne Llewllyn, *Joan of Arc: Heretic, Mystic, Shaman,* (Lewiston, NY: Edwin Miller Press, 1986), 50, 82 (adapted from both sources).

50. Quoted in Barstow, 1986, 25 ("Voice from God").

51. Burman, 106, quoting *Henry VI, Part I;* Barstow, 1986, xv ("a heroine of the French resistance").

52. Quoted in Burman, 114.

53. Coulton, 262–63.

54. Quoted in Coulton, 262–63.

55. Quoted in Barstow, 1986, 82.

56. Quoted in Barstow, 1986, 91.

57. Burman, 109.

58. Quoted in Barstow, 1986, 96.

59. Lambert, 56, 100 ("gave a voice . . ." and "quid pro quo"); Burman, 97 ("a wild orgy of plunder").

60. Lea, 49.

61. "Canons of the Fourth Lateran Council, 1215," Canon 1, in *Internet Medieval Sourcebook*, www. fordham. edu/halsall/basis/lateran4. html.

62. Quoted in Burman, 167–68.

63. De Santillana, 13 ("Mathematics are for mathematicians").

64. De Santillana, 128.
65. Quoted in Burman, 170.
66. Quoted in de Santillana, 315 (adapted).
67. Quoted in de Santillana, 124 (adapted).
68. Quoted in de Santillana, 129 ("foolish and absurd . . . ," etc.), 134 ("The said Galileo . . .") (adapted).
69. De Santillana, 195 ("provided the treatment . . ."); quoted in de Santillana, 196 ("Preface to the Judicious Reader").
70. De Santillana, 221.
71. Quoted in de Santillana, 276 (adapted).
72. De Santillana, 313.
73. Quoted in de Santillana, 338 (adapted).
74. Quoted in Burman, 174 ("the formal prison . . ."); quoted in de Santillana, 318 ("to all Inquisitors . . .").

6. PURITY OF BLOOD

1. The epigraph at the head of this chapter is quoted in David M. Gitlitz, *Secrecy and Deceit: The Religion of the Crypto-Jews* (Philadelphia and Jerusalem: Jewish Publication Society, 1996), 38. Juan de Salzedo is recalling the events of 1492 and quoting a remark made by a Jewish man named Fernando de Guernica to another Jewish man named Isaac the Portuguese.
2. Gui, 139–40.
3. Joshua Trachtenberg, *The Devil and the Jews: The Medieval Conception of the Jew and Its Relation to Modern Antisemitism* (New Haven: Yale Univ. Press, 1943), 180.
4. Trachtenberg, 180.
5. Quoted in Trachtenberg, 179.
6. Quoted in Kamen, 2.
7. Matt. 27:22, RSV.
8. "Wandering Jew," 259–63, in *Encyclopedia Judaica*, vols. 1–17, corrected ed. (Jerusalem: Keter Publishing House, Ltd. n.d.), 261.
9. Rev. 2:9, 39, KJV; Jewry Law of King Venceslas II for Brünn, quoted in Trachtenberg, 164 ("Because of the crime . . .").
10. Quoted in Trachtenberg, 187.
11. Quoted in Trachtenberg, 94, 110.
12. Trachtenberg, 190, 193.
13. Trachtenberg, 31.
14. Burman, 29–30, quoting Achille Luchaire, *Innocent III*.
15. From "Chronicle of Rabbi Eliezer bar Nathan," quoted in Armstrong, 73 (adapted).
16. Roth, 21.
17. Roth, 18 (adapted).
18. Quoted in Kamen, 6.
19. Estimates of the Jewish population in Spain are "based on pure speculation," according to revisionist historian Henry Kamen. But he agrees that the Jews of Aragón

"were reduced to one-fourth of their numbers as a result of the fateful year 1391."
Kamen, 23.

20. Roth, 26.

21. Kamen, 11.

22. Roth, 29.

23. Quoted in Kamen, 16 (adapted).

24. Roth, 52–53.

25. Kamen, 23, 25.

26. Quoted in Kamen, 20.

27. Quoted in Kamen, 20. The tale is probably fanciful, but Kamen observes: "There
is a grain of truth in the story of Torquemada and the pieces of silver."

28. Quoted in Kamen, 21 (adapted).

29. Quoted in Kamen, 70.

30. Kamen, 217.

31. Roth, 152.

32. Roth, 163.

33. Quoted in Roth, 164 ("Lutheran heretics"); Griffiths, 60 ("the vulgar tongues").

34. Quoted in Roth, 170.

35. Roth, 186, 188, 190.

36. Quoted in Kamen, 129.

37. Quoted in Burman, 203.

38. Quoted in Roth, 66.

39. Quoted in Roth, 67.

40. Quoted in Kamen, 256.

41. Kamen, 276.

42. Quoted in Roth, 193.

43. Quoted in Kamen, 262 ("Tithes are ours . . .") (adapted).

44. Kamen, 266.

45. Quoted in Kamen, 274.

46. Quoted in Roth, 76.

47. Quoted in Kamen, 174.

48. Quoted in Burman, 143.

49. Quoted in Roth, 100.

50. Quoted in Roth, 77 (adapted).

51. Kamen, 194 ("farcical"); quoted in Kamen, 194 ("a fellow who would do . . .").

52. Kamen, 196.

53. Quoted in Roth, 90.

54. Quoted in Kamen, 22.

55. Quoted in Kamen, 299 ("Moses, Moses").

56. B. Netanyahu, *The Origins of the Inquisition in Fifteenth Century Spain* (New
York: Random House, 1995), xvi.

57. Netanyahu, xvii.

58. Gitlitz, 84 ("along the spectrum . . ."), 85 ("idiosyncratic"), 87 ("syncretistic");
quoted in Kamen, 42 ("Holy Mary . . .").

59. Netanyahu, xvii.

60. Kamen, 40–41 (adapted).
61. Roth, 199.
62. Netanyahu, 984, 990.
63. Kamen, 205.
64. Quoted in Roth, 295, 296 (adapted).
65. Roth, 109 ("formal"); John Addington Symonds, quoted in Roth, 119 ("The procession presented . . .").
66. Quoted in Kamen, 208–9 ("the Wood with which the Criminals are burnt"); quoted in Griffiths, 101 ("*Justitia et misericordia*").
67. Kamen, 201.
68. Quoted in Burman, 154–55.
69. John Addington Symonds, quoted in Roth, 119 (adapted).
70. Roth, 137 ("the shrieks of dying heretics . . ."); quoted in Roth, 71 ("Noble Queen! . . .").
71. Quoted in Roth, 71.
72. Quoted in Kamen, 243.
73. Roth, 124.
74. Roth, 236.
75. Kamen, 213.
76. Roth, 261.
77. Roth, 91.
78. Quoted in Roth, 282 (adapted).
79. Quoted in Roth, 267.

7. THE ETERNAL INQUISITOR

1. Barstow, 1986, 125.
2. Quoted in Jack Langford, "The Condemnation of Galileo," *Reality* 8 (1960): 78 ("the greatest scandal . . ."); Cardinal Paul Poupard, Oct. 31, 1992, quoted in "John Paul II and Galileo," Pauline Books and Media, http:www/daughtersofstpaul.com/johnpaulpapacy/meetjp/thepope/jpgalileo.html ("subjective error . . .").
3. Quoted in Burman, 214. Burman notes that the decree against Freemasonry was withdrawn in 1983.
4. Burman, 214 (adapted).
5. De Santillana, 324 ("the great denouncer . . ."); Lea, 257 ("It was a system . . .").
6. Quoted in Roth, 100.
7. G.G. Coulton, *Inquisition and Liberty* (Boston: Beacon Hill, 1959), 311.
8. Roth, 274 (adapted).
9. Lea, 97 (adapted).
10. Kamen, 315.
11. Quoted in Kamen, 153.
12. Quoted in de Santillana, 324.
13. John and Anne Tedeschi, in Ginzburg, ix.
14. Quoted in Ginzburg, 2, 111.

15. Quoted in Ginzburg, 127.

16. John and Anne Tedeschi, in Ginzburg, ix ("moral justice . . .") (adapted); Moore, 3 ("with Spinoza, not to ridicule . . ."), 5 ("a persecuting society").

17. Edward Peters, *Inquisition* (Berkeley and Los Angeles: Univ. of California Press, 1989), 1, 2.

18. Norman F. Cantor, *Inventing the Middle Ages: The Lives, Works and Ideas of the Great Medievalists of the Twentieth Century* (New York: Quill William Morrow, 1991), 397.

19. Cantor, 397.

20. Cantor, xiv, referring to the phenomena described in Norman Cohn's *Europe's Inner Demons* (that is, the Witch Craze) and *The Pursuit of the Millennium* (millenarian movements).

21. G.G. Coulton, *The Inquisition* (New York: Jonathan Cape & Harrison Smith, 1929), 91 (adapted).

22. Quoted in Jochen von Lang, with Claus Sibyll, *Eichmann Interrogated: Transcripts from the Archives of the Israeli Police*, trans. Ralph Manheim (New York: Vintage Books, 1984), 21–22.

23. Quoted in von Lang, 23 ("the Jews department"), 24 ("to make an abstract . . ."); quoted in Saul Friedländer, *The Years of Extermination, 1939–1945*, vol. 2 of *Nazi Germany and the Jews* (New York: HarperPerennial, 1998), 199 ("for a successful internal struggle . . .").

24. Friedländer, 1998, 198 ("an entirely integrated system . . ."); Kamen, 213 ("combustible material").

25. World Committee for the Victims of German Fascism, *The Brown Book of the Hitler Terror and the Burning of the Reichstag*, intro. Lord Marley (London: Victor Gollancz, 1933), 200. The man behind *The Brown Book* was Willi Müntzenberg, later described by Arthur Koestler as "the 'Red Eminence' of international anti-Fascism." Russell Jacoby, "Willi the Red," *The Nation*, Feb. 16, 2004, posted Jan. 29, 2004, at http://www.thenation.com/doc/20040216/jacoby.

26. Quoted in Eric A. Johnson, *Nazi Terror: The Gestapo, Jews and Ordinary Germans* (New York: Basic Books, 2000), 15.

27. Quoted in Edward Crankshaw, *Gestapo: Instrument of Tyranny* (London: Wren's Park, 2002), 127 ("rigorous examination," etc.); quoted in von Lang, 71 ("redistribution"), 79 ("evacuation"); E. Johnson, 4 ("evacuation"), 383 ("deportation"); Friedländer, 1998, 484 ("resettlement.").

28. Quoted in Crankshaw, 28–29.

29. Eichmann, quoted in von Lang, 108 ("Special treatment . . .").

30. Burman, 29–30, quoting Achille Luchaire, *Innocent III*.

31. Anthony M. Platt, with Cecilia E. O'Leary, *Bloodlines: Recovering Hitler's Nuremberg Laws, From Patton's Trophy to Public Memorial* (Boulder, CO: Paradigm, 2006), 5 ("subjects"); Friedländer, 1998, 160, 229 ("mutual masturbation" and "purification").

32. Quoted in Friedländer, 1998, 197.

33. Quoted in Friedländer, 1998, 97 ("[W]e must recognize . . .").

34. Quoted in Friedländer, 1998, 184 ("Without fear, we want to point the finger . . ."), 182 ("This Jewish pestilence . . . ," referring to the events of the Spanish Civil War).

35. Jewry Law of King Venceslas II for Brünn, quoted in Trachtenberg, 164.

36. Friedländer, 1998, 51 ("full Jew"); 141 ("a *Mischlinge* of the second degree"); E. Johnson, 105 ("for most party officials. . .") (adapted).

37. Quoted in Friedländer, 1998, 4 (adapted).

38. Quoted in Friedländer, 1998, 254.

39. Quoted in Friedländer, 1998, 200.

40. Quoted in Friedländer, 1998, 121 ("The Jewish Murder Plot . . .").

41. E. Johnson, 398.

42. E. Johnson, quoting Emanuel Schäfer, 4 ("The Jews were placed . . .") .

43. Friedländer, 1998, 201. ("a strategic center . . .").

44. Friedländer, 1998, 201.

45. Gitlitz, 83.

46. Friedländer, 1998, 40 ("a confrontation . . .").

47. Quoted in E. Johnson, 382–83.

48. Quoted in Saul Friedländer, *The Years of Extermination, 1939–1945*, Vol. 2. of *Nazi Germany and the Jews* (New York: HarperCollins, 2007), 332 ("the most evil world enemy . . ."); quoted in E. Johnson, 385 ("parasites . . .").

49. Quoted in Friedländer, 2007, 332 ("the most evil world enemy . . .").

50. Roth, iii.

51. Roth, 274–75.

52. Quoted in Friedländer, 1998, 186.

53. Robert Conquest, *The Great Terror: Stalin's Purge of the Thirties* (New York: Macmillan, 1968), xii ("the whole alleged plot . . .").

54. Quoted in People's Commissariat of Justice of the U.S.S.R., *Report of Court Proceedings: The Case of the Trotskyite-Zinovievite Terrorist Centre* (Moscow: People's Commissariat of Justice of the U.S.S.R., 1936), 169.

55. G. E. Evdokimov, quoted in People's Commissariat, 166.

56. Martin, 119 ("proto-Stalinist"); Vishinsky, quoting Vladmir Lenin, in People's Commissariat, 118 ("filthy scum"); Conquest, 1968, 138 ("the swallow").

57. Quoted in People's Commissariat, 118.

58. Vishinsky, quoted in People's Commissariat, 136 ("sacrilege").

59. Quoted in Conquest, 1968, 127 ("None of us desires . . .") (adapted).

60. Conquest, 1968, 125 ("Their constant avowals," etc.).

61. Quoted in Conquest, 1968, 132. "Koestler's account is in fact well founded on the facts. . . . His 'Rubashov' is modeled on Bukharin in his thinking and Trotsky and [Karl] Radek in his personality and physical appearance." Conquest, 1968, 133, n. 29.

62. People's Commissariat, 137–38.

63. Quoted in People's Commissariat, 164 ("I demand . . ."); quoted in foreword to Leon Trotsky, *Stalin's Frame-Up System and the Moscow Trials* (New York: Pioneer, 1950), viii ("the supreme penalty . . . ," etc.).

64. Quoted in Donald Rayfield, *Stalin and His Hangmen: The Tyrant and Those Who Killed for Him* (New York: Random House, 2005), 319 ("It needs stylistic polishing").

65. Quoted in Rayfield, 317, 320 ("A Poem About Stalin . . ." and "Koba, why do you need my life?").

66. Anne Applebaum, *Gulag: A History of the Soviet Camps* (New York: Penguin, 2003), 3.

67. Quoted in Applebaum, 21 ("ongoing purification"), 64 ("wreckers"), 105 ("the second category," etc.), 109 ("isolation"), 111 ("enemies of the people" and "counter-revolutionaries").

68. Robert Conquest, *The Harvest of Sorrow: Soviet Collectivization and the Terror-Famine* (New York: Oxford Univ. Press, 1987), 284 ("traitor to the fatherland") (adapted); quoted in Applebaum, 111 ("crawl[ed] stealthily into socialism . . .").

69. Applebaum, 106 ("the Revolution devoured . . ."); Conquest, 1987, 284 ("Member of the Family . . .").

70. Quoted in Applebaum, 106.

71. Quoted in Conquest, 1968, 318–19.

72. Applebaum, 116.

73. Applebaum, 116.

74. Peters, 1985, 68 ("queen of torments.

75. Rayfield, 279.

76. Hannah Arendt, quoted in Applebaum, 21.

77. Applebaum, 117, 119.

8. AMERICAN INQUISITION

1. Lea, 49 ("a settled punishment . . ."); Lambert, 8 ("to buy faggots . . .").

2. Held, 80 ("tossed back . . .").

3. Burman, 150 ("The Spanish Inquisition . . .") (adapted); Ernest W. Pettifer, *Punishments of Former Days* (Hampshire, UK: Waterside Press, 1992), 124 ("strong and hard pain").

4. Marion L. Starkey, *The Devil in Massachusetts: A Modern Enquiry into the Salem Witch Trials* (New York: Anchor Books, 1969; orig. pub. 1949), 30 ("tricks and spells").

5. Quoted in Starkey, 47 ("Who torments you?"); Starkey, 50 ("shrewish . . .").

6. Quoted in Starkey, 87.

7. Quoted in Starkey, 94 ("Why he can pinch . . ."); Starkey, 94 ("the crazed fantasies . . .").

8. Arthur Miller, *The Crucible,* intro. Christopher Bigsby (New York: Penguin Books, 2003; orig. pub. 1952), 26.

9. Quoted in Starkey, 205.

10. Quoted in Starkey, 208.

11. Quoted in Starkey, 214 ("It is better . . ."); quoted in Armstrong, 396–97 ("Kill them all . . .").

12. Starkey, 228 ("melted like moonshine . . .").

13. Quoted in Starkey, 262 ("bring[ing] upon ourselves . . ."), 259–60 ("was a great delusion . . . ," etc.).

14. Quoted in Richard Francis, *Judge Sewall's Apology: The Salem Witch Trials and the Forming of an American Conscience* (New York: HarperCollins, 2005), 93–94.

15. De Santillana, 324.

16. Quoted in Roger Daniels, Sandra C. Taylor and Harry H. L. Kitani, eds., *Japanese Americans: From Relocation to Redress* (Rev. ed.) (Seattle: University of Washington Press, 1991), 57 ("enemy aliens"); quoted in Martin E. Marty, *One God, Indivisible, 1941–1960,*

vol. 3 of *Modern American Religion* (Chicago: University of Chicago Press, 1999), 77 ("one drop. . .");quoted in Douglas Brinkley, ed., *World War II: The Axis Assault, 1939 1942* (New York: Times Books, 2003), 279 ("A Jap's a Jap"); quoted in Shimon Shetreet, *Free Speech and National Security* (Leiden, The Netherlands: Marinus Nijhoff Publishers, 1991), 187 ("pressing public necessity").

17. Quoted in Victor S. Navasky, *Naming Names* (New York: Penguin Books, 1981), 22.

18. Lillian Hellman, *Scoundrel Time,* intro. Garry Wills (Boston: Little, Brown, 1976), 39 ("the fear of a Red tank . . ."); quoted in Ellen Schrecker, *Many Are the Crimes: McCarthyism in America* (Boston: Little, Brown, 1998), 135 ("almost a separate species . . ."), 144 ("the germ of death . . . ," etc.).

19. Quoted in Navasky, 74.

20. Quoted in Navasky, ix.

21. Navasky, 75 ("orgy of informing . . ."); Hellman, 93 ("inhuman and indecent . . . ," etc.).

22. Intro. to Hellman, 18–19, 20.

23. Quoted in Otto Friedrich, *City of Nets: A Portrait of Hollywood in the 1940s* (Berkeley and Los Angeles: Univ. of California Press, 1997; orig. pub. 1986), 321.

24. Quoted in Schrecker, 361.

25. Isaac Deutscher, biographer of Trotsky, quoted in Friedrich, 293 ("the Galileo of his drama . . .") (adapted); Brecht, *Galileo,* quoted in Friedrich, 295 ("I recanted because . . .").

26. Quoted in Friedrich, 330.

27. Quoted in Friedrich, 330 ("No, no, no . . . ," "based on the philosophy . . . ," and "a good example") (adapted).

28. Quoted in Navasky, 212 ("I speak my own sins," etc.), 215 ("I have had to go to hell . . .").

29. Quoted in Navasky, 212.

30. Schrecker, 317.

31. Schrecker, 360.

32. Quoted in Elaine Woo, "M. Radulovich, 81; Airman's Case Played Key Role in Helping to End McCarthy Era," *Los Angeles Times,* Nov. 21, 2007, B-8.

33. Miller, 111. The final line of dialogue is actually spoken by the character of Thomas Danforth: "Mr. Hale! Mr. Hale!"

34. Haynes Johnson, *The Age of Anxiety: McCarthyism to Terrorism* (Orlando, FL: Harcourt, 2005), xii ("what can happen . . ."), 4 ("devil's brew of fear . . . ," etc.).

35. Quoted in James Bovard, *Terrorism and Tyranny: Trampling Freedom, Justice, and Peace to Rid the World of Evil* (New York: Palgrave Macmillan, 2003), 1.

36. H. Johnson, 467.

37. H. Johnson, 469, 470 ("not a single one of these individuals . . ." and "not one was convicted. . . .").

38. Quoted in H. Johnson, 473.

39. Quoted in H. Johnson, 482 ("watch lists" and "no-fly lists"), 484 ("read your medical records . . ."); quoted in Bovard, 157 ("Total Information Awareness"); Phil Kent, Southeastern Legal Foundation, quoted in Bovard, 158 ("the most sweeping threat . . .").

40. Quoted in Bovard, 144–45 ("millions of American truckers . . ." and "snitch system").

41. Quoted in Bovard, 321.

42. Kamen, quoted in Burman, 150–51 ("called into existence . . ."); Cohn, 49 ("a monstrous, anti-human conspiracy"); Lambert, 151 ("a devoted underground elite"); John and Anne Tedeschi, in Ginzburg, ix ("legal justice"); Miller, quoted in Navasky, 212 ("murderous engine").

REFERENCES CONSULTED

Applebaum, Anne. *Gulag: A History of the Soviet Camps.* New York: Penguin Books, 2003.

Armstrong, Karen. *Holy War: The Crusades and Their Impact on Today's World.* New York: Anchor Books, 2001.

Barstow, Anne Llewellyn. *Joan of Arc: Heretic, Mystic, Shaman.* Studies in Women and Religion, vol. 17. Lewiston, NY: Edwin Mellen Press, 1986.

———. *Witchcraze: A New History of the European Witch Hunts.* New York: Pandora, 1994.

Bible Works 5: Software for Biblical Exegesis and Research. Norfolk, VA: Hermeneutika Bible Research, 2001.

Bovard, James. *Terrorism and Tyranny: Trampling Freedom, Justice, and Peace to Rid the World of Evil.* New York: Palgrave Macmillan, 2003.

Brecht, Bertolt. *Galileo.* Trans. by Charles Laughton. Ed. by Eric Bentley. New York: Grove Press, 1966.

Brinkley, Douglas, ed. *World War II: The Axis Assault, 1939–1942.* New York: Times Books, 2003.

Burman, Edward. *The Inquisition: The Hammer of Heresy.* New York: Dorset Press, 1992. (Orig. pub. 1984).

"The Canons of the Fourth Lateran Council, 1215." In *Internet Medieval Sourcebook,* ed. by Paul Halsall. Online Reference Book for Medieval Studies, Fordham University Center for Medieval Studies. http://www.fordham.edu/halsall/basis/lateran4.html.

Cantor, Norman F. *Inventing the Middle Ages: The Lives, Works and Ideas of the Great Medievalists of the Twentieth Century.* New York: Quill William Morrow, 1991.

Cawthorne, Nigel. *Witch Hunt: History of a Persecution.* New York: Barnes & Noble, 2004.

Chamberlin, E. R. *Everyday Life in Renaissance Times.* New York: Capricorn, 1967.

Chartier, Roger. "The Practical Impact of Writing." In *Passions of the Renaissance,* 123. Ed. by Roger Chartier. Trans. by Arthur Goldhammer. Vol. 3 of *A History of Private Life,* ed. by Phillipe Ariès and Georges Darby. Cambridge: Harvard Univ. Press, Belknap Press, 1989.

Cohn, Norman. *Europe's Inner Demons: An Enquiry Inspired by the Great Witch-Hunt.* New York: Basic Books, 1975.

Conquest, Robert. *The Great Terror: Stalin's Purge of the Thirties.* New York: Macmillan, 1968.

———. *The Harvest of Sorrow: Soviet Collectivization and the Terror-Famine.* New York: Oxford Univ. Press, 1987.

Coulton, G. G. *The Inquisition.* New York: Jonathan Cape & Harrison Smith, 1929.

———. *Inquisition and Liberty.* Boston: Beacon Press, 1959. (Orig. pub. 1938.)

———. *Medieval Village, Manor, and Monastery.* New York: Harper & Row, 1960. (Orig. pub. 1925.)

Crankshaw, Edward. *Gestapo: Instrument of Tyranny.* London: Wren's Park, 2002.

Daniels, Roger, Sandra C. Taylor, and Harry H.L. Kitani, eds. *Japanese Americans: From Relocation to Redress.* Rev. ed. Seattle: University of Washington Press, 1991.

De Cristofaro, Maria, and Tracy Wilkinson. "Vatican Lifts a 700-Year-Old Bum Rap." *Los Angeles Times,* Oct. 26, 2007, A-3.

Dershowitz, Alan M. *America on Trial: Inside the Legal Battles That Transformed Our Nation.* New York: Warner Books, 2004.

De Santillana, Giorgio. *The Crime of Galileo.* New York: Time Inc., 1955. (Orig. pub. Univ. of Chicago Press.)

Dostoyevsky, Fydor. *The Brothers Karamazov.* Trans. by Constance Garnett. New York: Modern Library, n.d.

Ehrenreich, Barbara, and Deidre English. *Witches, Midwives and Nurses: A History of Women Healers.* New York: Feminist Press at the City Univ. of New York, 1973.

Encyclopedia Judaica. Vols. 1-17. Corrected ed. Jerusalem: Keter Publishing House, Ltd., n.d.

Ferruolo, Stephen C. *The Origins of the University: The Schools of Paris and Their Critics, 1100–1125.* Stanford, CA: Stanford University Press, 1985.

Francis, Richard. *Judge Sewall's Apology: The Salem Witch Trials and the Forming of an American Conscience.* New York: HarperCollins, 2005.

Friedländer, Saul. *The Years of Persecution, 1933–1939.* Vol. 1 of *Nazi Germany and the Jews.* New York: HarperPerennial, 1998.

———. *The Years of Extermination, 1939–1945.* Vol. 2 of *Nazi Germany and the Jews.* New York: HarperCollins, 2007

Friedrich, Otto. *City of Nets: A Portrait of Hollywood in the 1940s.* Berkeley and Los Angeles: Univ. of California Press, 1997. (Orig. pub. 1986.)

Gibbon, Edward. *The Decline and Fall of the Roman Empire.* 3 vols. 1776–1789. Reprint, New York: Heritage, 1946.

Ginzburg, Carlo. *The Cheese and the Worms: The Cosmos of a Sixteenth-Century Miller.* Trans. by John and Anne Tedeschi. New York: Penguin Books, 1982.

Gitlitz, David M. *Secrecy and Deceit: The Religion of the Crypto-Jews.* Philadelphia and Jerusalem: Jewish Publication Society, 1996.

Grafton, Anthony. "Say Anything: What the Renaissance Teaches Us About Torture." *The New Republic,* Nov. 5, 2007, 22–24.

Greene, Graham. *The Power and the Glory.* New York: Penguin Books, 2003. (Orig. pub. 1940.)

Griffiths, Arthur (Major). *In Spanish Prisons: The Inquisition at Home and Abroad; Prisons Past and Present.* New York: Dorset Press, 1991. (Orig. pub. 1894.)

Gui, Bernard. *The Inquisitor's Guide: A Medieval Manual on Heretics.* Trans. and ed. by Janet Shirley. Welwyn Garden City, UK: Ravenhall Books, 2006.

Guitton, Jean. *Great Heresies and Church Councils.* Trans. by F. D. Wieck. New York: Harper & Row, 1965.

Hamilton, Bernard. *The Albigensian Crusade.* London: The Historical Association, 1974.

Held, Robert. *Inquisition: A Bilingual Guide to the Exhibition of Torture Instruments from the Middle Ages to the Industrial Era.* Florence: Qua d'Arno, 1985.

Hellman, Lillian. *Scoundrel Time.* Intro. by Garry Wills. Boston: Little, Brown, 1976.

Innes, Brian. *The History of Torture.* Leicester, England: Blitz Editions, 1999.

Jacoby, Russell. "Willi the Red." *The Nation,* Feb. 16, 2004. Posted Jan. 29, 2004, at http://www.thenation.com/doc/20040216/jacoby.

"John Paul II and Galileo," Pauline Books and Media. http:www/daughtersofstpaul.com/johnpaulpapacy/meetjp/thepope/jpgalileo.html.

Johnson, Eric A. *Nazi Terror: The Gestapo, Jews and Ordinary Germans.* New York: Basic Books, 2000.

Johnson, Haynes. *The Age of Anxiety: McCarthyism to Terrorism.* Orlando, FL: Harcourt, 2005.

Kafka, Franz. *The Complete Stories.* Ed. by Nahum N. Glatzer. New York: Schocken Books, 1976.

———. *The Trial.* Trans. by Edwin and Willa Muir. New York: Modern Library, 1956.

Kamen, Henry. *The Spanish Inquisition: A Historical Revision.* New Haven: Yale Univ. Press, 1997.

Kelly, Henry Ansgar. "Inquisition and the Prosecution of Heresy: Misconceptions and Abuses." *Church History* 58 (1989): 439–51.

Kirsch, Adam. *Benjamin Disraeli.* New York: Schocken Books, 2008.

Koestler, Arthur. *Darkness at Noon.* Trans. by Daphne Hardy. New York: Macmillan, 1958.

Ladurie, Emmanuel Le Roy. *Montaillou: Cathars and Catholics in a French Village, 1294–1324.* Trans. by Barbara Bray. New York: Penguin Books,1980.

Lambert, Malcolm. *Medieval Heresy: Popular Movements from the Gregorian Reform to the Reformation.* 2d ed. Cambridge, MA: Blackwell, 1992.

Langford, Jack. "The Condemnation of Galileo." *Reality* 8 (1960): 65–78.

Laursen, John Christian, and Cary J. Nederman. *Beyond the Persecuting Society: Religious Toleration Before the Enlightenment.* Philadelphia: Univ. of Pennsylvania Press, 1998.

Lea, Henry Charles. *A History of the Inquisition of Spain.* 4 vols. Louisville, KY: Bank of Wisdom, 2000 (CD-ROM).

———. *A History of the Inquisition of the Middle Ages.* 3 vols. Louisville, KY: Bank of Wisdom, 2000 (CD-ROM).

———. *The Inquisition of the Middle Ages: Its Organization and Operation.* New York: Citadel Press, 1961.

Llorente, D. Juan. *The Inquisition of Spain.* Louisville, KY: Bank of Wisdom, 2000 (CD-ROM).

Malone, Mary T. *Women and Christianity.* Vol. 1, *The First Thousand Years.* Dublin: Columbia Press, 2000. Vol. 2, *From 1000 to the Reformation.* Maryknoll, NY: Orbis Books, 2002.

Martin, Sean. *The Cathars: The Most Successful Heresy of the Middle Ages.* New York: Thunder's Mouth Press, 2005.

Marty, Martin E. *One God, Indivisible, 1941–1960.* Vol. 3 of *Modern American Religion.* Chicago: University of Chicago Press, 1999.

Miller, Arthur. *The Crucible.* Intro. by *Christopher* Bigsby. New York: Penguin Books, 2003. (Orig. pub. 1952.)

Moore, R. I. *The Formation of a Persecuting Society: Power and Deviance in Western Europe, 950–1250.* Oxford, UK, and Cambridge, MA: Blackwell, 1987.

Navasky, Victor S. *Naming Names.* New York: Penguin Books, 1981.

Netanyahu, B[enzian]. *The Origins of the Inquisition in Fifteenth Century Spain.* New York: Random House, 1995.

Oldenbourg, Zoé. *Massacre at Montségur.* Trans. by Peter Green. London: Phoenix Giant, 1998.

Orwell, George. *1984.* New York: Signet, 1981. (Orig. pub. 1949.)

Ozick, Cynthia. *Quarrel & Quandary.* New York: Alfred A. Knopf, 2000.

People's Commissariat of Justice of the U.S.S.R. *Report of Court Proceedings: The Case of the Trotskyite-Zinovievite Terrorist Centre.* Moscow: People's Commissariat of Justice of the U.S.S.R., 1936.

Peters, Edward. *Inquisition.* Berkeley and Los Angeles: Univ. of California Press, 1989.

———. *Torture.* New York: Basil Blackwell, 1985.

Pettifer, Ernest W. *Punishments of Former Days.* Hampshire, UK: W1992. (Orig. pub. 1947.)

Plaidy, Jean. *The Spanish Inquisition: Its Rise, Growth, and End.* New York: Citadel Press, 1969.

Platt, Anthony M., with Cecilia E. O'Leary. *Bloodlines: Recovering Hitler's Nuremberg Laws, From Patton's Trophy to Public Memorial.* Boulder, CO: Paradigm, 2006.

Purkiss, Diane. *The Witch in History: Early Modern and Twentieth-Century Representations.* New York: Routledge, 1996.

Rayfield, Donald. *Stalin and His Hangmen: The Tyrant and Those Who Killed for Him.* New York: Random House, 2005.

Redondi, Pietro. *Galileo: Heretic.* Trans. by Raymond Rosenthal. New York: Penguin Books, 1989.

Root, Deborah. "Speaking Christian: Orthodoxy and Difference in Sixteenth Century Spain." *Representations* 23 (Summer 1988): 118–134.

Roth, Cecil. *The Spanish Inquisition.* New York: Norton, 1964. (Orig. pub. 1937.)

Rürup, Reinhard, ed. *Topography of Terror: Gestapo, SS and Reichssicherheitshauptamt on the "Prinz-Albert-Terrain": A Documentation.* Trans. by Werner T. Angress. Berlin: Verlag Willmuth Arenhövel, 1989.

Ruthven, Malise. *Torture: The Grand Conspiracy.* London: Weidenfeld & Nicolson, 1978.

Schrecker, Ellen. *Many Are the Crimes: McCarthyism in America.* Boston: Little, Brown, 1998.

Segev, Tom. *The Seventh Million: The Israelis and the Holocaust.* Trans. by Haim Watzman. New York: Hill & Wang, 1993.

Shetreet, Shimon. *Free Speech and National Security.* Leiden, the Netherlands: Martinus Nijhoff Publishers, 1991.

Sommerfeldt, John R. *Bernard of Clairvaux: On the Spirituality of Relationship.* Mahwah, NJ: The Newman Press, 2004.

Starkey, Marion L. *The Devil in Massachusetts: A Modern Enquiry into the Salem Witch Trials.* New York: Anchor Books, 1969. (Orig. pub. 1949.)

Stockdale, J. J. *The History of the Inquisition: Including Its Secret Tribunals.* Louisville, KY: Bank of Wisdom, 2000 (CD-ROM).

Summers, Montague, ed. and trans. *The "Malleus Maleficarum" of Heinrich Kramer and James Sprenger.* New York: Dover, 1971. (Orig. pub. 1928.)

Trachtenberg, Joshua. *The Devil and the Jews: The Medieval Conception of the Jew and Its Relation to Modern Antisemitism.* New Haven: Yale Univ. Press, 1943.

Trotsky, Leon. *Stalin's Frame-Up System and the Moscow Trials.* New York: Pioneer, 1950.

Von Lang, Jochen, with Claus Sibyll. *Eichmann Interrogated: Transcripts from the Archives of the Israeli Police.* Trans. by Ralph Manheim. New York: Vintage Books, 1984.

Wakefield, Walter L. *Heresy, Crusade and Inquisition in Southern France, 1100–1250.* Berkeley and Los Angeles: Univ. of California Press, 1974.

Wakefield, Walter L., and Austin P. Evans. *Heresies of the High Middle Ages: Translated with Notes.* New York: Columbia Univ. Press, 1991.

Woo, Elaine. "M. Radulovich, 81; Airman's Case Played Key Role in Helping to End McCarthy Era." *Los Angeles Times,* Nov. 21, 2007, B-8.

World Committee for the Victims of German Fascism. *The Brown Book of the Hitler Terror and the Burning of the Reichstag.* Intro. by Lord Marley. London: Victor Gollancz, 1933.

INDEX

Spain: anti-Semitism, 173–76, 176n, 177–78, 180, 181, 182, 194–96; bishop of Segovia, 179; chilling effect of Inquisition, 210; Columbus's voyage, 165–66; *convivencia*, 169, 173, 181, 183; Muslims in, 173–74, 182–83; "purity of blood," 15, 194–96, 218; War of Spanish Succession, 185–86; witches/witchcraft in, 188

Spanish Inquisition, 5, 6, 80n, 166, 167–205; accused and legal counsel, 191; book banning, 183, 184, 187; burning of victims, 56, 85–86, 132, 180, 184, 186, 189, 196–202; charges against the dead, 178; confession and torture, 96–97; *consulta de fé*, 191; dates of, 55, 169, 177; death toll, 202; Edict of Grace, 189, 189n; ending, 202–5; Englishman burned alive, 184, 241; evidence against Jews and Muslims, 183; exotic heresies, 184–85; "first sketch of the Inquisition" and, 61; Freemasonry, 185, 208; as instrument of state terror, 185; interrogation, 167; Jewish persecution, 14, 55, 166, 174–84, 192–96; last victim, 204–5; *La Suprema*, 178, 188, 191, 210, 216; machinery of persecution, 55; manuals, 178–79, 201; mission of, 201; in the New World, 55; ordeal of Elvira del Campo, 210; persecution of sexual deviancy, 188; proceedings, 189–91; Protestants targeted, 183–84, 189; punishments, lesser, 199; "purity of blood" and *conversos*, 5, 55, 174–84, 176n, 186, 192, 193–96, 202, 210, 221, 247; *quemadero*, 197, 199; secrecy, 191; secular government's use of, 55, 185–89; *tierras de herejes*, 187; Torquemada, 64, 67, 173, 176, 179, 181–82; torture, 104, 190, 210; tribunals, 178; witches, 152, 188; women victimized, 202; as zenith and beginning of decline of Inquisition, 15

Spanish Inquisition, The (Roth), 6–7, 227, 229

Spengler, Johann, 146, 148, 153

Spinoza, Baruch, 180, 213
spirituali (Spirituals), 135–36, 137
Sprenger, Johann, 146
Stalin, Joseph, 6, 228, 230–33, 236, 237
Starkey, Marion L., 244, 245
Switzerland, 152–53, 154

Tack, John, 184
Tanchelm of Antwerp, 27, 28
Teresa of Ávila, 185
Toledo, Spain, 183, 184, 189, 202
Torquemada, Juan de, 192
Torquemada, Tomás de, 64, 67, 173, 175, 176, 179, 181–82, 192, 236, 247
torture, 6, 73, 76, 93–132; in America, 244, 256; of children, 76, 111; Church sanctions, 17, 89, 94; classic legal definition, 101; confessions under, 11, 81, 96–103, 110, 145; duration of, 16, 106; ecclesiastical courts and, 16; English, *peine forte et dure*, 242, 244–45; euphemisms, 97–98, 239; fire as, 105, 107, 216; five degrees of severity, 93–94, 98, 106, 153; Galileo and, 164; "heretic's fork," 108; *judicium secularum*, 9; *La Pera* (the Pear), 2–3, 109, 217; as lawful, 94, 111, 112; legitimized by the Inquisition, 210; Nazi Germany, 216–17; ordeal vs., 101–3; process, 103–5; psychological, 103–4; records, 103–4, 212, 217; red-hot iron, 97, 102; rope, 107; sadism and, 16, 95, 107–8, 109, 110, 153–54; secrecy of, 8, 112–13, 210; in secular courts, 16; sleep deprivation, 107; Spanish Inquisition, 104, 190, 210; Stalinist Russia, 230; standard operating procedures, 16; *stivaletto*, 106–7; strappado, 97, 105–6, 212, 216, 230, 236; terror and, 97, 103; theater of, 104, 108; tongs, 108–9; used on first Christians, 94; victims blamed for, 98; water/waterboarding, 4, 104–5, 107, 216, 239, 256; wheel and rack, 97, 106, 108, 110; of witches, 153–54
Toulouse, France, 45–46, 50–51, 69, 78, 90–91, 119, 145